The Science of Mystic Lights

HARVARD MIDDLE EASTERN MONOGRAPHS
XXVI

The Science · of · Mystic Lights

Quṭb al-Dīn Shīrāzī and the Illuminationist Tradition in Islamic Philosophy

JOHN WALBRIDGE

DISTRIBUTED FOR THE
CENTER FOR MIDDLE EASTERN STUDIES
OF HARVARD UNIVERSITY BY
HARVARD UNIVERSITY PRESS
CAMBRIDGE, MASSACHUSETTS
1992

ISBN 0-932885-06-3
Library of Congress Catalog Card Number 91-075860
Printed in the United States of America

To Linda, with love

Contents

List of Figures

Preface

I began this study interested in the influence of mysticism on Islamic philosophy, which, it seemed to me, found its distinctive form only when its Greek prototype had been thoroughly infused with Ṣūfī ideas. I was especially curious about how Ibn 'Arabī's ideas had been incorporated into later philosophical systems.

This eventually led me to Quṭb al-Dīn al-Shīrāzī (634/1236 to 710/1311). He was trained by Naṣīr al-Dīn al-Ṭūsī, the leading follower of Avicenna in his generation, and wrote the best-known commentary on Suhrawardī's *The Philosophy of Illumination*. For a time, at least, he was a student of Ṣadr al-Dīn al-Qūnawī, Ibn 'Arabī's closest disciple. Thus, modern historians have credited Quṭb al-Dīn with being the first to unite the three traditions that were to be the dominant influences on later Islamic philosophy: the "Peripatetic" philosophy of Avicenna, the Illuminationist philosophy of Suhrawardī, and the doctrine of the unity of existence of Ibn 'Arabī.

Unfortunately, this theory of Quṭb al-Dīn's significance was based on external bio-bibliographical information, not on a reading of his works. There the main frame of reference was clearly the system of Avicenna. I could find no internal evidence of a link with Ibn 'Arabī, apart from two quotations. The most interesting problem turned out to be his connection with Suhrawardī's Illuminationist philosophy.

In his long commentary on *The Philosophy of Illumination,* Quṭb al-Dīn by and large deals with Suhrawardī's philosophy in Avicennan terms—the "Peripatetic" or "physical mode," as he sometimes refers to it. In his other main philosophical work, *The Pearly Crown,* he often refers to Suhrawardī's Illuminationist doctrines, though he never cites him by name. Thus, it seems clear that Suhrawardī was the active influence on his thought, while Avicenna's philosophy provided the framework within which he worked.

Since there is no full and satisfactory account of *The Philosophy of Illumination* and its relation to Avicennan Neoplatonism, the first question I needed to answer was how this philosophy is distinctive. This problem was made more difficult by Suhrawardī's use of a strange symbolism of light. Quṭb al-Dīn and Suhrawardī himself in his other works had generally used conventional Avicennan terminology. Therefore, my first project was to analyze the structure and content of *The Philosophy of Illumination* in order to learn the significance of Suhrawardī's terms and language and their relation to "Peripatetic" terms. My approach has been to follow carefully the lines of argument in *The Philosophy of Illumination,* both in isolation and in the context of Quṭb al-Dīn's commentary, always keeping in mind what is said about method and scientific reasoning in the logic of Avicenna and Suhrawardī. The results of this are contained in Chapter 2 below. In the end, I found a systematic relation between Illuminationist and Avicennan concepts. Suhrawardī's philosophy, I concluded, does not differ from Avicenna's in terminology but in particular doctrines. The first set of doctrines concerns epistemology, ontology, and cosmology; the second, his concept of the World of Image.

Quṭb al-Dīn's other major philosophical work, *The Pearly Crown,* although virtually free of the distinguishing vocabulary of *The Philosophy of Illumination,* generally follows Suhrawardī in his most basic views. Quṭb al-Dīn develops them in a rather more subtle and sophisticated manner than Suhrawardī does in *The Philosophy of Illumination. The Pearly Crown* is thus fundamentally an Illuminationist book, despite its almost total lack of a terminology of light such as is found in *The Philosophy of Illumination.*

That done, I turned to the problem of the World of Image and the related questions of time, the Eternal Return, the pre-existence of the soul, and reincarnation. This has a special interest since some of Quṭb al-Dīn's ideas, especially those about reincarnation, were not followed by any later philosophers.

Thus, I have thoroughly examined only the relationship of Quṭb al-Dīn's thought with Suhrawardī's *Philosophy of Illumination.* Quṭb al-Dīn's connections with Avicenna are more obvious and less interesting since, it seems to me, he was modifying Avicennan ideas under Suhrawardian influence, rather than the other way around.

There are several major limitations in this study. First, I paid no attention to Quṭb al-Dīn's scientific works, which constitute the bulk of his writings. These would likely give us a clearer understanding of his view of the world and might well clarify some aspects of his philosophical views. They certainly are important for the history of science, especially in astronomy and medicine. Nor did I study most of Quṭb al-Dīn's minor philosophical works, most of which I did not have access to.

Second, I did not study the debates among Quṭb al-Dīn's Avicennan contemporaries: Ṭūsī's commentary on Avicenna's *Ishārāt,* the debate on being between Ṭūsī and Kātibī, the *Muḥākamāt* of Quṭb al-Dīn's student Taḥtānī, and other such works. I have no doubt that these would add to our understanding of Quṭb al-Dīn's philosophical views, if only by clarifying the extent to which his Illuminationist views diverged from the Avicennan tradition.

Third, I did not study Shahrazūrī's commentary on *The Philosophy of Illumination* or his *al-Shajara al-Ilāhīya,* which my friend Hossein Ziai tells me are the unmentioned sources of much of Quṭb al-Dīn's commentary. A reading of Shahrazūrī would probably demonstrate that Quṭb al-Dīn's views were derivative in many respects (and his commentary partly plagiarized), thus reducing his importance as an original philosopher though not, I think, affecting the accuracy of my portrayal of his philosophy or of Suhrawardī's.

NOTE ON TERMINOLOGY

I use the term *existence* systematically in place of *being* as an equivalent of *wujūd*. This allows me to distinguish *existence* and *existent* (*mawjūd*), a crucial distinction in the philosophy I am studying. It also avoids confusion with less technical uses of the English *being*.

I use *quiddity* rather than *essence* for *māhīya* since *quiddity* is, in fact, the English rendering of the Latin translation of exactly this Arabic word. If a distinction can be made between quiddity and essence, it is that quiddity is the mental nature of the thing, while essence is that nature as embodied in a concrete thing. Thus, I reserve *essence* as a translation of *dhāt,* a term that is virtually synonymous with *reality* (*ḥaqīqa*) and *identity* (*huwīya*) and is closely related to *nature* (*ṭabīʿa*).

Otherwise, terms are fairly clear, although the reader should carefully distinguish between adjectival—*one, necessary,* etc.—and nominal—*unity, necessity,* etc.—forms.

By *Islamic philosophy* I simply mean the philosophy done by philosophers living in the Islamic lands. All of the philosophers I am concerned with here were Muslims writing in Arabic or Persian. They were cut off by language or society from Greek, Latin, old Persian, Indian, and other types of philosophy.

Proper names are transliterated except in a few cases where a Latin form is well known. I often drop the initial *al-*.

Dates, where appropriate, are given in the form "428/1037," where the date is given first according to the Islamic lunar calendar and is followed by its common-era equivalent.

ACKNOWLEDGMENTS

There are a number of people and institutions whose assistance or tolerance helped make this study possible and whom I wish to thank. Prominent among them is my teacher Muhsin Mahdi, who first interested me in Islamic philosophy. I also owe thanks to my very good friends in the Middle East Department of the Harvard College Library, to the librarians at Yarmouk University and Bay de Noc College, and to various patient employers. Hossein Ziai, who knows much more about Suhrawardī than I do, encouraged me and shared his knowledge. Sheik Abdullatif Berry was kind enough to obtain a manuscript for me from the library of the Shrine of the Imām Riḍā in Mashhad.

I would like to thank the Millī Library in Tehran and the Āstān al-Quds Library in Mashhad for giving me copies of the manuscripts that form the basis of the text edited later in the book and to the Majlis Library in Tehran for a microfilm of an early manuscript of *The Pearly Crown*.

Special thanks are due to Diane Levy for service beyond the call of duty in preparing this book for publication.

For financial support at various points in my research, I am happy to thank the United States government and its programs to support foreign language study, as well as the National Spiritual Assembly of the Bahā'īs of Jordan.

Most of all I am grateful for the patience of my family.

The Science of Mystic Lights

·ONE·

Quṭb al-Dīn's Life and Times

ISLAMIC PHILOSOPHY BEFORE THE THIRTEENTH CENTURY

By the end of the tenth century, the works of Aristotle, synthesized into a school corpus and supplemented by Neoplatonic texts and a substantial edifice of commentary, had passed into the hands of Islamic philosophers,[1] who now faced the problem of finding a unifying interpretation of this literature. Fārābī, one of the earliest Islamic philosophers, took classical political theory as his point of departure. This approach did not find much favor, and Fārābī had few direct followers except in distant Spain and the cold, damp lands of the Latin West.

Islamic philosophy found its classic synthesis in the works of Avicenna (d. 428/1037). Deeply influenced by Fārābī, he built a coherent system based on the works of Aristotle and the

1. For a general account of the transmission of Greek philosophy to the Arabs, see F. E. Peters, *Aristotle and the Arabs,* New York University Studies in Near Eastern Civilization, no. 1 (New York: NYU Press, 1968). His *Aristoteles Arabus* (Leyden: E. J. Brill, 1968) is a bibliographical study of the Aristotelian and pseudo-Aristotelian works in Arabic. His "The Origins of Islamic Platonism: The School Tradition," in *Islamic Philosophical Theology,* ed. Parviz Morewedge, Studies in Islamic Philosophy and Science (Albany: State University of New York Press, 1979), 14–45, surveys current knowledge about Platonic and Neoplatonic works in Arabic.

Neoplatonic texts that had been translated in his name. In place of Fārābī's political framework was a Neoplatonic metaphysics. So successful was Avicenna's systematic synthesis that his works virtually supplanted those of Aristotle and Fārābī. From the eleventh century on, philosophers in the central and eastern Islamic lands worked in his shadow.[2]

In his metaphysics Avicenna distinguished between essence and existence—what a thing is and that it is—and between that whose existence is necessary in itself and that whose existence is necessary by another but contingent in itself. Based on these two distinctions, he proved the existence of a God whose essence was identical with his existence and whose existence was necessary in itself. He then traced the emanation of a series of immaterial intellects, each with an associated celestial sphere and soul. It was through contact with the last of these intellects that the human mind obtained the abstract intelligibles. Within this Neoplatonic structure the details of Avicenna's philosophy—subjects like logic and the nature of the physical body—were worked out in quite Aristotelian terms.[3]

Avicenna's position as a Muslim philosopher bequeathed to him the problems associated with prophecy and the afterlife. Adapting an approach explored by Fārābī, he explained these in terms of the imagination. His solution, however, had serious

2. The relative practical importance of Aristotle, Fārābī, and Avicenna may be roughly measured by the scarcity of manuscripts of Aristotle in Arabic, the loss of many of Fārābī's commentaries on Aristotle, and the abundance of manuscripts of and commentaries on many of Avicenna's works.
3. A readable account of Avicenna's cosmology and related ideas, along with a good bibliography, is found in Seyyed Hossein Nasr, *An Introduction to Islamic Cosmological Doctrines,* rev. ed. (Boulder: Shambhala, 1978), 177–274. The most recent major study of Avicenna in English is Dmitri Gutas, *Avicenna and the Aristotelian Tradition,* Islamic Philosophy and Theology: Texts and Studies 4 (Leiden: E. J. Brill, 1988).

weaknesses. As we will see, Islamic philosophers returned to these problems again and again.[4]

SUHRAWARDĪ

Shihāb al-Dīn Yaḥyā Suhrawardī (549/1154 to 587/1191), the influence of whose masterwork *The Philosophy of Illumination* is the main subject of this study, placed his own work in the context of a largely fictitious history of philosophy. He saw himself as the culmination of an "Illuminationist" tradition of philosophy that began with the legendary sages of the ancient past, was continued by certain of the pre-Socratics, and culminated with Plato in the West and with the Persian sages in the East. After Plato this tradition was carried on not by the philosophers but by the mystics.[5] Against them were arranged the

4. Avicenna, *Kitāb al-Shifā': al-Ilāhīyāt* (The Book of Healing: Metaphysica), ed. Ibrāhīm Madkūr (Cairo: al-Hay'a al-'Āmma li-Shu'ūn al-Maṭābi' al-Amīrīya, 1380/1960), 2:435–55; Fazlur Rahman, "Dream, Imagination, and 'Ālam al-Mithāl," *Islamic Studies* 3 (1964): 167–80.
5. Suhrawardī, "Ḥikmat al-Ishrāq" ("The philosophy of illumination"), *Œuvres philosophiques et mystiques,* ed. Henry Corbin, Bibliothèque Iranienne, n.s. (Tehran: Académie Imperiale Iranienne de Philosophie, 1976–77), 2:9–11. Quṭb al-Dīn al-Shīrāzī, *Sharḥ Ḥikmat al-Ishrāq (Commentary on "The Philosophy of Illumination"),* ed. Asad Allāh Harātī ([Tehran]:, 1313–15/1896–98), 4–5, 12–22.

   (Hereafter references to *The Philosophy of Illumination* are given in the form "*Illumination,* 9–11/12–22"—where the first set of page numbers refers to the Corbin edition and the second to the text of Suhrawardī in Quṭb al-Dīn's commentary. References specifically to the *Commentary,* and not to the text embedded in it, have the form "*Commentary,* 4–5." References to other works of Suhrawardī have the form "Suhrawardī, *Œuvres.*")

   This legendary history is summarized in Seyyed Hossein Nasr, *Three Muslim Sages* (Cambridge, Mass.: Harvard University Press, 1964), 60–63. It is treated thoroughly in Corbin's introductions to the three volumes of "followers of the Peripatetics"—the Aristotelians who had been blinded by their ambition and occupied themselves with hair-splitting and social climbing. Aristotle explained this personally to Suhrawardī in a dream:

> Then he began praising his teacher Plato so lavishly that I asked him in astonishment, "Have any of the philosophers of Islam attained to his rank?"
>
> "No," he said, "nor to a thousandth part of it."
>
> I mentioned several of them, but he refused to consider them. However when I mentioned Abū Yazīd al-Basṭamī, Abū Muḥammad Sahl b. 'Abd Allāh al-Tustarī, and others like them [i.e., the ecstatic mystics], he was delighted and said, "These are the true philosophers and sages, for they were not content with mere formal knowledge."[6]

This, of course, does not have much to do with history, especially if we take "Illuminationist" to mean "Platonic" and "Peripatetic" to mean "Aristotelian." Suhrawardī, for example, criticizes the "Peripatetics" for limiting the number of emanated celestial intellects to ten and for making a real distinction between essence and existence in concrete things, evidently meaning by "Peripatetics" Avicenna and his followers. "Illuminationist philosophy" does have some conspicuously Platonic elements, but its relation to classical Platonism—much less to Hermes and the pre-Socratics—is loose at best.

Suhrawardī's *Œuvres,* especially 1:xxvii–lxii and 2:31–38, and in Corbin's *En Islam iranien,* vol. 2, *Sohrawardī et les Platoniciens de Perse* (Paris: Gallimard, 1971), 19–80.

6. Suhrawardī, *Œuvres,* 1:70–74. Suhrawardī says he had been baffled by the problem of knowledge. In the dream Aristotle explains to him the theory of knowledge by presence, which resolved his difficulties and is in fact the basis of the philosophy of illumination. Aristotle's comments on Plato and Islamic philosophers and mystics are incidental to the main point of the dream.

This was a legendary history, but one quite real to the men involved. And since it is not my intention to trace the influence of classical philosophy in Islam (which, in any case, I have no special qualifications to do), but to trace the influence of Suhrawardī's thought within Islamic philosophy, I generally take this history as given. Thus I use *Peripatetic* to mean Avicennan, as my sources do. The reader should be aware of this.

Suhrawardī perhaps had never heard the name of Plotinus, although he had read the excerpts from the *Enneads* circulated under the title of *The Theology of Aristotle.* His knowledge of Aristotle was indirect, mainly filtered through Avicenna. Plato he probably knew only through doxographies and epitomes of such dialogues as the *Timaeus*. There are genuinely Platonic elements in his thought—a version of the doctrine of Forms, for example—and Pythagorean elements, such as universal cycles, as well as ideas that had more in common with the genuine thought of Aristotle, such as the approach to being. His work as a whole, however, was thoroughly within the framework of Islamic Neoplatonism.

ISLAMIC PHILOSOPHY IN THE THIRTEENTH CENTURY

In the late twelfth and early thirteenth centuries, the stage was set for the developments in Islamic philosophy that culminated in the so-called School of Iṣfahān in Ṣafavid Iran in the sixteenth and seventeenth centuries.

Although Avicenna's influence had by no means died out, interest in his thought had waned somewhat in the eleventh and twelfth centuries. In the late twelfth century attention was once again focused on him by two sharp attacks. On the one hand, Suhrawardī severely criticized Avicenna in the name of mysticism and the Illuminationist philosophy of Plato and the ancients. From the other side the theologian Fakhr al-Dīn Rāzī (d. 606/1209), while following Ghazālī's lead in adapting philosophical ideas to theological uses, nonetheless criticized Avicenna in a commentary on his *Book of Hints and Allusions.*[7] About half a century later Naṣīr al-Dīn Ṭūsī undertook to defend Avicenna against both camps in another commentary on the *Hints.*[8] His colleague at the observatory of Marāgha, Najm al-Dīn Kātibī Qazwīnī, also participated in Avicenna's defense in his two popular textbooks on philosophy and logic.[9]

A fourth influence beginning to be felt in the mid-thirteenth century was that of the great Ṣūfī theorist Ibn 'Arabī (d. 638/1240).[10] His works electrified many in the Islamic world who saw in them a supreme mystical synthesis that laid bare the inner heart of Islam. His students quickly began the task of systematizing their master's chaotic system and applying its ideas to the current issues of Islamic thought. In the mid-thirteenth century Ibn 'Arabī's closest student, Ṣadr al-Dīn Qūnawī, was writing on philosophical topics and corresponding with Ṭūsī on questions relating to Avicennan thought.[11]

7. *Sharḥ al-Ishārāt* (Constantinople: 1290/1873) contains Ṭūsī's commentary. See also *Encyclopedia of Islam,* 2d ed. (hereafter abbreviated as "*EI2*"), s.v. "Fakhr al-Dīn al-Rāzī," by G. C. Anawati.
8. In Avicenna, *Kitāb al-Ishārāt,* ed. Sulaymān Dunyā (Cairo: 1957–58).
9. Najm al-Dīn Kātibi Qazwīnī, *Al-Risāla al-Shamsīya fī al-Qawā'id al-Manṭiqīya* and *Kitāb Ḥikmat al-'Ayn.* See Carl Brockelmann, *Geschichte der Arabischen Literatur* (Leyden: E. J. Brill, 1937–49), G1:466–67, no. I, II; S1:845–48, no. I, 847, no. II.
10. In recent years there has been considerable interest in Ibn 'Arabī, including the formation of a scholarly society devoted to his work. The most recent major work is William C. Chittick, *The Ṣūfī Path of Knowledge: Ibn 'Arabī's Metaphysics of the Imagination* (Albany: SUNY Press, 1989).
11. William C. Chittick, "Mysticism versus Philosophy in Earlier Islamic History: The al-Ṭūsī, al-Qūnawī Correspondence," *Religious Studies* 17 (1981): 87–104. Chittick, unfortunately, does not deal in detail with the philosophical issues raised in the correspondence.

Later Iranian philosophy is generally held to have been a synthesis of these trends: the Peripatetic philosophy of Avicenna, the Illuminationist philosophy of Suhrawardī, and the theosophy of Ibn 'Arabī. And, of course, any philosophy in Islam was carried out in the shadow of dialectical theology. Quṭb al-Dīn Shīrāzī was in the midst of this activity and had connections with all these intellectual currents.

QUṬB AL-DĪN'S FAMILY AND EDUCATION

Even in an age when intellectual versatility among scholars was the rule rather than the exception, Quṭb al-Din Maḥmūd b. Mas'ūd al-Shīrāzī was a man of truly catholic breadth. He grew up in the years of the Mongol invasion, that difficult time when Islamic culture reached its mature height while its political manifestations collapsed in ruin, and he lived to play a small role in bringing the pagan invaders within the circle of Islam. He was of the first rank of the intelligentsia of his age.

In Shīrāz in the first half of the thirteenth century, the Kāzarūnī family was well known for its skill in medicine and its prominence in the Ṣūfī community.[12] Ḍiyā' al-Dīn Maḥmūd b. al-Muṣliḥ al-Kāzarūnī was a staff physician and ophthalmologist at the new Muẓaffarī Hospital.[13] His brother, Kamāl al-Dīn

12. Unless otherwise noted, my account of Quṭb al-Dīn's family and early life is based on the autobiography found in the introduction to *The Offering to Sa'd,* his commentary on Avicenna's *Canon of Medicine* (see App. C, no. 29, below), published by Muḥammad Mishkāt in the introduction to his edition of Quṭb al-Dīn's *Durrat al-Tāj li-Ghurrat al-Dubāj (The Pearly Crown for Dubāj's Brow)* (Tehran: Majlis, 1317–20/1938–42), 1/1/kh–z, n. 2. (The autobiography is referred to hereafter as *Offering. The Pearly Crown* is referred to as *Crown.*)
13. See Dawlatshāh Samarqandī, *The Tadhkiratu'sh-Shu'arā,* ed. E. G. Browne (London: Luzac, 1901).

Abū al-Khayr, was also a doctor in Shīrāz. The poet Sa'dī may have been their brother-in-law.[14]

Ḍiyā' al-Dīn's only known son, Quṭb al-Dīn Abū al-Thanā' Maḥmūd ibn Mas'ūd ibn al-Muṣliḥ al-Shīrāzī,[15] was born, probably in Shīrāz, in Ṣafar 634/October–November 1236. As a child he was his father's apprentice at the hospital. When the boy was fourteen, his father died, and he was given the vacant position at the hospital. Although he had learned the basics of medical practice (except for the treatment of glaucoma) from his father, he now began serious study of medical theory, especially the "General Principles" (*Kullīyāt*) of Avicenna's *Canon of Medicine,* first with his uncle and then with two other teachers of medicine, Shams al-Dīn Kīshī and Sharaf al-Dīn Būshkānī. Of the uncle we know no more than Quṭb al-Dīn tells us, but

14. Sa'dī was thirty years or more older than Quṭb al-Dīn, so he could not have been the son of Quṭb al-Dīn's sister, as Abū al-Qāsim Kāzarūnī would have it. See his *Sullam al-Samāwāt,* cited in Muḥammad-Bāqir Khwānsārī, *Rawḍāt al-Jannāt,* ed. Sa'īd Ṭabāṭabā'ī (Tehran, 1304–6), 509, 723. Cf. Shādrawān Mīnawī, "Mullā Quṭb al-Shīrāzī," in *Yād-Nāma-i Īrānī-i Mīnūrskī* ed. Mujtabā Mīnawī and Īraj Afshār (Tehran: Dānishgāh-i: Tehran 1969), 180, who does not believe the story told on p. 20–21 below and points out that "sister" (*ukht*) is likely to be a misreading for "brother" (*akhī*). On the other hand, the relationship with Sa'dī is only mentioned in one late, weak source and may be based only on the coincidence that some sources give Sa'dī's father's name as Muṣliḥ, which is also the name of Quṭb al-Dīn's grandfather. Sa'dī would thus have been his paternal uncle. Sa'dī and Quṭb al-Dīn's father were both students of 'Umar Suhrawardī in Baghdad at about the same time.

It is quite possible that the whole business is based on Khwānsārī's overly literal interpretation of one of the jokes told about Quṭb al-Dīn. See p. 26, n. 86 below.

15. Ibn al-Fuwaṭī, cited in Ibn Rāfi' al-Sallāmī, *Tārīkh 'Ulamā' Baghdād,* ed. al-Taqī al-Fāsī (Baghdad: Matba'at al-Ahālī 1357/1938), 219, gives his name thus. In his own books he usually called himself "Maḥmūd b. Mas'ūd b. al-Muṣliḥ al-Shīrāzī, of all God's creatures most in need of Him." He is also called "al-Fārisī," "al-Shāfi'ī," and "al-Ash'arī," though these last are really not proper names.

Kīshī and Būshkānī were well-known teachers of the religious and rational sciences in Shīrāz. Muḥammad b. Aḥmad Kīshī (d. 694/1294–95) was a Ṣūfī and later became a prominent professor at the Niẓāmīyah in Baghdad.[16] Būshkānī (d. 680/1281–82) taught Bayḍāwī, the author of the popular Qur'ān commentary.[17]

As well as working with these teachers, Quṭb al-Dīn at this time read a number of commentaries on Avicenna's "General Principles." Finding neither the commentaries nor the explanations of his teachers to be completely satisfactory, Quṭb al-Dīn realized he would have to go elsewhere for advanced study in medical theory.

In addition to his medical studies, Quṭb al-Dīn was learning to be a Ṣūfī. His father had been one of the Shīrāz mystics. He had studied in Baghdad with Shihāb al-Dīn 'Umar al-Suhrawardī (d. 632/1234–35), the author of a famous handbook of mysticism, and had received from him the *khirqa,* the patched woolen frock that was the symbol of a Ṣūfī's spiritual lineage. When Quṭb al-Dīn was ten, his father invested him with the *khirqa* of blessing.[18] He must also have had contact with Shaykh

16. Ibn al-Fuwaṭī, *al-Ḥawādith al-Jāmi'a* (Baghdad, Maktabat al-'Arabīya 1351/1932), 358; Muḥammad-Taqī Mīr, *Sharḥ-i Ḥāl wa-Āthār-i 'Allāma-yi Quṭb al-Dīn . . . Shīrāzī,* Intishārāt-i Dānishgāh-i Pahlawī, no. 91 (Shīrāz: Pahlavi University, 2535/1976), 5 n. 3; Mudarris Riḍawī, *Aḥwāl wa-Athār-i . . . Khwāja Naṣīr al-Dīn al-Ṭūsī,* Intishārāt-i Dānishgāh-i Tihrān, no. 282 (Tehran: Tehran University, 1334), 106–8. Possibly the work referred to in Brockelmann, S1: 92822*k*, is his. His name is also given as Kab(a)shī and Kayshī. He was also a teacher of the 'Allāma Ḥillī and corresponded with Ṭūsī, although he was not a Shī'ī. Perhaps he recommended Quṭb al-Dīn to Ṭūsī as a student.
17. Mīr, 5 n. 4. Other sources, reading *Offering* in various ways, give the name as Rakshāwī and Barkashāwī.
18. "*Tabarruk,*" *Crown,* "*khātima,*" quṭb 4, pt. 2, chap. 2. (This part has not been published. I have used the Majlis manuscript, no. 4720, for the unpublished sections. See App. C, no. 1, below.) The *khirqa* of blessing was given as a sign of favor, not as a token of completed discipleship.

Najīb al-Dīn 'Alī b. Buzghush al-Shīrāzī (594/1197–98 to 678/1279–80), also a student of Suhrawardī and the most important Ṣūfī in Shīrāz at that time.[19]

Quṭb al-Dīn remained in Shīrāz until he was twenty-four (658/1260), by which time he had absorbed all that the local teachers had to offer. Indeed, it would have been more usual for him to have left earlier; but in 651/1253, when he was about seventeen, Hülegü, the Mongol Īl-Khān, had marched from Karakoram to destroy the Assassins in their Iranian strongholds and the caliphate itself in Baghdad. By 654/1256 he controlled Iran and had captured the secret fortresses of the Assassins. On 10 February 1258, he sacked Baghdad, killing thousands of people including the caliph himself. Shīrāz was spared, being well out of the main line of attack and its governor having hastily offered his submission.

Among the spoils of the chief Assassin fortress of Alamūt was the astronomer Naṣīr al-Dīn Ṭūsī.[20] Possessed of a fine talent for changing sides, he soon became an advisor to the Īl-Khān. Shortly after the fall of Baghdad the Īl-Khān offered him an immense grant for an observatory where a new set of astronomical tables would be compiled, a project of interest to the Īl-Khān because of its application to astrology.

Construction of the observatory began 4 Jumādā I 657/30 April 1259 at Marāgha in northwestern Iran, then the Īl-Khānid capital. Ṭūsī soon attracted a glittering staff. Among its senior members were Najm al-Dīn Kātibī Qazwīnī, (d. 675/1276) known as Dabīrān, an excellent astronomer and mathematician

19. Ibid.; Zarkūb-i Shīrāzī, *Shīrāz-Nāma,* ed. Bahman Karīmī (Tehran: Aḥmadī, 1310/1331), 131–32.

20. See Riḍawī, 25–33, for the circumstances of the founding of the Marāgha observatory.

as well as philosopher;[21] and Mu'ayyad al-Dīn 'Urḍī (d. 664/1265–66) of Damascus, now thought to have been the most original astronomical theorist of his day and an expert on astronomical instruments.[22] Among the junior staff was the librarian Ibn al-Fuwaṭī (642/1244–723/1323), whose historical works are the main source for our knowledge of the observatory and its staff and students.[23] Ṭūsī also put together a scientific library—said to have included 400,000 volumes—and an outstanding collection of astronomical instruments.

Quṭb al-Dīn was among the first students attracted to the observatory, arriving a year or less after its foundation.[24] He came with the intention of studying medicine; but he found that although Ṭūsī was very helpful in theoretical matters, his understanding of medicine was limited by a lack of practical experience. In any event Quṭb al-Dīn was soon deeply involved in mathematics and philosophy[25] and quickly became Ṭūsī's most important student. Among other things he studied Avicenna's *Book of Hints and Allusions.*[26] Besides helping with the astronomical observations, he worked as a scribe. Manuscripts

21. *EI2*, s.v. "al-Kātibī," by M. Mohaghegh; Riḍawī, 130–31; Brockelmann, G1:466–67, S1:845–48.
22. Riḍawī, 131–32; Brockelmann, S1:869–70; George Saliba, "The First Non-Ptolemaic Astronomy at the Maraghah School," *Isis* 70 (1979):571–76.
23. *EI2*, s.v. "Ibn al-Fuwaṭī," by Franz Rosenthal; Riḍawī, 144–47; Brockelmann, G2:162, S2:202.
24. For reasons of chronology, as well as quality of sources, it is unlikely that Quṭb al-Dīn was first Kātibī's student in Qazwīn as Khwānsārī, 508, reports. See Mishkāt's introduction to Quṭb al-Dīn, *Crown,* 1/1/ṣ–ḍ, for a discussion of the evidence.
25. Ibn al-Fuwaṭī, *Talkhīṣ Majma' al-Ādāb fī-Mu'jam al-Alqāb* (Damascus: Mudīrīyat Iḥyā' al-Turāth al-Qadīm [1967?]), vol. 4, bk. 4:716–17.
26. Ibn Ḥajar al-'Asqalāni, *al-Durar al-Kāmina fī A'yān al-Mi'a al-Thāmina* (Haydarabad, 1350), 4:339.

of a number of Ṭūsī's minor works, presumably from this time, still exist in his hand.[27]

His next most important teacher was Kātibī, whose works he studied with him. The glosses he wrote on Kātibī's *Ḥikmat al-'Ayn*[28] probably date from this time. Kātibī thought well enough of him to take him as a teaching assistant when he was appointed professor at a new school at Juwayn in Afghanistan.[29] Quṭb al-Dīn also studied astronomy and geometry with 'Urḍī, whom he later referred to as "the master" (*al-shaykh al-imām*) in his own astronomical works.[30]

In 664 or 665/1266 or 1267, he received the *khirqa* of discipleship (*irāda*) from Muḥyī al-Dīn Aḥmad b. 'Alī b. Abī al-Ma'ālī, a disciple once removed of Najm al-Dīn Kubrā, the founder of a great family of Ṣūfī orders.[31]

In the period 665/1267 to 667/1269 Quṭb al-Dīn accompanied Ṭūsī on a long book-buying trip in Khurāsān and Quhistān and probably went on alone to Baghdad, where he may have stayed in the Niẓāmīyah.[32] Mīnawī, however, says that he stayed in Khurāsān to teach with Kātibī, as was mentioned above, then spent two or three years studying *fiqh* with Shaykh 'Alā' al-Dīn Tā'ūsī in Qazwīn. To Ḍiyā' al-Dīn Ṭūsī, who ran into him there, he explained that although his knowledge had grown greatly since he had left Shīrāz and medical practice, he was nonetheless still anxious to learn the religious sciences,

27. Ibn al-Fuwaṭī, *Talkhīṣ,* vol. 4, bk. 4:717; Riḍawī, 207–8, 221; Mīr, 38–40.
28. Ibn al-Fuwaṭī, *Talkhīṣ,* vol. 4, bk. 4:716–17. See App. C, no. 3, below.
29. Ibn al-Fuwaṭī, in Sallāmī, 222.
30. Ibn al-Fuwaṭī, *Talkhīṣ,* vol. 4, bk. 4:717; George Saliba, "The Original Source of Quṭb al-Dīn al-Shīrāzī's Planetary Model," *Journal for the History of Arabic Science* 3 (1979):5.
31. *Crown,* "khātima," quṭb 4, pt. 2, chap. 2. I have found no other mention of this man.
32. Sallāmī, 220; *Offering,* vol. 1, bk. 1:d.

especially *fiqh*. During his stay in Baghdad, he was greatly honored by Shams al-Dīn Juwaynī, the Ṣāḥib-Dīwān.[33] (It was not Quṭb al-Dīn but rather his source, Sa'īd Farghānī, who studied in Baghdad with the Ṣūfī Muḥammad b. Sukrān al-Baghdādī.[34])

The date and circumstances of Quṭb al-Dīn's final departure from Marāgha are not clear. He left in his mid-thirties, sometime between 667/1268 and 672/1274. There are reports he was estranged in the end from Ṭūsī (although on the occasions he mentioned Ṭūsī in his own works, it was always in terms of highest praise).[35] Most such accounts center on Ṭūsī's not having mentioned his name in the introduction to the *Īl-Khānid Astronomical Tables* eventually produced by the observatory team. One report, for example, relates that the tables, still incomplete at Hülegü's death, were barely finished as Ṭūsī himself was dying. His powers failing toward the end, he made a number of mistakes in the tables, so he provided in his will that Aṣīl al-Dīn, his son and successor at Marāgha, should collaborate with Quṭb al-Dīn in their correction. Quṭb al-Dīn, offended at not having received proper credit in the book, refused to do so. As a result, the tables remained uncorrected and were little used.[36]

Against this some argue that only Ṭūsī's four chief collaborators, all of them Quṭb al-Dīn's teachers and a generation senior to him, were thus mentioned and that Quṭb al-Dīn, still only a student, would not have expected to receive credit re-

33. Mīnawī, 169, 178. I do not know Mīnawī's source for Quṭb al-Dīn's stay in Qazwīn or his early relations with Juwaynī. On Ṭā'ūsī, a Ṣūfī, see Brockelmann, S1:806. Ḍiyā' al-Dīn Ṭūsī was probably Naṣīr al-Dīn's grandson. See Riḍavī, 40, 42.
34. *Crown*, "khātima," quṭb 4, pt. 2, chap. 2.
35. For example, "Thus argued the most learned of [the moderns] in his *Commentary on the 'Hints'*." *Commentary*, 42; *Offering*, vol. 1, bk. 1:d.
36. Riḍawī, 32. Riḍawī, unfortunately, does not give a source for this story except to say that it is "famous."

gardless of the work he had done.[37] There are other accounts that attribute the estrangement to his having embarrassed Ṭūsī in front of the Īl-Khān.[38]

By 673/1274 Quṭb al-Dīn had found his way to Konya. There he studied *ḥadīth* and the rational, religious, and mystical sciences with Ṣadr al-Dīn Qūnawī.[39] Part of the manuscript of Ibn al-Athīr's *Jāmiʿ al-Uṣūl,*[40] a popular collection of *ḥadīth,* which he wrote out and read to Qūnawī for correction, still survives in Istanbul.[41]

There is also an account of a meeting with the poet Jalāl al-Dīn Rūmī at this time. When Quṭb al-Dīn came into Rūmī's presence, the old poet ignored him for a long time and then

37. Riḍawī, 140–41.
38. Sallāmī, 220; Khwāndamīr in Riḍawī, 71, and Mīr, 53–54. If Khwāndamīr's anecdote is authentic (which Riḍavī doubts), then the Īl-Khān in question would certainly have been Abaqa, as Sallāmī's account implies—not Hülegü. Although Quṭb al-Dīn was a Sunnī (see his *Crown,* vol. 1, bk. 1:150), I have found no evidence that he resented Ṭūsī's Shīʿism.

    Later Shīʿite authorities debated whether he was to be considered a reliable authority in the transmission of Shīʿite ḥadīth. They concluded that although his testimony should be given weight, it would be irregular to rely on his unsupported word. See Khwānsārī, 509. In an anecdote widely reported in Shīʿite sources, he gives an answer of studied ambiguity when asked whether Abū Bakr or ʿAlī was the best man after the Prophet. See Mīr, 29.
39. *Crown,* "khātima," quṭb 4, pt. 2, chap. 2; Ibn Ḥajar, 1:340; Abd al-Raḥmān Jāmī, *Nafaḥāt al-Uns min Ḥaḍarāt al-Quds,* ed. Mahdī Tawḥīdīpūr ([Tehran]: Saʿdī, 1336), 555–56.
40. Brockelmann, G1:357, S1:608.
41. The second volume, dated 673/1274. According to Quṭb al-Dīn's colophon, Qūnawī had read the book to its author and received a license to teach it. (See Mīr, 39, citing Ritter, *Oriens* 6 (1953):71–77.) According to Sallāmī, however (219) Qūnawī had it via a certain Sharaf al-Dīn Yaʿqūb b. Muḥammad al-Hadhbānī. (The spelling of the last name is uncertain.) Sallāmī also reports that Quṭb al-Dīn transmitted Baghawī's *Sharḥ al-Sunna* (Brockelmann, G1:364, S1:622) on the authority of Muḥyī al-Dīn ʿAlī al-Farawī.

told a story. The scholar Ṣadr-i Jahān of Bukhara used to pass a beggar on the street each day but never gave him anything. One day after this happened, the beggar said to his friends, "Tomorrow I will lie down, and you cover me with my cloak and act as though I were dead." They did so, and when Ṣadr-i Jahān came by, he gave some money. The beggar abruptly sat up. Ṣadr-i Jahān said, "If you hadn't been dead, I wouldn't have given you anything." From this Quṭb al-Dīn understood that until he died to his self, Rūmī could give him nothing. He was silent and left. Regardless of the truth of this anecdote, there would not have been much sympathy between the proud and intellectual young scientist and the passionate old mystic.[42]

About this time Quṭb al-Dīn was appointed chief judge of Malatya and Sivas in Anatolia, either by the vizier Shams al-Dīn Juwaynī, who was well known as a patron of scholars—Ṭūsī, among others—or by Mu'īn al-Dīn Parwānah, the Saljūq governor of Anatolia whom Quṭb al-Dīn came to know in Konya.[43] In any event, the actual work of the position was done by his deputies,[44] so he spent his time teaching and writing. For some years he lived in Sivas, although this may have been interrupted by visits to the court in Tabrīz.[45] His first major

42. Muḥyī al-Dīn Ibn Abī al-Wafā', *al-Jawāhir al-Muḍī'a fī Ṭabaqāt al-Ḥanafīya* (Hyderabad: Niẓāmīyah, 1332), 2:124. Aflākī, Rūmī's biographer, gives a version in which Quṭb al-Dīn is converted and becomes a follower of Rūmī. See Mīr, 21.
43. Ibn al-Fuwaṭī, *Talkhīṣ*, vol. 4, bk. 4:717; Ibn al-Fuwaṭī, in Sallāmī, 222. Saljūq Anatolia had been a Mongol province for about thirty years. Juwaynī had recently turned his attention to strengthening the Mongol position in Anatolia. Juwaynī's wealth, prestige, and pro-Muslim policies eventually irritated the Mongols. He gradually fell from favor and was executed in 683/1284. See *EI2*, s.v. "Djuwaynī, Shams al-Dīn."
44. Jamāl al-Dīn Yūsuf Ibn Taghribirdī, *al-Nujūm al-Zāhira fī Mulūk Miṣr wa' l-Qāhira* (Cairo, n.d.), 9:213.
45. Ibn al-Fuwaṭī in Sallāmī, 222. It seems, for example, from this account that he was at court when Abaqa died in 680/1282.

work, a large book on astronomy called *The Highest Attainment in the Knowledge of the Spheres,* was completed in Sha'bān 680/November–December 1281 in Sivas and was dedicated to Shams al-Dīn Juwaynī.[46] This book is a classic synthesis of the astronomical theories of the Marāgha school. Another work dedicated to Juwaynī, a commentary on the abridged version of a famous text by Ibn al-Ḥājib on Mālikī law, must also have been written in this period.[47] A second, slightly shorter, astronomical work called *The King's Offering* was completed four years later in Sivas in Jumādā I 684/July–August 1285.[48] Two minor works are known to date from this period, a Persian translation of Ṭūsī's recension of Euclid's *Elements* completed in Sha'bān 681/November–December 1282[49] and a short note on the treatment of heretics and infidels, written in Konya in Rabī' II 685/May–June 1286.[50] This latter might have had something to do with his work as judge.

After their defeat at 'Ayn-Jālūṭ in 658/1260, the Mongols maintained uneasy relations with the Mamlūk sultanate in Egypt and Syria. However, when Aḥmad Tekūdar became Īl-Khān in the spring of 681/1282, Shams al-Dīn Juwaynī urged

46. Assuming the statement that it was finished in Shīrāz was based on a misreading of *Sivas.* Max Krause, "Stambuler Handschriften islamischer Mathematiker," *Quellen und Studien zur Geschichte der Mathematik, Astronomie, und Physik,* Abt. B, Studien 3 (1936):507; R. A. Dozy et al., *Catalogus codicum orientalium bibliothecae Academiae Lugdano-Batavae* (Leyden: 1851–90), 3:114–15. See App. C, no. 14, below.
47. Mīnawī, 195. See App. C, no. 41, below.
48. Krause, 507. See App. C, no. 15, below.
49. Aḥmad Munzawī, *Fihrist-i Nuskha-hā-i Khaṭṭī-i Fārsī* (Tehran: Mu'assasa-i Farhangī-i Manṭiqa'ī, 1348/1969–1353/1974) 1:147. See App. C, no. 25, below.
50. Wladimir Ivanow, et al., *Catalogue of the Arabic Manuscripts in the Collection of the Royal Asiatic Society of Bengal, 1st Supplement* (Calcutta: Royal Asiatic Society of Bengal 1939–49), 87. See App. C, no. 46, below.

him to make peace with the Mamlūks. Against the advice of the council of princes, he agreed; and Quṭb al-Dīn, who happened to be at court, was ordered to draft a letter to Sayf al-Dīn Qalāwūn, the ruler of Egypt, announcing Tekūdar's conversion to Islam and offering to take various measures to encourage Islam and establish friendly relations with Egypt. Quṭb al-Dīn—along with Kamāl al-Dīn Rāfi'ī, the Shaykh al-Islām, and Bahā' al-Dīn Pahlawān, the Atabek—set out at the head of an embassy in late summer, but the group was coolly received and left without achieving anything substantial. A later delegation, in fact, was thrown in prison where the ambassador died. The other Mongol princes resented Tekūdar's conversion and his overtures to Egypt. He was killed and replaced by Arghūn two years later. The final conversion of the Īl-Khāns did not take place until the reign of Maḥmūd Ghāzān (695/1295 to 703/1304).[51]

Quṭb al-Dīn took advantage of the trip to lecture in Damascus on Zamakhsharī's Qur'ān commentary and Avicenna's *Canon of Medicine* and *Book of Healing*.[52] More important, he was able to visit several libraries in Egypt where he found three complete commentaries on the "General Principles" of the *Canon* along with glosses and other material. Believing that he had the most comprehensive collection of material on Avicenna's "General Principles" ever assembled and that the new material solved the remaining difficulties in Avicenna's work, he now decided to write his own detailed commentary. He returned

51. For a general account of the episode, see J. A. Boyle, "Dynastic and Political History of the Īl-Khāns," *Cambridge History of Iran,* vol. 5, *The Saljūq and Mongol Periods* (Cambridge, Mass.: Cambridge University Press, 1968), 365. For Quṭb al-Dīn's role, see Abū al-Fidā, *Annales Muslemici,* ed. Jacobi Reiskii (Copenhagen, 1794), 5:62; Ibn al-Fuwaṭī in Sallāmī, 222–23.

52. Ibn Ḥajar, 4:340.

to Anatolia and published his commentary the following year 682/1283–84. He says the work met with immediate acclaim.[53]

QUṬB AL-DĪN'S HABITS AND CHARACTER

Quṭb al-Dīn had a sharp and quick mind and uncommon energy. As a teenager he undertook serious study of the theoretical parts of Avicenna's *Canon,* something probably not often done by ordinary physicians. Ibn al-Fuwaṭī, Quṭb al-Dīn's friend for more than fifty years, reported his intense application to his work as a student.[54] As a mature scholar, he said, Quṭb al-Dīn was continually thinking and writing, and people flocked to his lectures.[55] It was said that "his rough draft was a fair copy"—that his first draft was never in need of revision.[56] A modern reader of one of his astronomical works does, in fact, complain that he tends to work out problems in his books as he goes along—trying out one approach then abandoning it in favor of another and then another.[57] The books I have read are well organized and reasonably clear, despite long sentences and a tendency to discuss the obvious at length.

With his quick mind, as often happens, went both a brilliance and charm in company and an arrogant and sarcastic treatment of people who crossed him. On the one hand, he played chess brilliantly and often. He played the violin well. He liked wine, some said. He was an amateur magician (sleight of hand, not necromancy). He was full of stories, jokes, and bits of poetry in Arabic and Persian, which he interspersed in his lectures. He spoke to kings and ministers as equals but gave large parts of

53. *Offering,* 1:1:d–dh.
54. Ibn al-Fuwaṭī, *Talkhīṣ,* vol. 4, bk. 4:716–17.
55. Ibid. and in Sallāmī, 221.
56. Ibn Ḥajar, 4:340.
57. E. S. Kennedy, "Late Medieval Planetary Theory," *Isis* 57 (1966):371.

his income to his students, the poor, and orphans.[58] One of his contemporaries reported that whenever he was with a king, vizier, or judge, he would pull a sheaf of twenty or so sheets of paper from his pocket. These contained notes on the needs of worthy unfortunates, which he would present one by one. When his host showed signs of weariness, he would remark, "For what else has God created us and of what other use are rank and wealth save to fill the needs of people?"[59]

On the other hand, his wit was sharp and often malicious and made him enemies. "He sat with the scorners," one source says.[60] For example, the famous scholar and vizier Rashīd al-Dīn Faḍl Allāh, who came from a Jewish family, was working on a commentary on the Qur'ān. On hearing this, Quṭb al-Dīn remarked, "Then I shall write a commentary on the Torah," which he proceeded to do. (Although no such work exists as far as I know, Quṭb al-Dīn did have a good knowledge of the Bible.) When told that Rashīd al-Dīn had written a treatise on the verse "No knowledge have we save what Thou hast taught us," Quṭb al-Dīn remarked, "He should have stopped at the first half of the verse."[61] In 706/1306–7, Quṭb al-Dīn was invited to the dedication of a mosque Rashīd al-Dīn had built. When asked his opinion of the beautiful and expensive prayer niche, he said, "It is very fine except that it is skewed to the west of the prayer direction"—implying that it faced Jerusalem, not Mecca. Not surprisingly, he fell from official favor when Rashīd al-Dīn became vizier.[62]

58. Ibn Ḥajar, 4:340; Ibn al-Fuwaṭī, *Talkhīṣ,* vol. 4, bk. 4:717; Jamāl al-Dīn 'Abd al-Raḥman al-Asnawī, *Ṭabaqāt al-Shāfi'īyah,* ed. 'Abd Allāh al-Jubūrī (Baghdad, 1391), 2:120.
59. Mīnawī, 177–78.
60. Al-Asnawī, 2:120.
61. Ibn al-Fuwaṭī, in Sallāmī, 221.
62. Mīnawī, 174–75. See p. 22 below. Rashīd al-Dīn Faḍl Allāh (c. 645/1247 to 718/1318) was born in a Jewish family of Hamadān but converted to

He was apparently not altogether scrupulous. When he was a student before his love of books was matched by an income to buy them, he would copy books surreptitiously or borrow and not return them. When he left Qazwīn, he pocketed a book on *fiqh* that he particularly coveted belonging to his teacher 'Alā' al-Dīn Ṭā'ūsī. Some time later when Ṭā'ūsī happened to mention that he had mislaid the book, he was told that Quṭb al-Dīn must have stolen it. He indignantly denied that such a thing was possible. However, Muhadhdhib al-Dīn Shīrāzī, one of Quṭb al-Dīn's students, reports that Quṭb al-Dīn taught from that very copy in Sivas and remarked that he had stolen it from his teacher when he was a poor student. Later—out of guilt, we may suppose—Quṭb al-Dīn gave away many books, including a valuable collection of medical texts that he donated to a new hospital in Khwārizm.[63]

A famous and probably apocryphal story tells that when Quṭb al-Dīn traveled, he would sometimes let out that he was an infidel who wanted to become a Muslim. This would always result in lavish gifts and hospitality. One day his relative Sa'dī the poet came across an excited crowd in a village he was passing through. A villager explained to him that there was an infidel becoming a Muslim. Sa'dī pushed through the crowd, found Quṭb al-Dīn, and said to him in a Shīrāzī dialect that the

---

Islam. He was a physician by training. A letter survives that he wrote to Quṭb al-Dīn from Multan in India, where he had gone to do a diplomatic errand and to gather rare drugs. *Makātīb-i Rashīdī,* ed. Muḥammad Shafī' (Lahore: Punjab Educational Press, 1364/1945), 159–68. In another letter, written while he was vizier to a son who was governor of Baghdad, he listed Quṭb al-Dīn first among the scholars of the time and ordered that certain costly gifts be given to him. In two reviews written in 706/1306–7, Quṭb al-Dīn praised Rashīd al-Dīn's works. A poem exists by Humām al-Dīn Tabrīzī, a friend of both men, appealing for an end to the breach between them. See Mīr, 46–50.

63. Mīnawī, 178–79.

villagers could not understand, "So, Quṭb al-Dīn, you never were a Muslim!"[64] Perhaps this was the side of his character that Rūmī saw.

Nevertheless, Quṭb al-Dīn had a streak of religious seriousness. All his life he wore Ṣūfī garb, even at court. When he was working on a book, he would pray and fast during the day and write at night. Religion seems to have become more important for him in the last years of his life when he spent time teaching the Qur'ān and regularly taking part in congregational prayer. He was said to have "followed the religion of old women." He once remarked, "Would that I had lived in the time of the Prophet, even if I were blind and deaf, so that His glance might have fallen upon me." He took great pride in the *ḥadīth* he transmitted on the authority of Qūnawī.[65] In mysticism he made no claim to special attainments.

Almost nothing is known of his family life. One report might indicate that he had children when he was chief judge in Sivas and Malatya.[66] On the other hand one of his later books contains a passionate—and rather un-Islamic—defense of celibacy.[67] He had no family to arrange his funeral.[68]

THE LAST YEARS

Sometime around 690/1290 Quṭb al-Dīn settled in the Īl-Khānid capital Tabrīz[69] and eventually ceased to serve in government

64. Khwānsārī, 508–9. See n. 14.
65. Ibn Ḥajar, 1:340; Sallāmī, 224; Tāj al-Dīn al-Subkī, *Ṭabaqāt al-Shāfi'īya al-Kubrā*, ed. Aḥmad b. 'Abd al-Karīm al-Qādirī al-Ḥasanī (Cairo: Maṭba'at al-Ḥasaynīya al-Miṣrīya, n.d.), 248.
66. Sallāmī, 220–21: "*Jā'a bi al-awlād fī al-Rūm.*"
67. *Crown*, "khātima," quṭb 4, pt. 2, chap. 7.
68. See p. 24 below.
69. Ibn al-Fuwaṭī, *Talkhīṣ*, vol. 4, bk. 4:717. Mīr's assumption that Quṭb

positions, though he kept his ties with the Īl-Khāns.[70] In the summer of 689/1290 he had an interview with the Īl-Khān Arghūn in which he explained a map of the coast of Anatolia.[71] In 694/1294–95 he published a second edition of his commentary on Avicenna's *Canon.*[72] In Rajab of the same year (May–June 1295), he completed his *Commentary on "The Philosophy of Illumination,"* which he dedicated to Jamāl al-Dīn Dastjirdānī, who was twice grand vizier between 694/1295 and his final fall and execution in October of 696/1296.[73]

In 697/1298 Rashīd al-Dīn was appointed vizier. Although Quṭb al-Dīn was still in Tabrīz in 704/1304–5 when he published *The Book of "I Tried So Don't Blame Me,"* a statement of his distinctive views on astronomy,[74] he probably left soon after. Apparently Rashīd al-Dīn, once his position with the Īl-Khān Ghāzān was secure, went to him to complain that Quṭb al-Dīn, though a religious scholar and dervish, was nonetheless drawing an annual stipend of 30,000 dirhams. Ghāzān, something of a miser, happily reduced it to 12,000.[75] In any case by Rajab 705/January 1306 Quṭb al-Dīn seems to have been in the independent Isḥāqid principality of the Amīr Dubāj in western Gīlān, probably having arrived there the previous year. To this prince he dedicated his philosophical encyclopedia, *The Pearly*

al-Dīn settled in Tabrīz immediately after returning from Egypt is contradicted by various bits of information placing him in Anatolia as late as 689/1290. There is actually no definite evidence placing him in Tabrīz before 701/1302, but it seems likely he settled there in the early 690s/1290s.

70. Subkī, 248.
71. Boyle, 5:371.
72. Mīr, 97. Yūsuf I'tiṣāmī et al., *Fihrist-i Kitābkhāna-i Majlis-i Shūrā-i Millī dar Tihrān* (Tehran: 1305/1927 to 1353/1973), 2:289.
73. *Commentary,* 8–9; *Crown,* vol. 1, bk. 1:h.
74. Krause, 508. See App. C, no. 17, below.
75. Mīnawī, 175.

Crown for Dubāj's Brow.[76] Since the Mongols suppressed Dubāj's principality later that year, Quṭb al-Dīn was probably soon back in Tabrīz.

Between 700/1300 and 710/1311, he wrote several other works. In 701/1302 he published the first commentary on the rhetoric of a well-known text on language, Sakkākī's *Key to the Sciences.*[77] While in Gīlān he also published a commentary on an abridged edition by Jalāl al-Dīn Qazwīnī of the same work. This second commentary was intended to deal with certain problems raised but not solved by Qazwīnī's abridgement and commentary.[78] It was probably at this time that he wrote, most likely as a pious exercise, a forty-volume commentary on the Qur'ān.[79] He also wrote a work on difficult passages in the Qur'ān and glosses on Zamakhsharī's commentary. He was working on the latter around 700/1300.[80]

Although he had left government employment, his classes were still a meeting place for students and the learned. He spent less of his time teaching the rational sciences and more on such occupations as teaching the Qur'ān. In Ramaḍān he was in the habit of going to the mosque to recite his ḥadīth.[81]

He died ten weeks after completing a third edition of his commentary on Avicenna's *Canon.* The date was given variously as 14, 16, 17, or 24 Ramaḍān 710, equivalent to 4, 6, 7, or 14 February 1311, with Sunday, 7 February being the most likely.[82] Because the 36,000 dirhams he was to be paid for

76. *Crown,* 1:1:'ch–'kh, 1:1:9 ff.
77. *The Key to the Key.* See App. C, no. 43, below.
78. *Sharḥ Talkhīṣ al-Miftāḥ.* See App. C, no. 44, below.
79. See App. C, no. 40, below.
80. *The Key to the Key* mentions that it was not finished. Mīr, 107–8. See App. C, nos. 38–39, below.
81. Sallāmī, 224; Ibn Ḥajar, 4:340.
82. Khwāndamīr, 3:197; Ibn al-Fuwaṭī in Sallāmī, 227; Ibn Ḥajar, 4:340; Ḥamd Allāh Mustawfī, *Tārīkh-i Guzīda,* ed. 'Abd al-Ḥusayn Nawā'ī (Teh-

the commentary had not reached him, he was penniless at his death, having given away all he had left during his last illness. The expenses of his burial had to be met by Khwāja 'Izz al-Dīn Ṭībī—a student of his and the son of one of the richest men in Persia—who spent 7,200 dirhams on a lavish funeral.[83] He was buried in the prestigious cemetery of Charandāb, close to the grave of his fellow student Bayḍāwī.[84]

STUDENTS AND INFLUENCE

Quṭb al-Dīn is said to have had many students, beginning from his time in Sivas. Two, Quṭb al-Dīn al-Taḥtānī and Kamāl al-Dīn al-Fārisī, were of major importance, in philosophy and optics, respectively. In at least four cases, Quṭb al-Dīn was the

---

ran, 1336), 701; Jalāl al-Dīn Suyūṭī, *Bughyat al-Wu'āt fī Ṭabaqāt al-Lughawīyīn wa'l-Nuḥāt,* ed. Muḥammad Abū al-Faḍl Ibrāhīm (Cairo: Maṭba 'at al-Bābī al-Ḥalabī, 1384/1965), 282; Tāshküprüzāda, *Miftāḥ al-Sa'āda* (Hyderabad, 1328), 164. The British Museum manuscript of *The Key to the Sciences* has a note giving the date of his death as 14 Ramaḍān. Mīr, 17, cites a verse giving the date of Sunday, 17 Ramaḍān/7 February, a date confirmed by Abū al-Fidā and Mustawfī. Since the day of the week is accurate, there is a good possibility that the verse is contemporary. Quṭb al-Dīn's old friend Ibn al-Fuwaṭī gives 16 Ramaḍān, which could well be the same day, given the vagaries of lunar dating, particularly in Ramaḍān.

83. Mīr, 14–17. See App. C, no. 13, below. Sa'd al-Dīn Sāwujī, the vizier to whom the book was dedicated, paid the sum in spite of being under a 60 million dirham tax assessment. He was executed the following year at the Īl-Khān's orders. The money was eventually used to pay Quṭb al-Dīn's debts, and the remainder was distributed among his students and dependents. Mīnawī, 182–83.

84. Bayḍawī's grave was destroyed by the Ṣafavids in the sixteenth century, so I assume Quṭb al-Din's was destroyed at that time as well. *Encyclopedia Iranica,* 1985 ed., s. v. "Bayḍawī." Incidentally, the theory advanced in this article—that Quṭb al-Dīn may have died in 716/1316—is based on a single source and is clearly untenable.

catalyst for his students' undertaking major research projects. Philosophically, the most important was Taḥtānī's *The Book of Judgments,* which evaluated the arguments advanced by Rāzī and Ṭūsī in their commentaries on Avicenna's *Hints.* He was also responsible for bringing Ibn al-Haytham's *Optics* to Fārisī's attention.[85]

Quṭb al-Dīn was unquestionably the only major figure among Ṭūsī's students at Marāgha and was generally recognized as the outstanding authority on the rational sciences in his generation. Although his astronomical works are now known to be more dependent on earlier members of the Marāgha school than was thought a few years ago,[86] they were well regarded and widely used for several centuries in Turkey, Iran, and India. *The Highest Attainment* and *The King's Offering* each exist in more than thirty manuscripts. The commentary on Avicenna's *Canon of Medicine* was also well known and widely copied. His writings on religion were less important, only the commentary on Sakkākī's *Key* being widely used. He was not considered a major authority on religious subjects.

The Commentary on "The Philosophy of Illumination" was Quṭb al-Dīn's most popular philosophical work. It supplanted Shahrazūrī's earlier commentary and, with Mullā Ṣadrā's glosses, remains the vehicle through which *The Philosophy of Illumination* is studied in Iran up to today. *The Pearly Crown,* although widely circulated, never attained the same importance, at least partly because philosophy was normally studied in Arabic. Frequently, individual books were copied separately, especially those on mathematics. Still, as philosophy it was important enough for Ṣadrā to cite it several times in his *Four*

85. See App. B below for details on Quṭb al-Dīn's students.

86. E. S. Kennedy, "Late Medieval Planetary Theory," *Isis* 57 (1966): 366, 371–77; Saliba, "Original Source," 3–6; Saliba, "The First Non-Ptolemaic Astronomy at the Maraghah School," 571–72. See pp. 16, 22.

Journeys. With the rise of Persian linguistic nationalism in the twentieth century, it has regained some of its earlier fame through being mentioned in textbooks of Persian literature. Iranian college students are liable to cite it (although not to read it) as an example of an outstanding work of Iranian philosophy. Of Quṭb al-Dīn's minor philosophical works, only his glosses on Kātibī's *Ḥikmat al-'Ayn* were widely circulated, and these only because they happened to be included in what became the standard commentary on the work.

Later generations knew Quṭb al-Dīn as *'Allāma*, a title meaning "supremely learned" given to a few scholars in the later centuries of Islam. In later works he was often referred to simply by this title or as *'Allāma-i Shīrāzī*, *'Allāma-i Quṭb*, or *Mullā Quṭb*. His friends and students heaped praise on him in his old age and after his death. Generally, this reputation endured.[87] His lasting philosophical importance is discussed in the conclusion of this work.

87. He also became a stock figure in jokes, a sort of intellectual Mullā Naṣr al-Dīn, appearing in such works as 'Ubayd-i Zāqānī's *Dilgushā* and Fakhr al-Dīn 'Alī Ṣafī's *Laṭā'if al-Ṭawā'if*. One story in the latter (cited in Mīr, 35–36) tells that Quṭb al-Dīn was once the honored guest at a royal banquet. The king arranged for all the penises of the slaughtered rams to be cooked separately and served to Quṭb al-Dīn in a covered dish. When Quṭb al-Dīn saw what it was, he instantly said to the servant, "Take it away! Why have you brought me the dish prepared for the harem?"

·TWO·

Suhrawardī's Science of Lights

STRUCTURE AND METHOD OF SUHRAWARDĪ'S *THE PHILOSOPHY OF ILLUMINATION*

The Commentary on *The Philosophy of Illumination*

Although it must have been the product of earlier study and work, Quṭb al-Dīn finished his *Commentary on "The Philosophy of Illumination"* in Rajab 694/May–June 1295, when he was fifty-eight years old,[1] a few years before his other main philosophical work, *The Pearly Crown*. Quṭb al-Dīn intended to be a faithful commentator, clarifying the obscurities and lacunae of Suhrawardī's exposition from the master's other works and their commentaries, paying special attention to producing a sound text.[2] In general, that is what he does. He gives variant readings, glosses on the text, and expositions of topics mentioned briefly or not at all. Only occasionally does he intrude with criticisms of arguments he considers unsound. To judge from his introduction, he must have agreed with much of Suhrawardī's system. He does write at length on topics of special interest to him, most notably on the World of Image.[3]

1. According to the colophon of the Bursa MS. See Minawī, 191.
2. *Commentary,* 7.
3. Many of these are discussed in ch. 4 below.

Quṭb al-Dīn draws heavily on the earlier commentary of Shahrazūrī, as well as the latter's philosophical encyclopedia, *The Divine Tree* (*al-Shajara al-Ilāhīya*), a debt that he does not acknowledge.

Suhrawardī's System

The Philosophy of Illumination (*Ḥikmat al-Ishrāq*) is a work of 250 pages, written in 582/1186 during Suhrawardī's stay in Aleppo. He indicates that it is an esoteric book, written for his disciples and not really intended for others. It was based in part on intuition or mystical insight; its full comprehension was reserved for those who have achieved a certain level of spiritual comprehension. He refers to the method of this book as "Illuminationist" (*ishrāqī*) and contrasts it with the "Peripatetic" (*mashā'ī*) method that normally was employed by Islamic philosophers and that he himself uses in his other works.

The book itself consists of an introduction explaining the circumstances of the composition of the work and its two main parts—"On the rules of thought" (logic) and "On the divine lights" (physics, first philosophy, and metaphysics).

The first thirty pages of the logic consist of a simple introduction to logic. Although this contains some innovations, the only one of importance here is Suhrawardī's attack on the Aristotelean doctrine of real definition. The remaining sixty pages of the logic are labeled as a discussion of fallacies but are, in fact, an attack on a number of Peripatetic—i.e., Avicennan—views with which Suhrawardī disagreed. These include Avicennan views on existence and accidents, matter and form, substance, unity and multiplicity, definition, the Platonic forms, and sensation. As is shown below, each was an important area of disagreement between Suhrawardī and his predecessors.

The second part of the logic, "On the divine lights," contains Suhrawardī's positive doctrine and is the part of his work that has attracted the most scholarly attention. He asserts that reality is divided into four things—substantial and accidental light and darkness. Of these, substantial light, which I translate as *immaterial light* (*nūr mujarrad*), is prior to the others. The highest reality is the Light of Lights, God. From this One Light, another light emanates. From these lights emanate both other lights and darkness—both accidental darkness in lights and substantial darkness—the "dark barriers" or bodies. These lights differ in intensity and in accidents. Through very complex interactions among the lights on different levels there emanate both a vertical order of lights—the intellects corresponding to the spheres of the planets—and a horizontal order—lights of equal intensity differing by their accidents. This horizontal order of lights is what Plato refers to as the *Forms* and what the ancient Persians call *angels*. It is through their solicitude that the earthly kinds and species are maintained.

Within the framework of this metaphysics of light, Suhrawardī worked out solutions to classic problems of Islamic philosophy—the nature of reality, the composition of material bodies, the human soul and its immortality, the basis of scientific knowledge, and the nature of prophecy.

Modern Scholarship on *The Philosophy of Illumination*

Suhrawardī thus uses an exotic vocabulary of light to set apart his *Philosophy of Illumination* from all other works of Islamic philosophy. While Islamic philosophers agreed that the book marked a major departure in philosophy, neither Suhrawardī's followers nor his commentators nor even he himself in other works chose to use this terminology, making it difficult to trace his influence. We may infer Hegel's influence wherever we find his terms, for example; but this is not usually possible with Suhrawardī.

Nor is it easy to assess Suhrawardī's aim. Henry Corbin, the most eminent Western student of Suhrawardī, emphasized mystical and esoteric elements. He and his followers took the symbolism of *The Philosophy of Illumination* as the inner core of Suhrawardī's thought. In this interpretation his more conventional works form a critical propaedeutic—useful, perhaps, but ultimately unimportant. Corbin, for example, translates the title of *The Philosophy of Illumination* (*Ḥikmat al-Ishrāq*) as *Le Livre de la théosophie orientale,*[4] and he writes mainly of the symbolism of the Orient, the dawn, and the Zoroastrian angels.[5] He pays little attention to the hard philosophical content of Suhrawardī's thought or to the relation between *The Philosophy of Illumination* and the contemporary Peripatetic works. In such an interpretation Quṭb al-Dīn's commentary is of little value since it focuses on conventional exoteric aspects of *The Philosophy of Illumination.*

Such scholars as Fazlur Rahman and Toshihiko Izutsu, who are primarily interested in later Islamic philosophy, have dealt with Suhrawardī as he was cited and criticized by their sources. Following the example of the later Iranian philosophers, they have treated him as a part of the general tradition of Avicenna and paid little attention to the symbolic aspects of *The Philosophy of Illumination.* They are, in fact, more likely to cite the Peripatetic works or the first book of *The Philosophy of Illumination,* where Suhrawardī's views vis-à-vis the Peripatetics are more clearly expressed. These scholars know Suhrawardī as the great exponent of the primacy of quiddity. Since they are

4. Corbin, *En Islam iranien,* 2:19–20; "Prolègomène," in Suhrawardī, *Œuvres,* 2:5 ff. His translation renders the title *Le livre de la sagesse orientale.*

5. Corbin, *En Islam iranien,* 2:40 ff.; "Prolègomène," 2:31–55.

interested in later thinkers, they have not systematically analyzed Suhrawardī's thought or works.[6]

Suhrawardī and Quṭb al-Dīn on *The Philosophy of Illumination*

In the introduction to the *The Philosophy of Illumination* Suhrȧwardī explains the structure of the work, its place among his writings as a whole, and the nature of his project. He also wrote several books "in the mode of the Peripatetics in which I summarized their principles," some before and some during the composition of *The Philosophy of Illumination.* This book, however, differs from the Peripatetic (i.e., Avicennan) works in the following ways: (1) it contains a "science of lights" and matters dependent on it; (2) it uses a different and better method, based on intuition as well as rational thought.[7]

Nevertheless, Suhrawardī insists that study of the Peripatetic works is essential as preparation for reading *The Philosophy of Illumination.*[8] In the introduction to his commentary, Quṭb al-Dīn praises the book: "It is the Shaykh's philosophy [*ḥikmat*] and belief [*i'tiqād*]." It contains the "most useful and worthy part of speculative philosophy and the most exalted part of intuitive [*dhawqīyah*] philosophy." It summarizes "what he had come to know with certainty." It contains "the difficult problems."[9] Like Suhrawardī he points out the connection of Illu-

6. Toshihiko Izutsu, *The Concept and Reality of Existence* (Tokyo: Keio Institute of Cultural and Linguistic Studies, 1971), 61, 109–12; Fazlur Rahman, *The Philosophy of Mullā Ṣadrā* (Albany: State University of New York Press, 1975), 10–11, 27, 99–101. A notable study of Suhrawardī's logic and epistemology is Hossein Ziai, *Knowledge and Illumination: A study of Suhrawardī's Ḥikmat al-Ishrāq* (Brown University Judaic Studies Series 97) (Atlanta: Scholars Press, 1990).
7. *Illumination,* 10/15–16.
8. *Œuvres,* 1:194.
9. *Commentary,* 3.

minationist philosophy with the "ancient" philosophers of Greece and Persia.[10]

Quṭb al-Dīn assumes the continuity of the teachings of *The Philosophy of Illumination* with those of the master's other works: these are, in fact, one of his commentary's sources. Where Suhrawardī writes of a "science of lights," Quṭb al-Dīn writes of "difficult problems," and so forth—implying that the work was systematically related to the usual problems of Islamic philosophy.

The Structure of Sciences according to Classical Logic

However else we may translate *ḥikmat al-ishrāq,* it also means "the Science of Lights." Suhrawardī uses precisely that term (*'ilm al-anwār*) in the introduction as a description of the book's contents,[11] and he clearly considers the second section of his book to contain a new science whose subject matter is light.

In classical logic, a science is an organized and demonstrative body of knowledge about a homogeneous subject. Avicenna identifies three elements as necessary to demonstration and, therefore, to science:

1. *Subjects,* whose quiddities have to be defined if they are not self-evident. These have to be of a common genus. Thus, works of Islamic metaphysics typically start with a chapter expounding self-evident concepts.[12]
2. *Objects of inquiry or theorems,* the essential accidents whose existence in the subject is investigated.
3. *Principles,* whose validity has to be freely accepted. These are

10. *Commentary,* 4. See pp. 3–5 above.
11. *Illumination,* 10/16.
12. See pp. 83–84 below.

> the general rules by which deductions can be made: for example, that there cannot be an actual ordered infinity.[13]

Avicenna and his followers distinguish various types of principles, ranging from self-evident first principles to sense data to common assumptions, each with its own degree of certainty. Sciences are related according to the relations of their principles. One science can take principles from another, as medicine did from physics.

A science was built up from principles, either known directly or borrowed from another science, and definitions, essential or descriptive. These serve as major and minor premises in the syllogisms of demonstration. Sciences treating the same subject could differ in their principles. For example, physics and mathematics both treated of bodies, but mathematics considered them as abstracted from matter.

The Science of Lights

The Science of Lights was a new science in the Peripatetic tradition—although perhaps old among the "Oriental" philosophers. Its subject is light and darkness. Its principles are of two types: sound Peripatetic principles and mystical intuition (mukāshafāt, dhawq).

SOUND PERIPATETIC PRINCIPLES. Suhrawardī devotes the first book of *The Philosophy of Illumination* to Peripatetic logic and philosophy and explains that his other works treat Peripatetic principles in detail. In none of these does he discuss the lights in the manner of the second book. However, when I examined those subjects specifically identified as "Illuminationist," in each case the Peripatetic works follow the Illuminationist view—although the lights might not be discussed as such. Later

13. Avicenna, *Kitāb al-Najāt,* ed. Mājid Fakhrī (Beirut: Dār al-Āfāq al-Jadīda, 1985), 104.

Islamic philosophers understood this and drew freely on all his works.

Although Suhrawardī considers their methods and conclusions to be generally valid,[14] he differs with the Peripatetics on specific points—especially on fundamental principles. Therefore, sound Peripatetic principles can be taken as premises in the Science of Lights. This includes both matters generally accepted by Peripatetics, such as the impossibility of an actual ordered infinity, and matters in which Suhrawardī corrected Peripatetic views on the basis of their own principles, such as the fictitiousness of existence.[15]

Quṭb al-Dīn summarizes Suhrawardī's opinion of the Peripatetic philosophy as follows:

> [The philosophy of] the people of our time is diseased in its principles, divergent in its arguments. So great is its dispute and dissension that it has become like a fruitless science of dissension. . . . Moreover, they have entirely abandoned intuitive philosophy in their preoccupation with details at the expense of fundamentals. They have razed speculative philosophy with their excessive arguments—all because of their love of leadership and meddling.[16]

MYSTICAL INTUITION (*MUKĀSHAFĀT, DHAWQ*). The Science of Lights, however, is based first on mystical intuition, although Suhrawardī later sought rational proof for convictions based on this experience. For him, propositions based on such intuition are empirical. Aside from the later rational demonstration, these propositions are supported by the experience of the sages of the past who followed similar mystical paths and

14. *Illumination,* 13/26; *Commentary,* 563.
15. See pp. 45–48 below.
16. *Commentary,* 5.

came to hold similar views.[17] Although the ancient and modern philosophers differed in the presentation of their teachings, nonetheless all agreed on such fundamentals as the unity of God, however much they might have disagreed on derivative matters.[18]

Suhrawardī compares the relation of mystical experience with Illuminationist philosophy to that of observation with astronomy and comments that without mystical experience the seeker wallows in doubts.[19] Still, observations alone are not a sufficient basis for a science: a rational structure is needed as well. Suhrawardī wrote *The Philosophy of Illumination* as philosophy, not mysticism. Even though he mentions his experiences occasionally and appeals to the probative value of the consensus of the sages, he was recording the rational proofs he found after his mystical experiences, not those experiences themselves. Figure 2.1 summarizes the underlying elements of the Illuminationist philosophies.

Language and Symbols

The exposition and terms of *The Philosophy of Illumination* are symbolic, as was the custom of the ancient sages.[20] Symbolism both protected philosophy from the unworthy and sharpened the mind of the seeker. The reader to whom the book is addressed is the "seeker of divinity and speculation," "upon whom a flash of the divine has descended," and who has mastered the basics of Peripatetic philosophy.[21] Moreover, the inner

17. *Illumination,* 10/16–17.
18. *Illumination,* 10–11/16–17, 20–21.
19. *Illumination,* 13/26–27.
20. *Illumination,* 10–11/17–18, 12/25.
21. *Illumination,* 12–13/25.

Figure 2.1 The Distinctive Bases of the Science of Lights

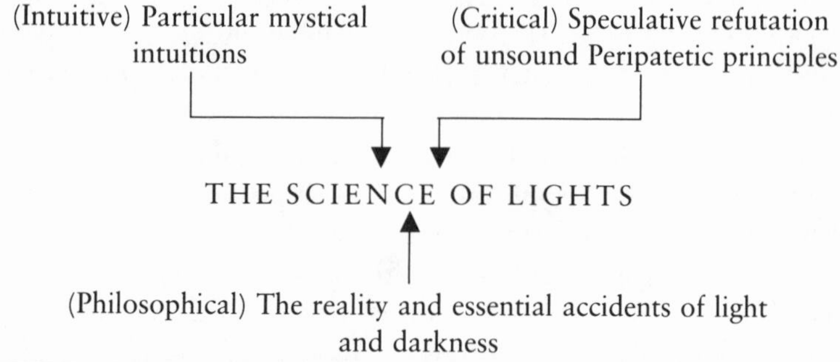

The Illuminationist philosophy was willing to use mystical intuition as a source of guidance and confirmation in the deduction of theorems; rejected certain philosophical principles and conclusions accepted by the Peripatetics; and investigated a new object of inquiry—namely, the concepts of light and darkness and their essential and accidental qualities. The Illuminationist philosophy shared with Peripatetic philosophy certain sound philosophical principles and was not concerned with all the subject areas covered by Peripatetic philosophy.

meaning of a statement can be true although the symbolic formulation is literally false.[22]

Quṭb al-Dīn sometimes refers to this symbolic terminology as "the mode of this book" (*naẓm al-kitāb*) in contrast to "the physical mode" (*al-naẓm* or *al-qānūn al-ṭabīʿī*)—standard Peripatetic terminology. For example, commenting on a passage in which Suhrawardī demonstrates that the soul cannot perish because it is an immaterial light, Quṭb al-Dīn writes: "This is a statement of the demonstration using the mode of this book; stating it in the physical mode."[23] He then restates the proof in more usual Avicennan form.

The symbolism of *The Philosophy of Illumination* is not just

22. *Illumination,* 10/17–18.
23. *Commentary,* 496; cf. 530.

a code in which Illuminationist symbols are used in place of Peripatetic terms. Although there is a systematic relation between them—*barrier* is equivalent to *body,* for instance—the Illuminationist symbols are the object of the science, not the Peripatetic terms that correspond to them. The properties of lights are investigated, not the properties of intellects or being—as when Suhrawardī deduces that a simple effect can result from a composite cause by taking the example of a table illumined by several lights. His symbolism is something like a new set of mathematical notations that in principle are reducible to simpler concepts but in practice acquire a certain autonomy and open up new mathematical possibilities.[24]

Thus, careful attention needs to be paid to the structure of Suhrawardī's argument on both levels—the level of the independent functioning of his Illuminationist symbols and the level of their systematic relation to Peripatetic concepts.

The Science of Lights and Peripatetic Philosophy

It is clear from what has gone before that the Science of Lights cannot be considered in isolation from Peripatetic philosophy (using *Peripatetic,* of course, in the sense of *Avicennan*). At one point in the introduction to *The Philosophy of Illumination* Suhrawardī implies that its contents can be divided into the Science of Lights, things that are based on it, and other things. Commenting on this Quṭb al-Dīn includes under the Science of Lights "knowledge [*ma'rifa*] of the First Origin, the intellects, the souls, the accidental lights and their conditions, and in general everything perceived by mystical intuition [*al-kashf wa'l-dhawq*]." "That which is based upon the Science of Lights" includes "most of physics and some of metaphysics [*al-'ilm al-ilāhī*] and in general most of that which is perceived by

24. My analogy, not Suhrawardī's.

thought." Things that are neither of the Science of Lights nor based on it are "certain questions of physics and theology."[25]

For example, commenting on the division of knowledge into conception and assent, Quṭb al-Dīn remarks that although this is the case for formal knowledge, there is also presential—Illuminationist—knowledge, occurring by the simple presence of the known to the knower. This is the kind of knowledge we have of the Creator, of the celestial intellects, and of our own selves; for it would be absurd to suppose that our self-knowledge is by the mediacy of a form.[26] Thus self-consciousness is an instance of a topic whose investigation depends on the Science of Lights.

The project of *The Philosophy of Illumination* was the rebuilding of the foundations of philosophy on firmer ground—mystical intuition guiding and confirmed by rational thought—although this was completely accessible only to those willing to follow the mystical path of the Illuminationists. But Suhrawardī was not concerned with replacing Peripatetic philosophy as a whole; he commended it to those without a portion of mystical insight.[27] It is wrong to exaggerate those passages in which he identifies himself with the ancient sages of Greece and the Orient. Ziai has shown that Suhrawardī's philosophy is contained within his Peripatetic works as well as *The Philosophy of Illumination* and that there is a clear structural relationship between *The Philosophy of Illumination* and Peripatetic philosophy.[28]

As Aristotle explains, the first principles of a science are not demonstrated within that science.[29] Suhrawardī's new Science of Lights is based on principles derived from his knowledge and

25. *Illumination,* 10/16.
26. *Commentary,* 38–39.
27. *Illumination,* 13/26.
28. Ziai, 2, 4, 9–11.
29. Aristotle, *Posterior Analytics,* 1:1, 3, 9.

criticism of Peripatetic philosophy. The form and conclusions of the science would, of course, be based on an investigation of the subject matter of the science and the inferences derived from it. Finally, the terms and expressions of this science are to some extent symbolic because of the abstrusity of the subject matter.

The Structure of *The Philosophy of Illumination*

Although most of the logic of *The Philosophy of Illumination* is no more than a compendium of essential rules of inference, it also includes a chapter on examples of fallacies that is, in fact, a list of Suhrawardī's main criticisms of Peripatetic philosophy. In this section, "On Deciding Certain Illuminationist Subtleties," he says that he will "examine particular principles, so that the truth thereof might be made known and thereby examples of fallacies might also be found."[30] In fact, this is his critique of Avicennan philosophy, a list of the chief erroneous opinions found in the philosophy of his predecessors with detailed refutations. Here he blasts down to philosophical bedrock to find firm foundations for the Science of Lights. He shows, for example, that the Peripatetic theory of definition makes knowledge impossible—preparing a basis for his presential theory of knowledge. This section also, directly and by elimination, provides positive principles needed for the exposition of the Science of Lights, such as the division of all things into the contingent and the necessary. To me, it shows beyond any question that the Science of Lights cannot be considered in isolation from Peripatetic philosophy and can be discussed validly in Peripatetic terms. I will regularly return to these criticisms as they are of relevance to Suhrawardī's main argument.

30. *Illumination,* 61/171.

THE ONTOLOGY OF *THE PHILOSOPHY OF ILLUMINATION*

In the second book of *The Philosophy of Illumination,* "On the Lights," Suhrawardī expounds the Science of Lights itself. This section does not follow the customary division into physics, mathematics, and metaphysics (or the alternate division into first philosophy, physics, mathematics, and metaphysics) simply because it is not any one of these sciences but a new science whose subject is the lights. As such, Quṭb al-Dīn remarks, it is the basis only of part of physics and part of metaphysics. Those who were interested in other matters were referred to the detailed works of Suhrawardī and others. Figure 2.2 shows the relation between the subjects of Peripatetic philosophy and the Illuminationist philosophy of Suhrawardī.

The Concept of Light

Later Islamic philosophers and some modern interpreters sometimes have said that Suhrawardī simply substituted light for existence.[31] It is true that in some places where we would expect to find existence discussed we find light. However, I treat this identification with caution in view of Suhrawardī's very clear denial that the concept of existence has any referent outside the mind. Thus, while Quṭb al-Dīn says that light is to darkness as existence is to nonexistence and manifestation to obscurity,[32] he does not as such identify light with existence; and in another place he identifies light with necessity and darkness with

31. For example, the contemporary Persian philosopher, Sayyid Muḥammad-Kāẓim ʿAṣṣār. See Seyyed Hossein Nasr, *Three Muslim Sages* (Cambridge, Mass.: Harvard University Press, 1964), 151–52 n. 27; and Izutsu, *Concept and Reality,* 144–45.
32. *Commentary,* 283–84.

Figure 2.2 Relation of Peripatetic and Illuminationist Principles in Philosophy

		KNOWN BY	EXAMPLE
THING	Matter in neither definition nor being (metaphysics)	Unsound Peripatetic principles	God is pure existence.
		Sound Peripatetic principles	God does not directly cause a body.
		Illuminationist principles	Platonic forms exist.
	Matter in definition and being (physics)	Unsound Peripatetic principles	Bodies are composed of form and matter.
		Sound Peripatetic principles	The spheres move in circles.
		Illuminationist principles	Bodies are absolute magnitude.
	Matter in being, but not definition (mathematics)	Sound Peripatetic principles	Pythagorean theorem

Suhrawardī's Illuminationist philosophy—the Science of Lights—overlaps Peripatetic philosophy. Certain conclusions of Peripatetic philosophy are based on unsound principles and thus are rejected. Peripatetic conclusions based on sound principles are to be accepted. Finally, there are philosophical truths that can be discovered only through the principles of the Illuminationist philosophy. The latter is concerned with "most of physics [i.e., questions relating to the material body and the soul] and some of rational theology [i.e., metaphysics, particularly God and the angels]." The Science of Lights does not deal with certain aspects of physics or metaphysics or with mathematics at all.

contingency[33] (although, as we will see, this cannot be taken literally). Moreover, darkness, in the form of bodies, exists no less than light. The question of why Suhrawardī chose to introduce light as a metaphysical concept must be asked and answered on several levels: mystical, symbolic, and critical.

MYSTICAL. Suhrawardī states that the truths of the Science of Lights are derived in the first instance from mystical intuition. Plato, for example, knew that the basis of all reality was light because he saw that this was so.[34] This tells us next to nothing until we know what is meant here by *light*. In *The Philosophy of Illumination* Suhrawardī states that immaterial light is only analogous to physical light.[35] From the point of view of immaterial light, physical light is light only accidentally. Moreover, he does not consider a mystical intuition in isolation to be a guarantee of the validity of the rational interpretation of that intuition or even a guarantee of the mystic's continued certitude about that experience. The mapmaker cannot just go to the top of the mountain to see the lay of the land; he must also return to the plain and, with the tools of surveying, establish distances, directions, and altitudes. The people of the plain cannot just accept the authority of the mapmaker; they must also understand how the symbols of the map express the landmarks they know.[36] *The Philosophy of Illumination* is philosophy, not mysticism; Suhrawardī constructs rational proofs of his intuitions both for the sake of his own continued certainty and correct interpretation of those intuitions and for the guidance of those without the experience.

SYMBOLIC. To know that light is a symbol only casts doubt on its real meaning. In isolation, we can see that it is a break

33. *Commentary,* 18.
34. *Illumination,* 162–65/378–81.
35. *Illumination,* 110/289–90.
36. The analogy is mine, not Suhrawardī's.

with customary Peripatetic philosophical terminology and thus presumably with that philosophy. It reminds us of the verse, "God is the light of heaven and earth."[37] But regardless of how evocative the symbol may be on a religious, historical, or magical plane, it cannot be significant to philosophy until it is brought into systematic relation with philosophical and scientific concepts and its structure and relationships are analyzed. If Suhrawardī's Science of Lights represents a genuine philosophical departure, then this will be reflected in the picture it shows us of reality. It must make some difference—in what we consider to be real, in what we can know, in the structure of the universe, or in some other way. And this in turn will tell us why he chose to begin philosophy with the symbol of light.

CRITICAL. We can answer the question negatively by looking at his criticisms of the conventional metaphysics of existence. In addition, these critiques furnished some of the first principles of the Science of Lights.

According to classical logic, the exposition of a science begins with the elucidation of the concepts of its subjects—not a matter of demonstration but of definition, whether strict or descriptive—and with its first principles, derived from another science or self-evident in themselves.[38] Therefore, we may begin to answer the question of why Suhrawardī chooses to explain reality in terms of light (1) *negatively,* by examining the criticisms of Peripatetic philosophy that are part of the logical prolegomena of *The Philosophy of Illumination,* and (2) *inductively,* as the structure and implications of the science emerge from an examination of his concepts and principles.

Therefore, after making a preliminary analysis of the concept of light, I examine several criticisms Suhrawardī makes of Peripatetic metaphysics. Then, I look at light, darkness, and the

37. Qur'ān 24:35.
38. Avicenna, *Najāt,* 108 ff.

related concepts that express the subject of the science. Finally, I examine the theorems of the Science of Lights and explain how they are related to Peripatetic metaphysics.

The Exposition of the Concepts of Light and Darkness

According to classical logic, the subject matter of a science is known by concepts that can be either acquired or self-evident. The fundamental concepts of a fundamental science thus have to be self-evident expressions of the essences of the subjects of that science. According to Suhrawardī these concepts cannot be defined strictly—he doubts that Peripatetic real definition has much application anyway—although they can be described in a looser sense (*rasm*) or simply pointed out (*ishāra, tanbīh*).

The first chapter of the second book of *The Philosophy of Illumination* introduces the concept of light:

> If there is anything in existence that does not need to be made known, it is the manifest. Since there is nothing more manifest than light, then there is nothing less in need of being made known.[39]

This was not a demonstration, but simply an explanation of a concept basic to the science—in this case, the manifest (not, note carefully, *manifestation*). As a choice of starting point it is significant. Normally, Islamic metaphysical works began with a statement such as

> "Existent," "thing," and "necessary" are ideas primordially engraved in the soul in such a way that they need not be acquired through ideas better known than them.[40]

39. *Illumination,* 106/283–84.
40. Avicenna, *Kitāb al-Shifā', al-Ilāhīyāt,* ed. Ibrāhīm Madkūr (Cairo: al-Hay'a al-'Āmma li-Shu'ūn al-Maṭābi' al-Amīrīya, 1960), 29.

Quṭb al-Dīn began his metaphysics with:

> "Existence" cannot be defined since it is a self-evident conception. There is nothing better known than it by which it might be made known.[41]

Suhrawardī's Peripatetic works contain similar statements.[42]

We will see that by basing his metaphysics on what is manifest, rather than on conceptions like *existent, thing,* and *necessity,* Suhrawardī begins with the structure of reality as we experience it rather than with the structure of our conceptual knowledge of reality, as he held Avicenna and his followers had. He begins from the best-known experience rather than from the most general concept. This difference of approach is the basis of Suhrawardī's distinctive views on metaphysics and epistemology.

His departure from traditional metaphysics is based both on mystical insight and on philosophical criticism of Peripatetic theory. Throughout his writings he attributes primary reality to concrete entities directly known, rather than to what he called "intellectual fictions": existence, unity, matter, form, and so on. Suhrawardī frequently identifies propositions reflecting this insight as *Illuminationist*—that is, based on mystical insight. This is in some ways more truly Peripatetic than the Avicennan Neoplatonism he was criticizing—although, of course, his idea of what can be directly known is rather different than Aristotle's.

He expresses his criticism of the Peripatetics in his account of these intellectual fictions (*i'tibārāt 'aqlīya*).[43] Suhrawardī

41. *Crown,* 1:3:1.
42. *Œuvres,* 1:4, 125, 199.
43. The term *i'tibārāt 'aqlīya* is difficult to translate. It refers to notions that the mind applies to reality but that do not have a specific external referrent. I use *fiction* as in *legal fiction,* something that is assumed for convenience

holds that such concepts as pure existence, pure quiddity, thingness, reality, essence, unity, contingency, necessity, substantiality, and color are mental fictions to which no external reality corresponded. Particular colors, particular single things, particular existents, of course, exist, but color in general, unity in general, and existence in general are only ideas in the mind. This notion in turn rests on a mystical basis, a fundamental attitude toward reality characteristic of his views as a whole. His view came to be known as *the primacy of quiddity* (*aṣālat al-māhīya*), a term that is not, as far as I know, found in his own writings. It might better be called *the primacy of the concrete*, for it is an intense awareness of the direct, tangible presence of specific concrete things, whether sensible or spiritual, and a disbelief in metaphysical substrates of any sort, such as existence, quiddity, substantiality, form, and matter.[44]

Quṭb al-Dīn succinctly summarizes the issue as Suhrawardī understood it as being

> between the followers of the Peripatetics who maintained that the existence [*wujūd*] of quiddities was additional to them [*zā'id 'alay-hā*] in the mind and in concrete things and their opponents who held that it was additional to them in minds but not in concrete things.[45]

The view Suhrawardī attributes to "the followers of the Peripatetics" is that because we can conceive the quiddity of something and doubt its external existence, there must be a real

---

but that does not really exist in the world. It is nearly equivalent to the term *secondary intelligibles* (*ma'qūlāt thāniya*) or *secondary intentions* of medieval logic, both Islamic and European, although with, I think, an additional implication that these notions are reified in a way that is not quite licit.

44. The role of the intellectual fictions as concepts is discussed in ch. 3 below.

45. *Commentary*, 182.

distinction in concrete things between existence and quiddity.[46] Moreover, the Peripatetic view that existence is the most general of things implies that it cannot be identified with existents.[47] These Peripatetics built their whole metaphysics on such a conception of existence.[48] He says that this was the popular understanding of the position of the Peripatetics.

Against this view he advances two main arguments. First, if there is a real distinction between an external substance and its existence, then if the substance exists by its existence, it exists by an accident. Therefore, the quiddity would have to exist in some way before its existence. Second, if there is a real, external distinction between existence and quiddity, then that existence would have existence, and then the existence of the existence would exist, and so on. The arguments are complex, and Suhrawardī repeats them in various places and forms in his works.[49]

We might ask whether these criticisms have anything to do with what Avicenna, clearly the principle target of this attack, and his followers actually said. It certainly is true that Avicenna fails to distinguish the concept and reality of existence as sharply as do later philosophers, who were aware of Suhrawardī's criticisms. Quṭb al-Dīn in fact accuses the Peripatetics of assuming that to every mental distinction corresponded a real distinction.[50] Qūnawī, in his correspondence with Ṭūsī, also asks

46. *Illumination,* 65/185–86.
47. *Illumination,* 64–65/183–184.
48. *Illumination,* 67/189–91. He adds that there is, in fact, another interpretation of existence in the Peripatetic tradition, one presumably more acceptable, but "the followers of the Peripatetics" do not speak of this but instead persist in talking about what they did not understand. He does not specify exactly who held to this better interpretation.
49. *Illumination,* 64–72/182–202; *Œuvres,* 1:21–26, 340–71.
50. *Commentary,* 185. For example, where Quṭb al-Dīn writes of existence, quiddity, unity, and so on as being "matters common to all notions [*mafhūmāt*]," Avicenna writes of "meanings common to all existents." See p. 84 below.

whether the distinction of quiddity and existence implies a real distinction in the concrete thing.[51] The latter, in his commentary on Avicenna's *Hints and Allusions,* denies this,[52] but this was certainly done in the awareness of Suhrawardī's criticisms.

Because Avicenna was not always clear about this distinction of the concept and reality of existence and the other "intellectual fictions," later philosophers made it explicit. In the East this development was especially associated with Suhrawardī.

Aquinas, following Averroes, understood Avicenna as teaching that existence is an accident of essence, an even more extreme interpretation of Avicenna.[53] This led to an important debate in thirteenth- and fourteenth-century Latin philosophy as to whether there is a real distinction between essence (more or less equivalent to what Suhrawardī meant by quiddity) and existence. Thomas held that there was; others, such as Duns Scotus, denied it. At least one philosopher, Giles of Rome, held that not only was there a real distinction between essence and existence, but they were actually separable, a view he held was essential to upholding the validity of theology.[54] Suhrawardī's criticisms, based as they are on the assumption that Avicenna made both a real and a mental distinction between quiddity and existence, certainly apply to Thomas's understanding of Avicenna.

51. Chittick, "Mysticism versus Philosophy," 99.
52. Cited in Izutsu, *Concept and Reality,* 109. Izutsu here argues that Suhrawardī misread Avicenna, whose ontology should be read as supporting the doctrine of the primacy of existence. See ibid., 109–12.
53. *Commentary on the Metaphysics of Aristotle,* tr. John P. Rowan, Library of Living Catholic Thought (Chicago: Henry Regnery Co., 1961), secs. 556, 558. Seyyed Hussein Nasr states that this was also Suhrawardī's view. It was not. See *Three Muslim Sages,* 67.
54. For an overview, see *New Catholic Encyclopedia,* 1967 ed., s.v. "essence and existence," by J. C. Taylor.

That the Fundamental Reality Is Light

Suhrawardī divides things into those that are light in their own reality and those that are not, each of which is either self-subsistent or accidental—dependent or independent, in Suhrawardī's terminology. This results in a fourfold division of reality into (1) self-subsistent *immaterial* or pure *lights* (*al-nūr al-mujarrad, al-nūr al-maḥḍ*), (2) *accidental lights* (*al-nūr al-'āriḍ*) inhering either in immaterial lights or in physical bodies, (3) *barriers* (*al-barzakh*) or *dusky substances* (*al-jawhar al-ghāsiq*), i.e., bodies, and (4) *dark modes* (*al-hay'a al-ẓulmānīya*)—accidents in either immaterial lights or physical bodies (see Figure 2.3). Immaterial light is the cause of the other three.[55]

Light is not, as some have thought, simply a substitute for existence. The Science of Lights is concerned with lights—not with light. The immaterial lights are individual, concrete things that are by essence manifest in themselves and make other things manifest. As such they are existents (*mawjūdāt*), and not existence (*wujūd*). They are monads—worlds in the void—and not waves of the sea of existence.

Moreover, although all things are caused by lights, not all of them are lights. Bodies and their nonluminous accidents are not lights, although their ultimate causes are the immaterial lights. Light is, however, the principle of the interrelationship of things. Quṭb al-Dīn, paraphrasing Suhrawardī, defines *light* (descriptively, not essentially) as "that which is manifest in itself and manifests another" (*al-jalī fī nafsihi al-muẓhir li-ghayrihi*) or, more simply, as "manifestation and its increase" (*al-ẓuhūr wa-*

55. *Illumination,* 107–9/284–88. Self-subsistent metaphysical light is called *immaterial* because it is free of matter. Another translation would be *abstract light*. I use *immaterial light* consistently in this work.

Figure 2.3 The Classes of Existents

	LIGHT IN ITS OWN REALITY	NOT LIGHT IN ITS OWN REALITY
INDEPENDENT (self-subsistent)	Immaterial or pure lights (intellects)	Dusky substances or barriers (material bodies)
DEPENDENT (inhering in another)	Accidental lights or luminous modes (physical light and some accidents in intellects and souls)	Dark modes (the nine accidental categories in bodies except physical light and some accidents of souls and intellects)

ziyādatuhu).[56] Things affect each other because it is in their nature to be manifest to each other or because they were made manifest to each other by something whose nature it is to do so. In themselves, however, they remain discrete and autonomous ontological blocks.

Neoplatonic philosophical systems such as Suhrawardī's are characterized by a hierarchy of causation, in which the continued existence of a thing is dependent on a cause of a higher order of being. Suhrawardī defines that relationship as being between the dependent (*faqīr*) and the independent (*ghanī*). If an immaterial light is dependent on another, it is clearly dependent on another immaterial light, not on a body or something

56. *Commentary,* 283; cf. *Illumination,* 113/295.

Figure 2.4 That Immaterial Light Is the Fundamental Reality

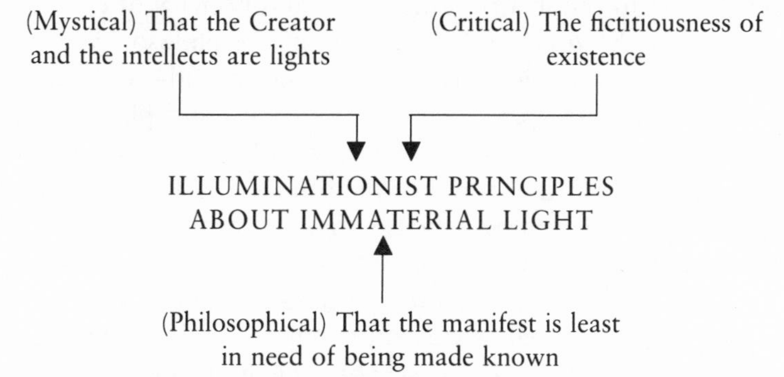

Suhrawardī supports his views about light as the fundamental reality in three ways: through mystical intuition of the lights, an attack on Peripatetic views about existence, and an analysis of existent things as manifest.

else of a lower order of being. Since there cannot be a hierarchy of causes with an infinity of levels, there has to be a light beyond which is no other light.[57] Figure 2.4 shows the three sources that Suhrawardī uses to derive his Illuminationist principles about immaterial light.

In summary, at the heart of the philosophy of illumination is an intuition of the concrete particularity of things. A human being or a rock or an intellect or God is a distinct, particular, and unitary thing. Although there is a mental distinction between a thing's existence—the act of its being real—and its quiddity or essence—what it is—this does not correspond to any real distinction in it. Only the particular and concrete in its particularity and concreteness is real. Each thing is absolutely discrete and discontinuous from other things.

57. *Illumination,* 121–23/306–10.

Later Islamic philosophers quite correctly place this view in opposition to the theory of the unity and primacy of existence and call it the *primacy of quiddity.* In the philosophy of the unity of existence, the universe is continuous, and—at the deepest level, at least—particulars are illusory. Later philosophers like Sabzawārī tend to refer to Suhrawardī's claim that existence is fictitious when they write of the primacy of quiddity.[58] This does not mean that we should make a distinction between existence and quiddity and maintain then that this quiddity is what is fundamental, for Suhrawardī holds that quiddity in this sense is just as unreal as existence. What is real is the thing in its particularity and wholeness, not some part of it.

The proponents of the primacy of existence held that existence alone is truly real and that quiddities—things in their particularity—are determinations of existence. Considered alone, the quiddities are mental fictions. The doctrine of the primacy of existence owes much to Suhrawardī. In addition to the use of the term *light* and related terms as symbols, certain of its main features were borrowed from or responded to his ideas—for example, the systematic ambiguity of existence, which is the notion that things can exist in different degrees of intensity. Nevertheless, these philosophers considered themselves distinctly opposed to Suhrawardī, although to go beyond his arguments they had to make yet another basic distinction, between the self-evident concept and hidden reality of existence:

> Its notion is one of the best-known things,
> But its deepest reality is in the extremity
> of hiddenness.[59]

58. *The Metaphysics of Sabzāwārī,* tr. Mehdi Mohaghegh and Toshihiko Izutsu, Wisdom of Persia 10 (Delmar, N.Y.: Caravan Books, 1977), p. 33.
59. Sabzlawārī, 31–32.

The importance of light in Suhrawardī's thought comes from the other aspect of his intuition of the concreteness of things: the fact that we are aware of them. What is best known to us is the manifest—not manifestation as some sort of immaterial entity, but just the concrete particular things we see and touch. Since physical light is the most conspicuous example of what is manifest and makes other things manifest, it is the best symbol for the fundamental knowability of things. In our world, the knowability of things is accidental. Substances are not essentially manifest but are manifested by other things. However, according to the principle of sufficient reason, we must eventually come to things manifest in themselves. These are the immaterial lights.

In Illuminationist terms, self-consciousness is to be understood as a thing's being manifest to itself. Now, a body cannot be self-conscious because it is not manifest in its essence. Nor, obviously, can even a luminous accident know itself since it is not a light to itself (*nūr li-dhātihi*).[60] In other words, self-consciousness cannot be identified with the image of the self in the mind. We know this image as another, except insofar as it is known to be an image of the self through some prior direct knowledge of the self. Suhrawardī distinguishes between this sort of discursive knowledge of the self, in which the self is known as one thing in the world among many, and direct awareness of one's own existence and experience. The latter cannot be explained without some direct self-awareness, unmediated by any concept or material or spiritual organ.[61]

60. *Illumination,* 110–11/290–91.

61. *Illumination,* 111–13/292–95. The question arises in philosophical discussion of artificial intelligence. See, for example, Douglas R. Hofstadter, *Gödel, Escher, Bach* (New York: Vintage Books, 1980), esp. 708–10, in which the position attacked by Suhrawardī—that self-consciousness is a form of the self in the mind—is defended.

This direct self-awareness is in turn the basis of life, perception, activity, and knowledge—each of which thus implies consciousness and the presence of a soul. Therefore, every living thing has to be an immaterial light.[62]

Vision happens simply by the presence of a lighted object before a healthy eye. That by *light* Suhrawardī means manifestation in a broader sense is shown by the fact that he criticizes the Peripatetic theory of sound as vibrations in the air with arguments very similar to those he advances against the conventional theories of vision. Although the Illuminationists would admit that hearing might be conditioned in some way on the vibration of air, sounds and other sensibles are experienced as simple subjective phenomena.[63]

Peripatetic real definition (*ḥadd*)—definition that captures the essence of the thing—crosses the boundary between concept and reality in that it purports to indicate the quiddity of the thing with all its essential attributes and the matters within its reality. By contrast, Peripatetic descriptive definition (*rasm*) defines a reality by matters external to it,[64] and nominal definition merely defines the concept in the mind,[65] both easier tasks. Suhrawardī himself uses the term *making known* (*ta'rīf*), a more general term.

While real definitions clearly would be very useful in sciences, it is doubtful whether any have ever been constructed.[66] There

62. Quṭb al-Dīn points out that this implies that the souls of animals are immaterial lights. *Commentary,* 290. He presumably mentions this because of his own special interest in animals and the transmigration of souls. See pp. 146 ff. below.
63. *Illumination,* 103–5/276–80.
64. *Illumination,* 19/56–57; cf. Avicenna, *Kitāb al-Ḥudūd,* in Amélie-Marie Goichon, *Lexique de la langue philosophique d'Ibn Sinā* (Paris: Desclée de Brouwer, 1938), 143. Quṭb al-Dīn quotes these definitions from Avicenna's *Ishārāt.*
65. *Commentary,* 61–62.
66. *Illumination,* 21/60–61.

is no way to know whether a property is in fact peculiar to a given essence, and, once in possession of certain essentials, there is no way to know for certain that others were not overlooked. Finally, there were some things, like bodies, which everyone knew perfectly well, but where there was no general agreement about their essential parts or whether indeed they had any.[67]

Moreover, whenever the Peripatetics actually advanced examples of their real definitions—for example, "Black is a color that gathers vision"—the definition in every case used intellectual fictions, such as *color,* or differences less known than what was defined, such as *gathers vision.* In fact, black was a simple reality, directly known to whomever saw it and unknowable to anyone who had not.[68] Concepts went back to such directly known simple realities. Composite concepts were known by compounding simple realities.

COSMOLOGY: THE GENERATION OF THE MANY FROM THE ONE

The Problems of Cosmology

The first chapter of the second book of *The Philosophy of Illumination,* "On Light and Its Reality," deduces the highest and simplest things from self-evident concepts in order of knowing. The second chapter, "On the Arrangement of Existence"—that is, cosmology—traces the actual emergence of the universe in order of being. The problem cosmology must address is why the universe exists as it does. In Muslim Neoplatonic systems this problem resolves itself into several interrelated questions:

67. *Illumination,* 19–20/58.
68. *Illumination,* 73–74/203–5.

- Why does being come from the One?
- How do the many kinds and individuals result from the One?
- Why is there order and disorder in the physical universe?

As in his ontology, Suhrawardī's answers emerge from the concept of light with the aid of certain axioms of pure reason shared with the Peripatetics.[69] The most important of these are the principle of sufficient reason and the impossibility of an actual ordered infinity.

THE PRINCIPLE OF SUFFICIENT REASON. For any existent fact there has to be a cause. If an entity of a higher order of being is the cause of two lower entities, there have to be two distinct aspects of the higher entity to explain the separate existence of each of the lower entities. Moreover, a lower entity cannot be the ontological cause of a higher entity since there would be no sufficient cause for its superiority. Therefore, causation proceeds downward.[70]

THE IMPOSSIBILITY OF AN ACTUAL ORDERED INFINITY. The medieval philosophical theory of infinity allows only potential or unordered infinities, a principle going back to Aristotle. "Any sequence in which there is an arrangement of any kind and whose individuals exist together must be finite."[71] For example, time can be infinite because all its moments do not exist simultaneously, and the number of individuals in the world of image can be infinite because they cannot be counted simultaneously. However, the number of levels of existence has to be finite.

Since Suhrawardī's and the Peripatetics' systems share the conclusion that the highest entity is simple in every respect, it is clear why Suhrawardī's universe has the familiar pyramidal

69. *Illumination,* 61–64/171–82.
70. *Illumination,* 62–63/175–80; 154/367–69.
71. *Illumination,* 63/180.

structure of levels of being gradually decreasing in complexity from the chaotic multiplicity of the physical world to an absolutely simple highest level.

Illuminationist Bases of Cosmology

As with ontology, we cannot conclude that because the axioms Suhrawardī shares with the Peripatetics give his system a structure similar to theirs, that the content of the two systems therefore is the same. The Science of Lights is distinct from the Peripatetic science of theology. Not only does Suhrawardī identify the subject matter as light rather than existence, but the internal structure and range of the concept of light are different from those of existence, as we have seen. As Suhrawardī develops his arguments, the principles derived from the concept of light differ more and more from comparable Peripatetic principles, and major differences of structure begin to appear. Suhrawardī is precise about this. He labels only certain principles and conclusions as *Illuminationist* (*ishrāqī*); others he does not. Those he labels as *Illuminationist* mark major divergences from Peripatetic doctrines. Although his symbolic terminology sometimes conceals the similarity of certain of his conclusions with Peripatetic views, his medieval commentators and critics were well aware that Suhrawardī's doctrines differ not by their language but by their content from Peripatetic ideas. This was why Suhrawardī's ideas were normally discussed in Peripatetic terms.

Suhrawardī claims that the principles of the Science of Lights are based on mystical experience. Mystical experience is not philosophy as such, but an empirical phenomenon to be explained by philosophy. Like any other empirical phemonenon it cannot be contravened by the conclusions of philosophy. Just as philosophy cannot conclude that the universe is simple and homogeneous—we can see that it is not—so too it cannot contravene the observations of the true mystic.

Suhrawardī is specific about the main mystical observations that apply to cosmology:

1. That the Creator is a light;
2. That the immaterial intellects are lights;
3. That each species has a lord of idols[72]—its Platonic Form—that is a self-subsistent immaterial light. There are therefore more than ten intellects.

Suhrawardī argues that the ancient philosophers of the Illuminationist tradition all agreed about these on the basis of their mystical experiences. Should not their testimony, he argues, receive at least as much credence as the astronomical observations of one or two individuals long dead? Suhrawardī relates that he himself held firmly to the Peripatetic view that there are but ten intellects until "he saw the proof of his Lord."[73] Those who doubt are to apply themselves to mystical exercise and the service of the contemplatives until they are granted this vision.

The Science of Lights, however, is based on these observations only indirectly. As a science it has to be deduced from necessary principles. Empirical observation can guide the scientist, but it cannot directly furnish the principles of his science. Those principles have to come from a higher science or be known as certain by reason.

72. *Arbāb al-aṣnām,* literally, *lords of idols* or *things that there are images of.* I think this may derive from old pagan Arabian usage in which a god was said to be "lord" of a particular idol. In any case, the philosophical sense is clear enough: the Platonic form is an angel, not the ideal exemplar of a thing. Suhrawardī would certainly deny that the *rabb ṣanam* of a rabbit was an ideal rabbit. *Archetype,* the rendering that my good friend Professor Ziai urges on me, is therefore misleading, apart from lacking the flavor of Suhrawardī's colorful terminology.

73. *Illumination,* 156/371.

The Emanation of the Cosmos from the One

Suhrawardī claims that the ontological basis of all things is immaterial light, light in itself for itself—in other words, what is self-subsistent, is manifest itself, and makes other things manifest. Immaterial light, moreover, is manifest to itself—that is, it is self-conscious.[74]

Visible light is accidental and manifests the other accidentally by creating an accidental illumination of the body, which is dark in itself. Immaterial light is substantial—light in itself—and its manifestation is both substantial and accidental: accidental in that it can illuminate other existing things, and substantial in that it can bring other things into being.

In contrast to the medieval and modern scientific notion of light as rays that traverse an intervening space and fall on a surface to illuminate it by reflecting from it, Suhrawardī holds that there are no intervening rays. Any surface not veiled from a light in some way becomes manifest. There is no transfer of an accident or division of the substance of the light. *Rays* (*ashi"ah*) refers not to lines of light emerging from a light but to the illumination of the surface of the illumined thing.[75]

The concept of light also differs from the concept of existence in that it accepts difference in intensity. Thus Suhrawardī disagrees with the Peripatetics, who maintain that what is self-subsistent does not differ in perfection and deficiency.[76] However, apart from difference of intensity and difference of accidents, the immaterial lights do not differ in kind.

Having previously shown that it is one in every respect, Suhrawardī concludes through the principle of sufficient reason that from the Light of Lights in isolation there can be but one

74. *Illumination,* 110–13/290–95.
75. *Illumination,* 97–103/261–74.
76. *Illumination,* 119–20/303–6.

effect.[77] Otherwise, there would have to be more than one aspect in the Light of Lights. The reasoning is familiar from Avicenna. The first creature could not be darkness (i.e., body) since this darkness could not create more light or darkness. Since there is light and multiplicity in the universe, the first creature had to be something that could itself create other beings: an immaterial light. This first light is called the proximate light.[78]

Suhrawardī's conclusions here do not differ in any significant way from those of the Islamic Peripatetics—nor did he or his commentators claim that they did. Quṭb al-Dīn, in fact, gives the Peripatetic equivalents of the relevant terms.[79] Immaterial light, it should be noted, is not equivalent to existence but to intellect, and its accidental light equivalent to intellection.

When we think about the emanation of things from the Light of Lights, it is easy to be misled by our imaginations. We think of a ray from a lamp shining into space with another lamp materializing at the end of that ray. From that lamp other rays come forth, at the end of which other lamps appear. The process seems quite arbitrary. However, we must remember two things: first, pure light is not in space or time; second, its manifestation is substantial. It is the nature of the Light of Lights, like the sun, to pour out its light; but by the very act of pouring out its light another light comes into existence. It is as though the sun has no body except its very light; but its light is a substance, not an accident. In that case, there would be no difference in reality between the sun and the light it gives off, but only a difference in intensity. In the case of the Light of Lights there is no space—so space cannot be the basis of division. Light can be differentiated only by intensity or by accidents—by color, we might say. Since there is no time or choice involved, merely

77. *Illumination,* 125/314–17.
78. *Illumination,* 126–29/317–22; cf. *Œuvres,* 1:61–62, 165–66.
79. *Commentary,* 317–18: "*al-ʿunṣur al-awwal,*" "*ʿaql al-kull.*"

the absence of veils, we must put aside any thought of the Light of Lights "deciding" to "create" other lights. The Light of Lights is like a brilliant lamp in a crystal cave. There is no choice on the part of the lamp: it illumines the cave, which reflects and sparkles—not by the choice of the lamp but simply by its nature. But in the case of the Light of Lights, whose manifestation is substantial, the cave and the crystals are themselves the product of the lamp.[80]

The Bases of the Doctrine of the Platonic Forms

The main difference between Illuminationist and Peripatetic/Avicennan cosmology is the number of intellects: the Peripatetics held that there is a single series of immaterial intellects, probably ten in all, ordered by rank. The Illuminationists thought there are many more, not all of which are responsible for heavenly spheres:

> The author of these lines was once zealous in defence of the Peripatetic school in its denial of these things [i.e., the multiplicity of the vertical and horizontal lights, the lords of idols, and the rays and their reflections, according to the opinions of the ancients—Quṭb al-Dīn.], strongly inclined towards the Peripatetic view, and definitely decided upon it. But he saw the demonstration of his Lord. Whosoever does not acknowledge this and is not convinced by the proof, let him engage in mystical exercises and serve the masters of contemplation. Haply he will be seized with a vision of the light shining in the World of Glory, and he will see the angelic essences and the lights that Hermes and Plato beheld.[81]

80. The analogies of this paragraph are mine, not Suhrawardī's.
81. *Illumination,* 156–57/371–72.

Figure 2.5 The Bases of the Doctrine of Forms

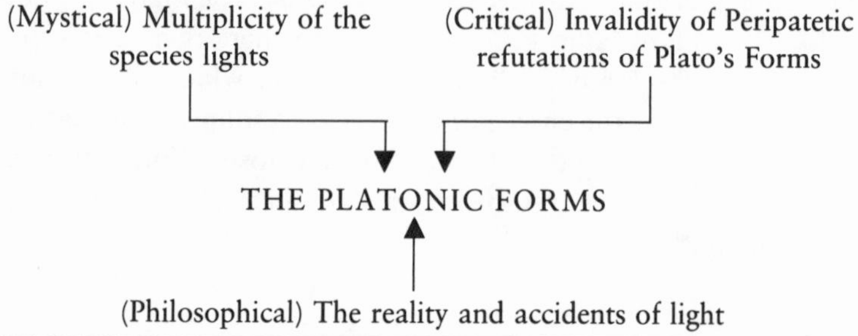

Suhrawardī's argument in defense of the existence of the Platonic Forms has three aspects: (1) through mystical intuition he has seen proof that these Forms exist; (2) the Peripatetic arguments against the Forms are unsound; (3) the existence of the Forms can be deduced from what is known about the properties of the immaterial lights.

Mystical experience here does not supply a positive principle—but an empirical brute fact sufficient to refute the Peripatetic doctrine and to point the direction for Illuminationist deductions. It also marks the second significant positive departure from Peripatetic views—the first being the division of reality by light/manifestation and darkness. Figure 2.5 shows Suhrawardī's argument for the existence of the Platonic forms.

Quṭb al-Dīn summarizes Suhrawardī's understanding of the Platonic doctrine of Forms as follows:

> Plato held that each bodily species in the sensible world has a Form [*mithāl*] in the intelligible world—a simple, luminous, self-subsistent, non-spatial form [*ṣūra*]. These, in truth, are the realities, since they are like spirits for the bodily forms of species. The latter are like idols of them—that is, shadows and droplets from them, because of the subtlety of the former and coarseness of the latter.[82]

82. *Illumination,* 92n/251.

He goes on to say that these are called *Forms* not because they are less real than the things we know but because they are more hidden.

Suhrawardī cites the Peripatetic argument questioning how the Platonic Form can be incarnated in material things. To this he replies that it is possible for the form of a substance to be present accidentally in the mind. In just such a way, self-subsistent Forms in the intelligible world can have idols [*aṣnām*] in the physical world.[83]

The flaw in the Peripatetic argument is to assume that what is true of the thing also is true of what resembles it [*mithāl*]. The truth is that what is true of the self-subsistent Form is not necessarily true of its form imprinted in a body. It is, in fact, a correlate of Suhrawardī's doctrine of the fictitiousness of general concepts such as existence (one agreed to by the Peripatetics) that accidentality is not part of the reality of the accident. Suhrawardī goes on to criticize the Peripatetics for inconsistently allowing existence to be considered substantial in the Necessary Existent and accidental in everything else.[84]

This is not a demonstration of the existence of the Platonic Forms. Rather it is a rejection of the arguments against them—a negative preparation for the demonstration, just as the mystical experience of the multiplicity of lights is a positive preparation. Thus we find this argument in the chapter on sophistry, along with refutations of other objectionable Peripatetic doctrines.

Unless Suhrawardī could show that a simple entity can be the product of a composite cause, he could not derive the horizontal order of intellects—the Platonic Forms—from the higher lights alone. He agrees with the Peripatetics that there is a vertical

83. *Illumination,* 92–93/251–52; cf. Aristotle, *Metaphysics* 1:9. Avicenna, *Ilāhīyāt,* 310–24, also refutes Pythagorean doctrines on number.

84. *Illumination,* 93–94/253–54.

series of lights—intellects—each the greatest possible emanation of the light above it in rank. In Peripatetic philosophy these are the only such intellects, since a simple effect has to be the product of a simple cause. An intellect cannot come into existence through the combined effects of two higher intellects. In the case of the emanation of the (simple) individual soul in response to the occurrence of matter with a suitable constitution, the cause is not compounded of the emanating intellect and the constitution. Rather, the intellect alone is the cause, and the constitution is merely the precondition of its causal efficacy.

The argument for the Peripatetic view is that each part of the composite cause is responsible for none, or part, or all of the effect. If it were not responsible for any of the effect, it would not be part of the cause. If it were responsible for part of the effect, then the effect would be composite. If it were responsible for all of the effect, then the other parts of the cause would not be truly so.

The fallacy is the assumption that what is true of the whole has to apply to each part. A thousand men may move a heavy stone, but each individual man may not be able to move it at all—yet each man is unquestionably part of the cause of the stone's movement.[85]

Suhrawardī later proved the same principle with Illuminationist arguments. If the rays from different lights interact, then the effect could be simple. The rays from different lights could fall on the surface of a table, but the illumination of the surface at any given point would not be composite. But if the different lights in the vertical series could interact directly and indirectly to produce further derived lights, and these in turn interact, then the number of distinct, simple lights would be very great.

85. *Illumination*, 94–95/254–58.

These would differ accidentally without necessarily differing in rank.[86]

Although the realities of the immaterial lights are always the same, the lights differ not only in their intensities but in accidental luminous or dark modes. The lights so distinguished are called the horizontal order—as opposed to the vertical order of lights, distinguished by intensity.[87] The horizontal lights cannot be systematically ordered. They are, however, finite in number (although very numerous), since the fact of diminishing luminosity applies to them as well as to the triumphal lights.

Each possible combination of accidents causes a light through substantial manifestation. Since this light in turn is illuminated by all the higher lights, it thereby acquires their accidents and the accidents of the higher lights reflected in them. This in turn results in further lights on an even lower level.[88] Obviously, the number of possible lights and the complexity of their accidental structures have multiplied greatly by the time we reach the lowest level of pure lights, where their intensity is too weak to result in a lower level of self-subsisting lights.

Among the Illuminationist principles Suhrawardī lists as the "most noble contingency" (*al-imkān al-ashraf*) that "the existence of a baser contingent implies the prior existence of a nobler contingent."[89] This notion—that any orderliness in the universe has to have been caused by a preexistent, isomorphic orderliness among the lights—is an application of the principle of sufficient reason. It implies that the Peripatetic limitation of the number of the intellects to ten has to be wrong.

Each light in the horizontal order is the lord of an idol: that

86. *Illumination,* 165/381–82.
87. *Illumination,* 138/343 ff.
88. *Illumination,* 139–43/344–48.
89. *Illumination,* 154/367.

is, the Platonic Form of a particular species. (Only species have Forms, according to Suhrawardī—not accidents, qualities, etc.)[90] The relation between these Forms and their idols has to be understood correctly. The Form does not somehow participate in each of its idols; to do so, the Form would have to be both in and out of matter, and one thing would have to be in many different material things. Moreover, the Form could not be created because of what is below it. Aside from leaving the question of causality unanswered, this would lead to an infinite regress of Forms of Forms, and so on.[91] This is Suhrawardī's answer to the third-man argument that always plagued Plato's theory of Forms.

Nor are the Forms corruptible composites. They are luminous simple essences whose shadows are the species. The material thing has a Form and accidents corresponding to the accidents of its immaterial lord.[92] In addition, the relations among the species and their relative ranks reflect the relations among the lights that are their lords.

The Form is only metaphorically a universal—it is certainly not a universal of logic in the sense of being an idea in the mind. It is, in fact, a self-conscious intellect—an angel. It is universal only in the sense that it has the same relation of care and solicitude to all the members of the species.[93] Figure 2.6 shows the classes of material lights.

The Lights as Causes of the Physical Universe

Suhrawardī's deductions about the origin of the spheres are based on the principle of sufficient reason. He does not claim to know how many spheres there are or how many lights in the

90. *Illumination,* 159/375.
91. *Illumination,* 158–59/373–74.
92. *Illumination,* 159–60/374–75.
93. *Illumination,* 160–61/375–76.

Figure 2.6 The Classes of Immaterial Lights

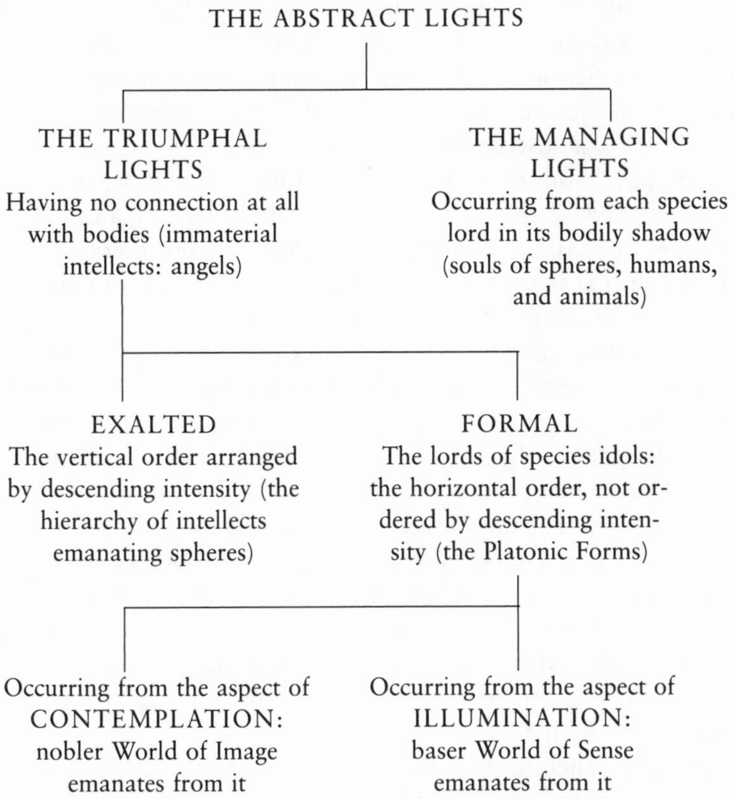

vertical order. On the one hand, since the motions of the planets are composite, each must have several spheres.[94] On the other, there could be additional spheres and planets veiled from us

94. *Illumination,* 132/333.

beyond those we can see.[95] He may have been thinking here of the World of Image, with its heavens surrounding ours.

Although the sphere of the fixed stars is higher than the spheres of the planets, it is actually more complex. Since there is no disorder in the heavens of Suhrawardī's universe, the patterns of the stars have to be the shadow of some intelligible order: the shadow of the horizontal order of lights or, more exactly, the result of the interaction of the aspect of dependence with the rays of the lights, especially of the weaker and lower ones.[96] We may not comprehend the pattern, but there can be no doubt that it is there. It is, in fact, empirical proof that the spheres have to number more than nine or ten.

Suhrawardī's demonstrations about the causes of the movements of the spheres illustrate the relation between the Science of Lights and Peripatetic philosophy. He uses principles drawn from Peripatetic physics to prove by elimination that whatever moves the spheres has to be alive. Then, the Science of Lights demonstrates that the movers of the spheres have to be immaterial managing lights. The managing lights—that is, souls—of the spheres, like the souls of men and animals, emanate from the light that is the lord of that species. Since the celestial souls obviously do not have any desires of appetite or passion, their movement has to be for the sake of illumination from the immaterial lights.[97]

Although there is an intelligible order among the immaterial lights and their mutual illuminations, it is far too complex to be expressed by any one state of the spheres and planets, particularly since the spheres veil each other. Therefore, the spheres expressed, through their movements and interrelationships, over

95. *Illumination,* 149/357.
96. *Illumination,* 142–43/347–48.
97. *Illumination,* 132/333.

a very long though finite time, the relationships among the immaterial lights and their rays.[98]

According to the principle of sufficient reason, everything has a distinct and sufficient cause for its existence. According to the Science of Lights, its ultimate cause is immaterial light. From this it is evident that the efficient cause of all sublunar events is ultimately the movements the spheres. This was the reason certain stars were considered lucky and others unlucky.[99]

The lowest of the vertical order of lights, lower in rank than the lights causing the spheres, are the lights that cause the elements. These lights emanate barriers submissive to the spheres and sharing a common matter (i.e., magnitude).[100] These are the material cause of the things of this world.

The formal cause of bodies is the horizontal order of lights—the lords of species idols, or the Platonic Forms. These lights cannot be ordered completely by rank, since not all such lights differ in luminosity. Unlike the vertical order of lights, which are distinguished solely by luminosity, the horizontal lights vary both in luminosity and in luminous and dark accidents. Therefore, the species they control can have the same or different ranks.[101] We may assume that the lights that are the species lords of maple and birch trees, for example, have the same rank, whereas they would have a higher rank than the lights of the grasses and a lower rank than the lights of the palm or any animal.

The difference in rank among the lights that are the lords of species explains the presence or absence of a managing light—the soul—and animal spirit. In the higher creatures—plants, animals, and human beings—the species light is relatively ex-

98. *Illumination,* 175/398–99.
99. *Illumination,* 143/348.
100. *Illumination,* 177–78/401–3.
101. *Illumination,* 178–79/403–4.

alted and the capacity of the constitution requires the mediacy of another light, the soul, to manage the individual creature. In animals and human beings this light is sufficiently exalted to require the mediacy of a subtle substance—the animal spirit—to manage the body. In the inanimate species, however, the species light is so low that it approaches the condition of accidental light, and the capacity of the body so limited that no mediating managing light is possible.[102]

Thus, Suhrawardī explains how the immaterial lights cause material bodies: the lowest vertical lights cause the elements, which are the material cause of the bodies of this world. The species lords—the horizontal order of immaterial lights—are the formal causes of their species. The movements of the spheres, caused in turn by the accidental relations among the immaterial lights, are the efficient cause of the bodies and their accidents. Figure 2.7 shows the causes of material creatures.

God's Knowledge and Providence

The question of God's knowledge of particulars, and therefore of individual providence, was important in Islamic philosophy in large part because it was a key dispute with the theologians.[103] The natural interpretation of the Qur'ān was that God knew and could act on particulars. Suhrawardī quotes the verse, "In the heavens and earth, not even the weight of an atom escapes Him."[104] However, it was not easy to reconcile the personal God of the monotheistic religions with the remote and utterly simple God of the Greek philosophical tradition. Theologians, with some reason, accused the philosophers of believing that God can know only universals—scientific theory, as it were.

102. *Illumination,* 165–67/383–85.

103. Avicenna, *Ilāhīyāt,* 398–99, 414 ff.; Averroes, *Tahāfut al-Tahāfut,* ed. Sulaymān Dunyā, 2d ed. (Cairo: Dār al-Ma'ārif, 1968), 690–711.

104. Qur'ān 34:3.

Figure 2.7 The Causes of Material Creatures

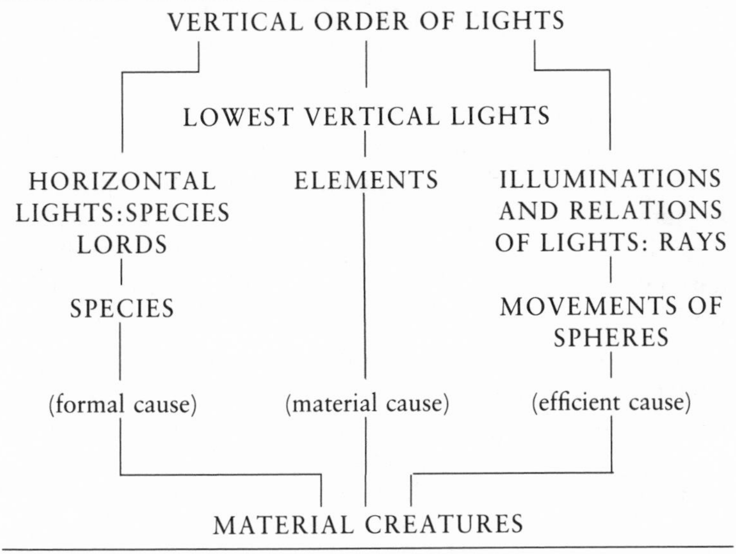

According to the Peripatetics, knowledge is the occurrence of the form of the known in the knower. However, God's knowledge cannot be of this sort since it implies the existence of multiplicity in the Divine Essence. The knowledge of God therefore has to be explained in some other manner. Suhrawardī summarizes the Peripatetic theory as follows:

> The Peripatetics and their followers say that the knowledge of the Necessary Existent is not something additional to it; rather it is its lack of absence from its own immaterial essence. They argue that the existence of things results from the Necessary Existent's knowledge of them.[105]

105. *Illumination,* 150–51/358–59.

Quṭb al-Dīn explains that they held this view because otherwise the essence of the Necessary Existent would have to contain multiplicity.[106] Because the essence of God is the cause of all things, the knowledge of all things is to be found in His knowledge of His own essence.[107]

Suhrawardī was unimpressed with this explanation. For one thing, he held that detailed knowledge cannot be implied by a negation. For another, knowledge of properties and accidents is not bound up in the knowledge of the essence. It certainly is not an adequate basis for a providential ordering of the world.[108]

Suhrawardī's solution to this problem employs his theory of knowledge by presence. The Peripatetics, like modern scientists, held that knowledge, sensation, and the like occur through the acquisition of a form: the imprinting of a shape on the retina, for example. Suhrawardī, however, insists on the primary role of consciousness. According to the Illuminationists, vision is simply the unobstructed presence of the lighted object before a sound eye—a relation, not an accident in the mind or eye. The knowledge of the Light of Lights is of this sort. The Light of Lights is manifest in itself and to itself. It is therefore self-conscious. Since all other things are in its presence, all other things are manifest to it. Therefore, the Light of Lights knows all things. This does not imply any multiplicity in the Light of Lights, as it is conditioned on a relation—manifestation—and a negation—the lack of obstruction. Thus, God's vision and knowledge are the same, as are His power and luminosity.

There is, however, no providence based on this divine knowl-

106. *Commentary,* 359.
107. *Illumination,* 151/359.
108. *Illumination,* 151–52/359–62.

edge. The Light of Lights does not learn the conditions of its creatures and then act so as to benefit them. The providential order we find in the world is not based on such ad hoc efficient causality but on the relationships among the immaterial lights.[109] The universe in all its complexity reflects the incomprehensibly complex but utterly rational relationships among the immaterial lights. Suhrawardī's universe is deterministic, fixed, and perfected in every particular by the relentless logic of the interplay of the divine lights.

PHYSICAL QUESTIONS

Suhrawardī also tries to apply the Science of Lights to questions of physics, particularly to the question of the composition of the body. Suhrawardī and his opponents needed to explain two aspects of bodies: divisibility and unity. The Peripatetics attribute the former to matter, the latter to form. Matter, however, has only the haziest sort of reality and is not directly perceptible. Form also includes several levels of universals: species, nature, and so on, all considered substances.[110] Against this Suhrawardī advances the view he attributes to the ancients—that body is a self-subsistent magnitude and its accidents. Through tortuous arguments, he tries to demonstrate that matter is a concept we apply to body in view of its changing states but whose reality we cannot assert. Thus we are left with magnitude—a sensible and concrete reality—as a constituent of body in place of a ghostly and unknowable prime matter.[111]

In the Peripatetic system, the bodily form, constituting with

109. *Illumination,* 150/358, 152–53/362–66.
110. *Illumination,* 82/225.
111. *Illumination,* 74–82/206–25.

matter the individual body, is constituted by other forms—of species, elements, and so on. Since these constitute substances, they have to be substances. Particular bodies, for example, are divisible or indivisible, soft or hard. The Peripatetics assert that this is due to other forms, which thereby particularize the body and constitute the species form. Suhrawardī suggests and then demonstrates that accidents can participate in the constitution of substance.[112] Thus, a body is just self-subsistent magnitude and accidents. Constitutions, for example, are qualities mediating qualities—not forms mediating forms, as was the case for the Peripatetics.[113] Likewise, the elements are only sensible forms and bodiliness.[114]

In the Peripatetic system, the form is the functional organization of the thing embodied its nature. According to Aristotle, nature is "the source from which the primary movement in each natural object is present in it in virtue of its own essence."[115] In Suhrawardī's system, the nature is the immaterial light that is the lord of the thing's species.[116] The material thing and its accidents are the recipient causes of the light's efficacy, but the efficient cause of the thing's essential movements is the angel of that species, which is thus the nature of the thing. Quṭb al-Dīn quotes John Philoponus's rejection of the Aristotelean interpretation of nature: "This does not indicate nature, but its action. Nature is a spiritual power acting in bodies."[117] In the higher creatures this power might be mediated by a soul or a soul and an animal spirit, but in the mineral realm it is effective directly.

112. *Illumination,* 82–83/225–28.
113. *Illumination,* 198/436–37.
114. *Illumination,* 193/428.
115. *Metaphysics* 5.4 (trans. Ross).
116. *Illumination,* 199–200/439.
117. *Commentary,* 439.

SUMMARY: THE STRUCTURE OF THE SCIENCE OF LIGHTS

Suhrawardī claimed that *The Philosophy of Illumination* was superior to works in the Peripatetic mode, whether his own or others', since it is based originally on mystical experience, not thought. It is not a book of mysticism, however, nor the record of his mystical experiences; it is a book of philosophy, whose conclusions are derived by rational demonstration from prior necessary premises. It is based on mystical experience only in the sense that (1) mystical experience first convinced Suhrawardī of the truth of his premises and conclusions and (2) the ultimate goal of the Science of Lights is the seeker's mystical attainment. Suhrawardī sometimes appeals directly to mystical experience, but this is only to increase the seeker's inner conviction or as a short-cut to his conclusion: the truth of the doctrine is sufficiently established by rational argument.

In fact, since Suhrawardī's demonstrations are usually causal, not merely assertoric, mystical and sensible experiences play only an indirect role in the demonstration.[118] Suhrawardī mainly works from the Creator to the creatures to explain why the universe is as it is. The congruence of experience with the results of the demonstration can only prove the possibility of the truth of the explanations. Experience can *disprove* a scientific model but cannot demonstrate its truth.

118. An assertoric demonstration proves that something is the case; a causal demonstration proves it through a middle term that is also the actual cause of the fact. See Aristotle, *Posterior Analytics,* 1.13 ("The nephew must have killed him because no one else had access to the murder weapon" vs. "The nephew killed him to keep him from changing his will," as it were).

In practice, Suhrawardī builds the Science of Lights on three bases. The first is his critical purging of Peripatetic philosophy, the project of his Peripatetic works and of considerable parts of *The Philosophy of Illumination.*

The second basis of the Science of Lights is the concept of light. Metaphysics supplies the foundations of all other sciences, so its subject has to be self-evident. If existence has no reality and its concept is ineluctably obscure, Suhrawardī must look elsewhere. Obviously, whatever does not need definition will be manifest. Therefore, the proper subject of metaphysics is the manifest—not manifestation, which presumably is an intellectual fiction. The symbols Suhrawardī chooses to represent these qualities are light and darkness.

Suhrawardī gives fair warning in the introduction to *The Philosophy of Illumination* that the work is symbolic. The commentators, and even Suhrawardī himself, lapse into Peripatetic terms—the "physical mode"—whenever it suits their purposes. That the key concept is the manifest rather than light is shown by the accounts of hearing and the other minor senses. Suhrawardī explains them in precisely the same way as sight, only without the obviously inappropriate symbol of light. Therefore, the real subject is things as manifest, either in themselves or by another.

This concept, as Suhrawardī works it out, implies the denial of any real substratum linking things. Instead, things are independent and autonomous, and their reality is precisely their individuality. Their interconnection consists in their being manifest to each other. Even the immaterial lights, which all share the common reality of light, are each autonomous monads, distinct and individual. Light certainly cannot be the substratum of Suhrawardī's universe, both because of the discontinuity of the immaterial lights and because the material world is not light in its substance. The subject of *The Philosophy of Illumination* is the lights, not light.

The third basis of *The Philosophy of Illumination* is the collection of metaphysical axioms shared with Peripatetic philosophy. Of these, the two most important are the principle of sufficient reason and the impossibility of an actual ordered infinity. These, of course, are used by other Islamic philosophers and explain why Suhrawardī's system includes the familiar pyramidal universe, culminating in an absolutely simple, necessary first cause. Nevertheless, the difference in content of the fundamental concepts of the system ensures that there are real differences in doctrine between the two systems.

Suhrawardī's contribution to Islamic ontology and thus to the other areas of philosophy dependent on it lies in his sharp distinction between the mental and the concrete. Before him Avicenna could operate on the casual assumption that the structure of reality corresponds to the structure of thought. Suhrawardī denies this, and thereafter all Islamic philosophers have to keep this distinction in mind. On this distinction rests the denial of the extramental reality of existence. After Suhrawardī what we might call "naive Avicennism" was unquestionably dead. Even the philosophers who upheld the primacy of existence accepted the validity of Suhrawardī's argument within its sphere. Sabzawārī, for example, cites it and escapes it only by making a further distinction between the concept and reality of existence. The concept of existence, he says, is self-evident to ordinary human consciousness. The reality of existence is primary but accessible only to mystical intuition.

In one sense, then, the Illuminationist philosophy was equivalent to the philosophy of the primacy of existence in that it was subsumed into it. On the other hand, it differed from it in that the philosophy of the primacy of existence was possible only on the basis of a further distinction that Suhrawardī did not make.

The point of this rather lengthy exercise has been to establish a basis for evaluating Quṭb al-Dīn's philosophy. I hope it is apparent from what has been discussed so far that Suhrawardī's contribution to Islamic philosophy is not his symbolism of light but a set of philosophical doctrines that have something quite precise to do with the philosophies that came before and after them. What they have to do with Quṭb al-Dīn's philosophy is examined in the next chapter.

·THREE·

Illuminationist Elements in Quṭb al-Dīn's The Pearly Crown

THE PEARLY CROWN

When the books of Aristotle reached the Arabs, they were taken as chapters of a systematic philosophical and scientific compendium, works such as Porphyry's *Isogoge* being added to fill perceived gaps. From their subjects was derived a scheme for the systematic division of the sciences, which the Islamic philosophers then took as the outline for their own encyclopedic works.

The pattern most later Islamic philosophers followed was set—here as in so many other areas—by Avicenna, especially in his *Book of Healing,* his most comprehensive work.[1] Such philosophically oriented encyclopedias covered logic, physics, and metaphysics. The more comprehensive, like the *Healing,* also included mathematics (including astronomy and music), practical philosophy, and natural history. The sciences were usually divided into speculative and practical, and the speculative into physics, mathematics, and metaphysics. Logic, being a tool of all the sciences, came first. The study of prophecy and the

1. Peters, in *Aristotle and the Arabs,* 105–20, gives outlines of the *Shifā* and several other encyclopedic works of various viewpoints.

supernatural was often included at the end of metaphysics. Although this outline was generally followed, subjects could be abridged or omitted, depending on the scope of the work and the author's interests and expertise. In philosophical works mathematics was often omitted, as were ethics, economics, and natural history, even sometimes logic. Such works could also be written on various levels of sophistication.

Quṭb al-Dīn composed *The Pearly Crown* according to a slightly different division of sciences in which metaphysics is divided into two—first philosophy coming after logic, and rational theology after mathematics. After an introduction on knowledge, the five main books cover logic, first philosophy, physics, mathematics, and metaphysics. An appendix (*khātima*) of four books covers the principles of Islam (*uṣūl-i dīn,* i.e., dogmatic theology), Islamic practice (*furū'-i dīn,* i.e., jurisprudence), practical philosophy, and mysticism. The book was considered noteworthy not only because it was written in Persian—unusual for a book of this scope—but also because it included the religious sciences.

Quṭb al-Dīn most likely published *The Pearly Crown* in 705/1306, eleven years after the *Commentary on "The Philosophy of Illumination."* Thus, Quṭb al-Dīn must have begun *The Pearly Crown* at the latest shortly after the publication of the *Commentary* in 694/1295. Two such substantial books, published late in his career, may be assumed to be considered expressions of his mature views.

There are problems connected with the interpretation of *The Pearly Crown.* First, parts of the work are translations: the astronomy is a translation of an Arabic epitome of Ptolemy, although Quṭb al-Dīn himself wrote extensively and creatively on astronomy. A translation of Fārābī's *Selected Aphorisms* and on ethical work by Avicenna were included in the chapter on practical philosophy, beside a systematic treatment of the same subjects by Quṭb al-Dīn himself. The rational theology is a translation of Fakhr al-Dīn Rāzī's *Book of Forty Chapters.* There was no attempt to relate Fārābī's, Avicenna's or Rāzī's works to the rest of the book.

Second, the philosophical books of *The Pearly Crown* are totally Peripatetic in their language, with virtually no use of distinctively Illuminationist terms. Moreover, they provide no discussion of topics such as the preexistence of the soul and the world of image, which we know Quṭb al-Dīn to have been particularly interested in. Nor is there any explicit reference to the *Commentary.*

The following, I think, may be known or surmised about *The Pearly Crown* based on historical evidence and the work itself:

1. It was a popular work intended for the educated layman: it was in Persian.[2] The more esoteric controversial philosophical topics were omitted. Even the chapter on mysticism was written for the novice.
2. As the rest of this chapter shows, the five philosophical books form a coherent whole, which can be systematically related to the *Commentary* and to Suhrawardī's *Philosophy of Illumination.*
3. The original plan of the book included the introduction, logic, physics, mathematics, and rational theology.[3]
4. In keeping with the work's general audience, Quṭb al-Dīn provided in two cases translations of classic works of mathematics. Possibly he supplied his own arithmetic and music because there were no recognized classics available or because he had not already published on these subjects.
5. The supplement on religion, practical philosophy, and mysticism was an addition to the original plan, perhaps suggested by the patron or his interests.[4]

2. *Crown,* 1:1:21.
3. *Crown,* 1:1:121.
4. *Crown,* 1:1:72.

It is conceivable that Quṭb al-Dīn retired to Gīlān with a manuscript consisting of the philosophical books of *The Pearly Crown* and that the other chapters were either added at the request of the Amīr or were quickly inserted to produce a finished work for which Quṭb al-Dīn might be paid. Nevertheless, none of the philosophically important chapters, with the exception of parts of the practical philosophy and the mysticism, were direct translations.

THE ILLUMINATIONIST THEORY OF REALITY

Illuminationist Themes in *The Pearly Crown*

Within the constraints imposed by the intended audience of *The Pearly Crown,* Quṭb al-Dīn explores several major Illuminationist themes, treating them in "the physical mode"—that is to say, in Peripatetic terms—elaborating them and bringing them into systematic connection with the mainstream of Islamic philosophy. There is, to begin with, the problem of the fundamental nature of reality: the fictitiousness of existence, the primacy of the concrete, and the discontinuity and manifestness of reality. There is also the problem of the basis of knowledge. Quṭb al-Dīn deals with this on several levels: in first philosophy in connection with the problem of quiddities; in logic in his discussion of definition; in physics in the discussion of bodily forms; and in rational theology in the discussion of the intellects and the Platonic Forms. The analysis on each level centers around the tension between the role of presence as the basis of knowledge and the need to establish the validity of universals and scientific knowledge.

In *The Pearly Crown* Quṭb al-Dīn does not address controversial matters such as the esoteric philosophical interpretation of religious dogmas. These he left for works of more limited circulation. He also does not use the symbolism of *The Philos-*

ophy of Illumination—aside from incidental contexts, such as prayers, where symbolism is especially appropriate. This symbolism probably had less to do with Illuminationist philosophy than it did with the instructional method of a single book, *The Philosophy of Illumination*.

The First Philosophy

The third book of *The Pearly Crown,* following Quṭb al-Dīn's fourfold division of philosophy, deals with the first philosophy, whose subject is universals. This, in turn, is divided into two chapters—one on "matters common to all conceptions" (existence, quiddity, unity, necessity, eternity, cause, and substance, along with their contraries and related terms—that is to say, the basic concepts of metaphysics) and another on the classes of accidents. The subjects roughly correspond to those covered in the first half of Avicenna's *Rational Theology*[5] or Aristotle's *Metaphysics* 4–10.

Suhrawardī's Science of Lights begins with an analysis of the structure of experience, starting with what is best known: light, or more generally, the manifest. Our knowledge, he holds, is not in the first place mediated by concepts but occurs by a direct relation with its object—presence. Our conceptual knowledge is once or twice removed from the thing. His symbols of light and darkness are the means by which he can rationally explore a realm known in the first instance by intuition.[6]

Quṭb al-Dīn, on the other hand, begins with the conceptual structure of our knowledge—with the concepts of existence, quiddity, unity, and so on. Then he moves from concept to reality following the same path as Avicenna but remaining always conscious of the distinction between concept and reality.

5. *Ilāhīyāt,* bks. 1–7.
6. See pp. 44 ff. above.

In the *Commentary* he remarks that Avicenna assumes that to every conceptual distinction corresponds a real distinction.[7] Although Ṭūsī denied this,[8] the line between concept and reality of metaphysical secondary intelligibles certainly is often blurred in Avicenna. Suhrawardī, on the other hand, makes a sharp and consistent distinction between the structure of the conceptual world and the structure of the real world. Quṭb al-Dīn thus followed Suhrawardī when he titled this chapter "matters common to all concepts [*mafhūmāt*]."[9] Avicenna called this branch of knowledge "matters common to all *things*."[10]

This conceptual system, however, was not arbitrary but had a systematic relation to experience and reality. The program of Quṭb al-Dīn's first philosophy is the exploration of this conceptual structure, its relation to reality, and the structure of reality insofar as it relates to the secondary intelligibles that are correlates of all our thoughts.

Existence

Quṭb al-Dīn begins his discussion of existence with the statement that the concept of existence is self-evident and undefinable since there is nothing better known by which it can be defined.[11] On a purely conceptual level, the concept of existence can be used in various ways: existence can be said to be in the mind, it can in different ways be said to be more or less general than "thing" or to be synonymous with it.[12] Existence in con-

7. *Commentary,* 185.
8. *Sharḥ al-Ishārāt,* in Izutsu, *Concept and Reality,* 109.
9. *Crown,* 1:3:1.
10. "*al-naẓar fī ma'rifat al-ma'ānī al-'āmma jamī' al-mawjūdāt,*" "Fī Aqsām al-'Ulūm al-'Aqlīya," *Majmū'at al-Rasā'il,* ed. Muḥyī al-Dīn Ṣabrī al-Kurdī (Cairo: Kurdistān al-'Ilmīya, 1338), 236.
11. *Crown,* 1:3:1.
12. *Crown,* 1:3:2.

crete things is simply that something is a concrete thing—not something by which it is a concrete thing.[13] Otherwise, Suhrawardī's third-man argument would apply: this existence would have existence, and so on, regressing to infinity. Therefore, concrete existence is simply the fact that something is existent. The concept, he warns us, is misleading in this respect.[14]

Moreover, existence is predicated equivocally of its instances, the particular existents. For example, the existence of the cause is stronger than and prior to the existence of the effect, and so on.[15]

In the world, everything is concrete and particular: "Those concrete things that are existent are particular existents" (*mawjūd-i mā'ī*). The existence of a particular thing is a concrete attribute—in the mind, a primary intelligible—but it is not the same as the existence of something else. These then are just meanings without names and are referred to as "the existence of" this or that. In other words, existence as a concept that applies directly to the thing is specific to that thing, and existence in general is a correlate of all of them in the mind[16]—a genus, perhaps, of the particular varieties of existence. This is not like redness, a concept really derived from its particular instances, since it is particularized not by a subject but by something acting like a difference: the "existence of" this or that. Existence in general presumably corresponds to color in general.

The *concept of existence,* however, is one. If it were not one, it could not be applied to absolutely any existent, nor could it be self-evident. The source of the general concept of existence

13. He said this was like life: life is a thing's being alive, not something by which it is alive. *Crown,* 1:4:75.

14. *Crown,* 1:3:2.

15. *Crown,* 1:3:2–3.

16. *Crown,* 1:3:3.

is the mind, not external reality. However, when it is universal, it has to be purely mental and apply only to things in the mind.

> When existence is general, this existence must be from the soul, for existence in the soul is existent just like all the rest of the meanings existent in the soul. . . . General existence is a correlate of everything in the mind.[17]

The implications of Quṭb al-Dīn's argument so far are these: If something is said to exist, this simply refers to its being existent, not to its having something that made it existent. Second, the relation between the concept of existence and existing things is mediated by primary intelligibles, the particular existences: the existence of Socrates or the existence of a relation. The primary intelligible relates to the thing in its particularity. Any commonality between existents as existents occurs on the level of the mind. There is nothing in the concrete things that specifically corresponds to existence in general.

From here he moves to his detailed proof of the fictitiousness of general existence.[18] If existence were not a purely intellectual predicate, it would have to belong to one of the classes of external things.

If it were the concrete quiddities themselves, it would be contraries: substance and accident, black and white. Moreover, in that case, the concept would be empty: "The substance is existent" would be equivalent to "The substance is substance" and "The existent is existent."

If it were something more general than any particular quiddity, it would either be self-subsistent or would occur in the concrete quiddity. In the former case, substance could not be

17. *Crown,* 1:3:3.
18. *Crown,* 1:3:3–5.

described by it, since it would have the same relation to substance as to everything else. If it occurred in the substance, the existence would be existent and would therefore not be applied univocally to all its instances. Moreover, in this case existence would be an accident and would be essentially posterior to its locus. Accident, in at least one sense, would be more general than existence. Also, if the quiddity and the existence were separate, then the contemplation of a nonexistent quiddity would lead us to consider the existence of the existence of the quiddity, which would not be the same as its existence. Thus, an infinite regress would result. This was Suhrawardī's argument and was commonly identified with him in later discussions of the fictitiousness or reality of existence.[19]

Therefore, the concrete quiddity and its existence are not two things outside the mind. The concrete quiddity itself is caused by its efficient cause. Existence is not added to it. "Existence" and "thing" are secondary intelligibles dependent on primary intelligibles: there is nothing in concrete reality that is existence or thing. These are just correlates of the intelligibility of the thing as an existent or as something—a rather Kantian view.

While rejecting Avicenna's distinction of quiddity and existence on the concrete level, Quṭb al-Dīn retains it on a conceptual level—as does Suhrawardī in his Peripatetic works. These concepts are not arbitrary constructions but necessary correlates of our knowledge of real things. Existence and quiddity are distinct only in the mind, where the paradoxes connected with them did not arise. Within their proper sphere, these concepts were a legitimate area of philosophical investigation.

Existence, although an intellectual fiction, relates to concrete quiddities in the following ways:

19. See pp. 45–48 above; Sabzawārī, *Metaphysics,* 33.

1. As a thing's relation to things, in which case existence is synonymous with *in:* Something is existent in the house or in the mind or among concrete things.
2. As a copula: Zayd is existent writing.
3. As the thing's concrete reality.[20]

In these cases the concept is related to the external quiddity. It should be noted, however, that in the first two cases *existence* is said of external relations, which themselves have a very tenuous reality, whereas in the third it just is said of the thing itself.

Quṭb al-Dīn has here worked out Suhrawardī's position in detail within the Avicennan/Peripatetic framework. Also, whereas Suhrawardī in *The Philosophy of Illumination* criticizes the application of the concept of existence to external reality, Quṭb al-Dīn investigates its role in our conceptual systems.

In summary, Avicenna makes a distinction between existence and quiddity, the precise significance of which is not altogether clear. Suhrawardī then argues that this distinction can be made only on the level of concept, not on the level of external reality.

If we take Sabzawārī as typical of those who in opposition to Suhrawardī maintained that existence is fundamentally real (*aṣīl*), we still find that Suhrawardī's distinction of the concept and reality of existence and his arguments about the fictitiousness of existence have been accepted, although subsumed into a larger framework. Sabziwārī first distinguished between the self-evident notion of existence and its hidden reality.[21] His account of the reality of existence then addresses Suhrawardī's criticisms: The reality of existence is analogical so that it is not found in the same way in different things;[22] the individual thing

20. *Crown,* 1:3:5.
21. Sabzawārī, 31–32.
22. Sabzawārī, 39.

is an ontological unity; existence in concept is an accident of quiddity.[23] It is only the distinction of the hidden reality and manifest concept of existence that prevents his position from collapsing into Suhrawardī's.

Thus, even the later philosophers who considered Suhrawardī fundamentally wrong thought that his criticisms of Avicenna were justified. His criticisms could be disposed of only by reinterpreting them in the light of a deeper mystical insight into the unity of reality.

THE STATUS OF UNIVERSALS

Quiddity

The second "matter common to all concepts" is quiddity, the other half of Avicenna's great division. The term *quiddity* (*māhīya, quidditas*) in Arabic and Latin means simply "the answer to the question 'What is it?'" This concept in English and Latin is closely related to *essence* (*essentia*) and in the Arabic of this context to *reality* (*ḥaqīqa*) and *essence* (*dhāt*).[24] Whereas *essence* and *reality* generally refer to what the thing is in its concrete reality,[25] *quiddity* tends to refer to its concept in the mind. There is not, however, any sharp distinction maintained among these terms (see Figure 3.1).

The philosophical issue is the status of universals. Quṭb al-Dīn defines *reality* as follows:

23. Sabzawārī, 43.
24. Soheil Afnan, *A Philosophical Lexicon in Persian and Arabic* (Beirut: Dar El-Mashreq, [1968]), s.v. "ḥaqīqat," "dhāt," "māhīyat;" Goichon, *Lexique,* s.v. "ḥaqīqa," "Dāt," "māhīya."
25. *Crown,* 1:5:72: "The reality of something is the particularity [*khuṣūṣīyat*] of its existence." This definition is from Avicenna.

Figure 3.1 Levels of Abstraction of Quiddity and Existence

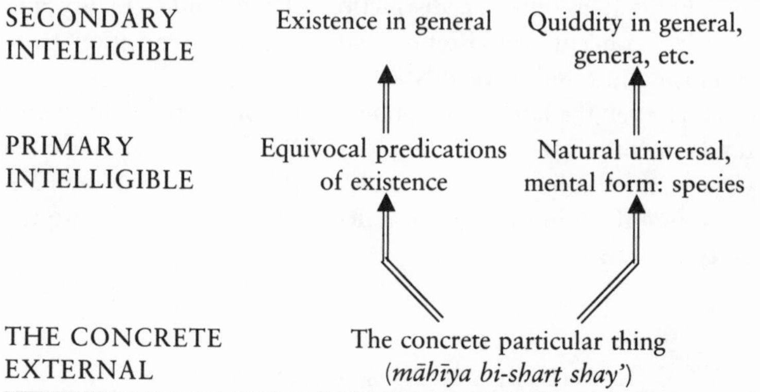

In the Illuminationist philosophy of Suhrawardī and Quṭb al-Dīn, the concrete individual thing is the primal reality—the doctrine later called the *primacy of quiddity*. A concept abstracted directly from concrete things is a primary intelligible and exists only in the mind, although it shares a concept with the concrete things. Secondary intelligibles are abstractions from ideas and have no existence in any sense outside the mind.

> Each thing has a reality such that that thing is that thing by that reality and by that reality it is different than what is other than it. . . . For example, humanity, in that respect in which it is humanity, has within its concept neither existence nor non-existence, nor unity nor multiplicity, nor generality nor specificity, nor any other one of the intellectual fictions.[26]

On a conceptual level the reality or quiddity of something is distinct from its existence, unity, universality, and so on. Quiddity can be considered on three levels. As *quiddity conditioned on something* (*māhīya bi-sharṭ shay'*), it is quiddity as it actually is (*min ḥaythu hiya hiya*)—*humanity* existing as a concrete thing. As *quiddity conditioned on nothing* (*bi-sharṭ lā shay'*), it

26. *Crown*, 1:3:10–11.

is abstracted from all connections and, strictly speaking, has no existence in objects or in minds. The third level is quiddity abstracted from all external connections but existent in the mind. This shares the concept of humanity with the external quiddity. But the external quiddity is not one: the humanity of *X* is not the humanity of *Y*. One might be learned, the other ignorant.[27] This is analogous to the distinction between general existence (a secondary intelligible) and the particular existences (primary intelligibles).

Concerning universals Quṭb al-Dīn states,

> [*X* and *Y*] share [*mushtarika*] in the notion [*mafhūm*] of humanity. What they share is the natural universal [*kullī ṭabīʿī*] and the imaginal mental form [*ṣūrat-i dhihnī-i mithālī*] having the same relation to all the external particulars of that form and corresponding [*muṭābiq*] to each one. For this reason it is called the "universal" [*kullī*].[28]

So far, then, there are six related concepts:

1. The concrete quiddity, *quiddity conditioned on something;*
2. The utterly pure quiddity, *quiddity conditioned on nothing;*
3. The mentally existent quiddity;
4. The natural universal, or nature;
5. The mental form in the imagination;
6. The notion of the quiddity.

The first, the concrete quiddity, is simply the concrete thing itself, something particular. The second is the absolutely pure quiddity, not even considered in relation to existence, particularity, and so on. There is no such thing. The third through fifth are all the idea of the thing in the mind, considered in different

27. *Crown,* 1:3:11–12.
28. *Crown,* 1:3:12.

ways. The last is the idea of the idea of the thing—a secondary intelligible.

The philosophical problem is to give universals sufficient reality to underpin science without stripping particulars of their primary reality. As a follower of Suhrawardī, Quṭb al-Dīn's first concern was with particular and tangible entities. Thus he reiterates his proof of the particularity of concrete things. External humanity is always individual, he says, and therefore can never be universal. Thus, the universal is rational and logical, not concrete. The natural universal has an identity, since it is existent in the mind. Its universality does not consist solely in its correspondence to many, since particulars can in some sense correspond to others, nor in its lack of particularization, since it is particularized in the mind. Rather, it is universal

> in respect of its being an imaginal essence [*kih ū dhātī'st mithālī*] which does not originate [*muta'aṣṣil*] in existence so that it would have been an original quiddity in itself. Instead, it is an image [*mithālī*]—not any image but a perceptual [*idrākī*] image—belonging to something that was, is, or will be.[29]

Insofar as this image corresponds to something external in some or all ways, it can be called a universal. This universal or image can be either prior or posterior to its concrete particulars. In the former case, it is the pattern according to which we create an external form. In the latter, it is a form acquired from external particulars. Thus, you can see Zayd and in your mind acquire a form of humanity from the particular qualities of Zayd. Then when you see 'Amr, you have no need to acquire a further form.

29. *Crown*, 1:3:12.

As the term *natural universal* implies, Quṭb al-Dīn here assumes there really are different kinds of things in the world. The basis for this is not yet established. Universals are known through the particulars. He makes no distinction between the natural and artificial. He returns to this problem in his physics when he discusses the material forms and in his metaphysics where he traces the basis of these forms and thus of universals back to the intellects.[30]

The next problem was how things differ and are distinguished: how quiddities and universals differ from each other and how individuals differ, both as concrete things and in the mind. Like the quiddities, the natural universals are not single or multiple in themselves. They have to have a cause for their multiplicity. Blackness is multiple by virtue of two bodies or conditions. Quṭb al-Dīn calls what makes them multiple a *distinguisher* (*mumayyiza*). This has to be something additional to the shared quiddity. This distinguisher is an aspect of the actual thing considered in relation to the knower:

> Thus, when an instance [*'adadī*] of the species of that nature is pointed out in sense, imagination, or the intellect, the one pointing it out knows that it is different from another. Therefore, there is something known in it by which he is acquainted with it and which distinguishes it from what is other than it. This thing is additional to its shared quiddity.[31]

Things, in fact, are distinguished by genus, difference, noncorrelate accident, and intensity, the last being an obvious reference to Suhrawardī.

This is only the structure of our knowledge of things, not the structure of the concrete things themselves: "The distinguisher

30. See pp. 98–100, 110 ff. below.
31. *Crown,* 1:3:14.

is not the individualizer."[32] A thing is individual by reason of its concrete identity—with respect to itself. Its distinction arises only from its participation in the shared meaning. A thing is individual because it is a particular thing. It is distinguished only in respect of its being known.

Quṭb al-Dīn now offers an analysis of quiddity, species, genus, and related concepts. The concepts of thing, reality, and quiddity in themselves—not as horse or man—are secondary intelligibles and intellectual fictions. Thing, reality, and quiddity *qua* being horse or man are the universal natures or natural universals. These are primary intelligibles but have in themselves no existence among concrete things.[33]

His problem here was to justify the objectivity of universals—of genus and species, difference, correlate accident, and so on—in the light of a metaphysics based on the concrete particular thing. It is possible, once it is admitted that quiddities in the mind do not have exact equivalents in external things, to produce an epistemology like that of Ibn Taymīya[34] or Hume, for example, in which concepts are arbitrary constructions and true science is impossible.

On the conceptual side, Quṭb al-Dīn divides quiddities into simple and compound, and the latter into arbitrary (*i'tibārī*)[35] compounds, like *white animal,* and real compounds. Within this schema he explains the five predicables of Porphyry.[36]

Externally, the situation is different. While an external quiddity can be compound—such as man, which has soul and body

32. *Crown,* 1:3:14.
33. *Crown,* 1:3:15.
34. Ibn Taymīya, *Naqḍ al-Manṭiq,* ed. Maḥammad b. 'Abd al-Razzāq al-Sanī' et al. (Cairo: Maṭba'at al-Sunna al-Muḥammadī, 1370/1951), 187. Ibn Taymīya was a vicious enemy of Greek logic and philosophy.
35. This is the same term that I translate by *fictitious* elsewhere.
36. *Crown,* 1:3:15–16.

as parts—the parts of the quiddity may exist only in the mind. Black, for example, is a simple sensible outside the mind, but in the mind it is composed of a genus—*color*—and a difference—*holding vision*. Externally, its being a color is the same as its being black. The genus, species, reality, and particularity of a concrete thing exist only in the mind. Genus and difference are only parts of the thing in the sense that they are parts of the definition. Here Quṭb al-Dīn restates his principle that the structure of things in the mind does not necessarily correspond to the structure of the external thing. That the concept of man is composite does not imply that the species man is composite in external reality. A real part of something, in fact, is not predicated of it.[37]

In this analysis, Quṭb al-Dīn refines Suhrawardī's criticism of the supposed Peripatetic reification of the concepts of existence and quiddity. His purpose in discussing universals is to define the relations between the conceptual structures explored by the Peripatetics and the unitary concrete object of Suhrawardī. In these two chapters and the following chapters on unity, necessity, and so on, he describes how this conceptual structure arises out of the concrete things.

To make real science possible, however, it is still necessary to explore the sources of regularity in the concrete things themselves. Within the structure of thing and knowledge as we have seen it so far, it would be natural to erect a Taymian/Humean epistemology in which species and genus are arbitrary concatenations of sensible qualities and natural laws nothing but the habits of God. To preserve the possibility of real science, Quṭb al-Dīn had to show that in real objects there is a basis for his distinction between real (*ḥaqīqī*) and fictitious compound quiddities.

37. *Crown,* 1:3:16–18

Other General Concepts

What it means for existence or quiddity to be fictitious may be better understood by considering the simpler case of unity and multiplicity. According to Quṭb al-Dīn, unity is the mind's intellection of the indivisibility of the concrete thing (*huwīyat*). The conception of this meaning is self-evident. Unity is an added mental notion since it has no existence among concrete things.

From this it may be seen that unity is neither part of the thing nor wholly arbitrary. If we consider a thing as an indivisible whole, we see it as one, but its unity is not part of its reality. On the other hand, the concept is not arbitrary, for we cannot look at it in this respect and say that it is actually two or three.[38]

Multiplicity, as well, was fictitious, the product of the mind considering several things together. Thus, one thing may be one or many, but not in the same sense.[39]

One, like *exists*, was used ambiguously (*bi-tashkīk*) by Quṭb al-Dīn. What is most truly one is what is said to be one in all respects—that is, the individual.[40]

The case of necessity, contingency, and impossibility is similar.[41] Their notions are self-evident and indefinable. These are conceptions occurring in the mind on the basis of external things, but they are not external existents. In the mind they are added to the conception of the thing. If they also were added to the thing, then the necessity of the necessary would be contingent, and so on. These were accidents of the intellect, not of the thing.

On the other hand, the conception of the necessity, contingency, or impossibility of something has a basis in reality in the

38. *Crown*, 1:3:18–19.
39. *Crown*, 1:3:19.
40. *Crown*, 1:3:20.
41. *Crown*, 1:3:24–29.

relation between the concrete thing and its cause, but not in such a way as to cause the multiplicity of the thing in its essence. Man is necessarily an animal, contingently literate, and impossibly a rock. He is also contingently existent. It is not arbitrary to say this, for each of these statements has a basis in actual fact. But these are relations and do not imply multiplicity in the reality of the thing. To say that a thing is contingent is to say something about its relation to its cause. The structure of the concrete thing does not mirror its structure in the mind. The concrete thing is unitary; the mental concept of it is not and is compounded of various aspects.

Quṭb al-Dīn, following Suhrawardī in a variation of Avicenna's famous distinction between necessary and contingent existence, thus divides existents as follows:

1. Existent essentially (*mawjūd bi'l-dhāt*) among concrete things:
   - Existent in itself and by itself (*li-dhātihi wa-bi-dhātihi*): the Necessary Existent;
   - In itself, not by itself: created substances;
   - Not in itself, not by itself: external accidents;
2. Existent accidentally:
   - Privations: rest, weakness;
   - Fictions not realized in objects: blindness.[42]

I assume this last category also includes intellectual fictions and mental existence. Existence in writing or in speech is actually metaphorical. Existence in this sense is mental.

Temporal (in the sense of having a beginning in time) is also an intellectual idea arising in the mind from the contemplation of nonexistence followed by existence. Again, it has no distinctive referrent in external reality.[43]

42. *Crown,* 1:3:24–26; *Œuvres,* 1:212–13.
43. *Crown,* 1:3:33.

Quṭb al-Dīn does not say in *The Pearly Crown* whether substantiality and accidentality are intellectual fictions or not. It may be assumed that he felt that they are, since the same sort of arguments apply to them as to the concepts discussed above.

What Difference Does It Make?

This view of the relation of universal concepts to particular things is basic to the doctrine of the *primacy of quiddity*—what I have called the *primacy of the concrete*. It is basic to the Illuminationist philosophy since it places ultimate reality with the concrete particular—that is, with what is manifest to us.

It is also significant in that it sharply defines the relations of concept and reality: Quibbles about issues such as the existence and nonexistence of existence, the existence of quiddity before its realization, and the existence of nonexistence come from assuming that the structure of the concrete thing corresponds to the structure of its concept in the mind.

On the other hand, if the force of these concepts is understood and if they are not improperly reified, they can be metaphysically fruitful. Thus, for example, the principle of sufficient reason was derived from notions of cause and necessity.[44] Various conclusions about time and motion could be drawn.

Forms and Bodies

Closely related to the problem of universals is the question of form and matter. Normally in Islamic philosophy a body is considered to be a composite of matter and form, neither of which can exist independently. Following Aristotle, the form of a body is considered to be individual, but from it is abstracted the universal. In *The Philosophy of Illumination* Suhrawardī

44. *Crown,* 1:3:27–28.

makes a radical attack on this theory, denying that there is any such thing as matter or bodily form. According to that work, bodies consist of self-subsistent magnitude and concatenations of accidents. The reality of the species and elements resides in the intellects—the Platonic Forms that are their lords and whose solicitude maintains the continuity and order of the individuals of the world. The lords of species idols, which are the horizontal order of intellects, are to be identified with the Forms of Plato.[45]

Quṭb al-Dīn takes a more conservative position. While retaining the intellects as the (at least probable) basis of species, he accepts the reality of matter and form and identifies four parts for each body:

1. Matter: something that bears the form (*ū ma'nī'st ki ḥamil-i ṣūrat-i ū'st*);
2. Form: its quiddity by which it is what it is;
3. Nature: the potency from which arises its essential change or changelessness;
4. Accidents, whether correlates of its species or not.[46]

It is easy to confuse the distinction of form and matter with that of quiddity and existence. For the simple abstract intellects—for which there is no matter—obviously existence cannot be identified with matter. In the sublunar world there is a real distinction between matter and form, although the two are not actually separable and neither alone is substance. Matter is the potentiality for division, while form is the actual connection. Each exists separately and has its own quiddity, although in a rather feeble way. Together they form body, but body has its own existence and quiddity. That existence and quiddity do not correspond to matter and form may be clearly seen from the fact that the quiddity of body would include its materiality.

45. See pp. 61–66 above.
46. *Crown,* 1:4:14.

Although Quṭb al-Dīn describes form as "the quiddity of a [body] by which it is what it is," form cannot be identified with the "quiddity conditioned on something" discussed in the first philosophy. This latter concrete quiddity would be the entire body with its matter, form, nature, and accidents.

Nor can the natural universal abstracted from the physical body relate solely to the form. The concept of man in its fullness refers to man's materiality, nature, and correlate accidents.

Nevertheless, Quṭb al-Dīn clearly departs from Suhrawardī's ideas about the sources of order in the world in that he gives material forms an independent causal efficacy, although their ultimate cause is still the higher intellects. For Suhrawardī, material bodies are just magnitude and accidents whose orderliness results directly from the solicitude of the intellects.

This is characteristic of Quṭb al-Dīn's use of Suhrawardī's ideas. He accepts the most basic metaphysical points but takes more careful notice of scientific data. Thus while accepting the fictitiousness of existence, Quṭb al-Dīn retains a hylomorphic theory of bodies in which forms are real. This difference of approach also is apparent in his treatment of such topics as perception and cosmology.

He notes Suhrawardī's division of the elements into opaque, translucent, and transparent, but he treats these as qualities of elements, parallel to the hot/cold and wet/dry divisions, and retains the theory of the four elements in which fire is an independent element rather than a state of air.

Knowledge

The positive counterpart in Suhrawardī's philosophy of illumination to the critical theory of the fictitiousness of existence is the theory of knowledge by presence (*'ilm ḥuḍurī*): that is, that knowledge occurs by the unveiled presence of the known to the knower, not by the imprinting of a form. In Suhrawardī's *Phi-*

losophy of Illumination this matter is treated on several levels. In the critique of the Peripatetics, he argues that the Peripatetic approach to definition makes it impossible to know anything, and in his own logic he substitutes a theory of definition based on direct knowledge of things. In his new Science of Lights he uses a theory of vision based on simple presence in place of Peripatetic theories requiring an intermediate entity. This, in turn, becomes the model for the knowledge of the intellects and, in fact, for his whole cosmology.

Quṭb al-Dīn in *The Pearly Crown* confronts a slightly different set of problems. He does not use the model of the Science of Lights; and since he is dealing with the whole of science, he systematically treats the problems of the Peripatetics. Although, as we will see, he does not accept all of Suhrawardī's more specific criticisms, especially in such fields as physics, he accepts his basic critique of Islamic Neoplatonism, including his notions about knowledge. Because the logical structure of *The Pearly Crown* is so different from that of *The Philosophy of Illumination,* the passages relating to knowledge must be gathered from widely separated points, although the theory of knowledge by presence was as fundamental for Quṭb al-Dīn as it was for Suhrawardī.

Definition

Although his division of the sciences follows Avicenna's division into the nine books of the Organon, Quṭb al-Dīn's logic more closely follows the outline based on "explanatory expressions" and "proof" used in Suhrawardī's works.[47]

Because of its implications for the relation between concept and reality in an essentialist frame of reference and for the theory of knowledge in general, the most important topic in

47. *Crown,* 1:1:76; Ziai, 46–90.

Illuminationist logic was definition. Definition, it should be remembered, is one of the areas in which Suhrawardī specifically criticizes the Peripatetics in the chapter on sophistical refutations in *The Philosophy of Illumination*.

The purpose of Peripatetic definition as it developed among the Islamic philosophers was to acquire the conception of the thing through an expression that captured the thing's essence.[48] A complete essential definition (*ḥadd tāmm*) was composed of the proximate genus of the thing and the differentia by which that species differs from other species of the genus. Essential description (*rasm*) used essentials other than the combination of proximate genus and differentia. There was also definition of the concept (*mafhūm*) of the thing, although this was less desirable for science.[49]

The trouble with the essentialist theory of definition was that it is very difficult, even in theory, to produce definitions that capture a thing's essence. It is easy to make a definition of the concept *man,* but there is no guarantee that it will correspond to the concrete essence. Nor is it hard to find a definition that distinguishes *humans* from everything else, but it is very difficult to produce a definition that captures what *humans* are in themselves, containing everything that cannot be otherwise and omitting everything that could be different. Suhrawardī deepened the difficulty by arguing that if the object of definition is to convey the essence to the mind, it is not enough just to supply terms that enable one to pick out that essence in the world. Rather, the definition has to list everything essential in that concrete essence, omitting nothing, so that the reader can synthesize these in the mind into an organic whole exactly corre-

48. *Crown,* 1:2:44; *Illumination,* 19/56–58; Ziai, 107–12.
49. *Crown,* 1:2:44–48; *Illumination,* 19–20/56–59; Ziai, 92–96.

sponding to the concrete whole. This, he maintains, is impossible.[50]

Quṭb al-Dīn, as usual, accepts the major criticisms of the Peripatetics but applies them cautiously and with more attention to the practical problems of science. Thus he defines a complete definition as

> an expression indicating the quiddity of the thing by correspondence [*muṭābaqa*]. It is composed of the genus and difference. . . . The genus contains all the common essentials and the difference all the distinguishing essentials if the genus and species are composite. Just as the creation of the thing outside is incomplete without the creation of all its parts, so too is its creation in the mind—i.e., its complete conception—without the creation of all the essentials in the mind.[51]

Constructing such a definition was, at least, extremely difficult. Finally, definition required a synthesis by which the parts of the definition are unified in the mind in a new concept.[52]

If a complete definition according to the concrete essence of the thing is difficult or impossible, other definitions are not. Although the medieval scientist adhered to an ideal of certainty in science, his practice was often more tentative and modest. Quṭb al-Dīn offers two alternative approaches to definition that are less ambitious and therefore more accessible. The first is essential description—replacing either or both genus and difference with common accident and property, respectively. Thus, for example, *humans* might be defined as splay-fingered bipeds. The former is a property specific but not essential to humans, while the latter is an accident common to various species taking

50. *Illumination,* 20–21/59–63.
51. *Crown,* 1:2:44–45.
52. *Crown,* 1:2:45.

the place of the genus. The mind then seeks what combines these.[53] An easier approach is definition of concept. Its limitation is that being purely formal, it has no necessary relation to the thing and has to be used in precisely the same form each time.[54]

The use of these in science is indicated in the final lines of his chapter on definition.[55] The terms used in definitions cannot be completely unknown but only unknown in their relations to what is defined. Therefore, definition is concerned not with the completely unknown (or the completely known) but with what is partially apprehended (*idrāk*) and is to be apprehended more perfectly. Definition, then, is not the static process that appears in textbooks on logic, but a living process in which definitions of increasing perfection interact with the experience of things. An essential description enables us to identify species in the world. By apprehension of the concrete thing, we are led to apprehend its other properties. From conceptual definitions we may make deductions that lead us to more perfect essential definitions. This has something in common with the process of "pointing and indication" (*ishāra, tanbīh*), which leads to the apprehension of the self-evident and indefinable conceptions.

Sense Perception

The theory of sensation tends to have a close relation to epistemology. In Suhrawardī's *Philosophy of Illumination* vision serves as an analog of knowledge in general. There vision occurs by the presence of a lighted and unveiled thing before a sound eye. A lighted thing is simply manifest: There is no intermediate

53. *Crown,* 1:2:44.
54. *Crown,* 1:2:46–47.
55. *Crown,* 1:2:47–48.

entity carrying vision. Insofar as he developed it, he applies this theory to other sensibles, notably sound. The main rival theory of perception—like the modern scientific theory—held that perception, imagination, and other processes in which forms are present in the mind take place by the imprinting of a form in the sense organ or brain. Suhrawardī held a special scorn for this. He thought that it was self-evident that we perceive things as they are. This being so, how can a mountain be contained in the eye? More important, if we do not have some direct access to the world, knowledge would be impossible.[56]

The scientific evidence for some sort of imprinting in perception is, of course, very strong; and Quṭb al-Dīn, with his scientific sophistication, could not ignore it. On the other hand, he was generally convinced by Suhrawardī's arguments about the centrality of presence in perception as the link between consciousness and physical process. If there was doubt, he remarked, it concerned imprinting, not presence.[57]

Given the scope of the work and the interests of the author, Quṭb al-Dīn's account of sensation in *The Pearly Crown* is much more thorough than Suhrawardī's in *The Philosophy of Illumination*. Quṭb al-Dīn defines perception (*idrāk*) as being when

> the reality of something is present in itself or in an image before that thing said to be the perceiver . . . whether that by which the perception occurs is its essence or an organ and whether the form is extracted from something external or is present from the beginning or is imprinted in the essence of the perceiver or in its organ or whether it is present without imprinting or inscribing in something.[58]

56. See pp. 53–54 above.
57. *Crown,* 1:3:82–83.
58. *Crown,* 1:3:80. Perception is a quality of the mind, knowledge in the broadest sense, encompassing all forms of mental activity.

Perception has to encompass both what involves imprinting of a form and what does not. We can say something about hypothetical mathematical figures, for example, but they have no concrete existence. Therefore, since something has to be present to the soul, there has to be a form imprinted in the soul. Self-consciousness, on the other hand, requires no imprinted form. For any sort of knowledge that changes, in fact, there has to be an acquired form of some sort occurring in us corresponding to the thing perceived.[59] Perception is also not just a relation between the perceiver and the perceived, although it involves one. Ultimately any sort of perception depends on presence. There has to be some stage where knowledge is direct and not mediated by a form. The forms of things perceived can be states in the soul, but the act of perception depends on the subject's direct consciousness of them. In his treatment of vision,[60] for example, Quṭb al-Dīn shows his relationship to other theories:

1. There is imprinting in the retina and the optic nerve. This is not true imprinting in that the object is imprinted to perspective and not in true size. (This is the physicist and physician writing.)
2. This imprinting does not occur from something being detached from the object seen—that is, the object is manifest.
3. The capacity for vision arises from the eye being opposite the thing with a transparent intermediary.
4. There are not really visual rays, such as optics was based on.
5. The optical ray theory works well enough mathematically if distances are not too great or small, although it is physically false.

59. *Crown,* 1:3:80.
60. *Crown,* 1:4:89–92.

The first and fifth points reflect scientific observation; the second, third, and fourth, Suhrawardī's presence theory of vision.

Suhrawardī uses light in two ways. First, in physics he advances his presence theory of vision, where the subject is physical light. Second, as a symbol light is a basic concept of his Science of Lights. Although Quṭb al-Dīn does not use light as a concept in his metaphysics, he does deal seriously with the presence theory of light in physical contexts.[61]

Light, according to Quṭb al-Dīn and Suhrawardī, is manifestation to vision. Its opposite is darkness—absolute obscurity. Light differs in intensity. It is neither an emanated transparent body nor color. This can be proven on several grounds, among which is that shaded snow still appears whiter than illuminated ivory. Light is not transferred from the illuminator to the illumined, but simply occurs there without movement. Like Suhrawardī and unlike most others, Quṭb al-Dīn defines *darkness* as simple absence of light, not absence of light in what might be illuminated. Light, then, is a sensible perfection by which things are illumined. Light, as Suhrawardī put it, is simply the manifestness of things and their ability to manifest other things.[62] With Quṭb al-Dīn, however, this concept is restricted to physical light.

In Illuminationist thought, sensations like color are simple experiences. Since Suhrawardī denies the reality of nonsensible physical realities, the actual objects of sensation are simple as well. Quṭb al-Dīn admits that each color is simple in sense, though perhaps not in actuality. The existence of the color is conditioned on light, not just on our seeing it. If dark air prevented us from seeing color in the dark, we could not see

61. *Crown,* 1:3:74–78.
62. See p. 62 above.

out of a dark cave. Color is not a substance and cannot be separated from its locus. This may have been directed against the ray theory of light in some form. Otherwise, color held many mysteries for Quṭb al-Dīn. He did not know whether all colors were simple in actuality or only in sense or, if they were not simple, which were primary and which compound. Nor could he tell whether the number of colors was finite or not.[63]

These discussions illustrate the relation between Quṭb al-Dīn's method and Suhrawardī's. Quṭb al-Dīn accepted Suhrawardī's most basic metaphysical and physical arguments. He understood the Science of Lights to be symbolic and chose to work within the terminological and conceptual framework of Islamic Neoplatonism. He was much more interested in science and some of the less central by-ways of philosophy than Suhrawardī had been. In general, he worked from a basis of Illuminationist metaphysical ideas, elaborated in the light of scientific data. Thus he reinterpreted the presence theory of vision with the aid of a much more sophisticated knowledge of optics and the physiology of the eye. He accepted the theory of light as manifestation and sensibles as simple, but dealt in a more complex and less dogmatic way with the problems of color. And as we will see, his account of the physical world was much more developed than that of Suhrawardī in *The Philosophy of Illumination.*

Self-Consciousness

In the Science of Lights a correlate of the manifestness of the abstract lights is their manifestness to themselves—that is,

63. His discussion of color in his commentary on Avicenna's *Canon* did apparently influence Kamāl al-Dīn Fārisī. See *Dictionary of Scientific Biography,* s.v. "Kamāl al-Dīn . . . al-Fārisī."

their self-consciousness. As such, abstract light equals self-knowledge, life, and so on. These are not separate parts of a composite entity, but rather each is itself the essence of the abstract light.[64]

In *The Pearly Crown,* as was implicitly the case in *The Commentary on "The Philosophy of Illumination,"* the place of abstract light is taken by intellect. Quṭb al-Dīn deals seriously with the question of self-consciousness twice. In the first case he was proving that the ego (*anīya,* that is, self-consciousness) is the only thing that meets the definition of the soul. There he shows that our awareness of ourselves is of a different character than our knowledge of anything else and that our self-consciousness can thus only be our essence itself. The soul/self-consciousness, moreover, is also life, since life is simply the presence of the soul. Finally, self-consciousness is the basic ingredient of knowledge. No matter what series of mechanisms we may posit to explain the process of learning and knowledge, ultimately an act of knowing reduces to an "I know" in which a form is manifest to an ego. Otherwise, there would be an infinite chain of forms but no knowledge. The argument is not without modern applications.[65]

Quṭb al-Dīn returns to discuss this problem in more detail in the discussion of intellects, in his rational theology. Beginning from the premise proven previously that the existence of the perceived for the perceiver constitutes its perceptibility, he proceeds to demonstrate that material things cannot be self-conscious and that whatever is self-conscious also has to know others.[66]

64. See pp. 53–54 above.
65. *Crown,* 1:4:70–75.
66. *Crown,* 1:5:34–36.

THE PLATONIC FORMS AS THE BASIS OF ORDER IN THE UNIVERSE

The Intellects and the Creation of the Cosmos

There are, it is to be recalled, two aspects to Suhrawardī's argument in *The Philosophy of Illumination:* critical and positive. The former involves the refutation and reformulation of certain Peripatetic doctrines; the latter, the concept of light. Suhrawardī's most important criticism concerns first philosophy: the intellectual fictions. The positive aspect of *The Philosophy of Illumination* concerns light, darkness, and related topics. Quṭb al-Dīn deals with these matters in the rational theology of *The Pearly Crown.*

In this work he approaches philosophy in order of knowing—rather than in order of being, as Suhrawardī had in *The Philosophy of Illumination.* Topics are treated from the bottom up rather than the top down. Moreover, he uses conventional Peripatetic terminology rather than terminology of light, so that *intellect* replaces *light.* Nevertheless, cosmology reflects Suhrawardī's ideas.

Stripped of its symbolic terminology, *The Philosophy of Illumination* makes the following basic points about the cosmos:

1. Intellects are the basic—although not the only—reality, the proximate or remote causes of all existents.
2. The One is of the same reality as the intellects, although infinite.
3. The intellects are very great in number and not all of them were associated with the spheres.
4. The intellects are manifest in their reality.
5. The intellects differ by intensity and accidents.
6. The souls of men and animals are of the same reality as intellects.

These philosophical theorems are derived deductively from basic concepts rooted in a critical study of Peripatetic philosophy. That they were deduced within the Science of Lights is not of central importance since they are systematically reducible to a Peripatetic conceptual framework. Nor, except in a biographical sense, are they based on mystical experience. Stripped of Illuminationist terminology, Suhrawardī's cosmology does not differ greatly in structure from Avicenna's. In the logic of *The Philosophy of Illumination* he identifies his major points of disagreement with the Peripatetics. There are only two points of disagreement that relate directly to cosmology: Suhrawardī's defense of the Platonic forms and the possibility of the emanation of a simple substance from a composite cause.

Quṭb al-Dīn's Demonstrative Method

Quṭb al-Dīn was careful about his method and the validity of his arguments. After demonstrating the existence of a substantial immaterial soul, for example, he gives rhetorical (*iqnāʿī*) proofs to the same effect, commenting that some individuals do not have the capacity to appreciate demonstration (*burhān*) and for them rhetorical proofs are more suitable.[67] Occasionally in the *Commentary* he also notes that he considers one of Suhrawardī's proofs to be only rhetorical. It is noteworthy that the most conspicuous example of this concerns Suhrawardī's proofs that the soul is not preexistent.[68] This is closely related to the problem of reincarnation, about which Suhrawardī himself remarked that "proofs on both sides are weak"[69] and which was the most famous area of disagreement between them.

The logical structure of *The Philosophy of Illumination* is outlined in Figure 3.2.

67. *Crown,* 1:4:76–78.
68. See pp. 137–38 below.
69. *Illumination,* 230/511.

Figure 3.2 The Logical Structure of *The Philosophy of Illumination*

TOPIC	METHOD
Critique of Peripatetic theories	Logical criticism
Light and darkness	Identification and explication of basic concepts by "indication and pointing"
Ontology	Demonstration of causal dependence of classes of existents on the Light of Lights, in order of knowledge
Cosmology, physics, religion	Demonstration of the properties of the Light of Lights and of the emanation of the universe from It, in order of being

Starting from basic concepts, Suhrawardī demonstrates first the existence of soul and intellect, and from that the existence and nature of the ultimate intellect, God. From God, Suhrawardī holds, we can in principle strictly deduce all that is or was or ever will be.

Quṭb al-Dīn's approach is different and suited to his more tentative approach to metaphysics. In this sort of philosophy, there has to be an ascent to the highest cause—the order of knowing—followed by a descent tracing the operation of cosmological causes—the order of being. Whereas Suhrawardī emphasizes the descent, Quṭb al-Dīn emphasizes the ascent, becoming more cautious as he nears the top. He begins with an examination of basic concepts such as existence, quiddity, unity, quality, and so on.[70] This is not so much demonstration as

70. *Crown,* 1:3.

explication and clarification of concepts. From there he gradually works upward. The main path up begins with the soul.

He first offers an *a priori* definition of the soul as an immaterial substance controlling the body and shows that nothing else can account for perception and voluntary movement.[71] The soul's existence established, other deductions reveal its properties, intellection, relation to bodies and various faculties and types. He then repeats this process with intellects, demonstrating by elimination that the cause of the soul's existence and intellection, the cause of the unending succession of temporal beings and events, the cause of bodies and celestial movements, all are the intellect—or more exactly, neither souls nor bodies nor their accidents.[72] Having delineated the effects of the intellects, Quṭb al-Dīn passes on to demonstrate the properties of the things that can cause such effects: their knowledge, life, and self-consciousness and their numbers, degrees, and manners of action.[73] Finally, he is in a position to demonstrate that there has to be a necessary intellect that is directly or indirectly the cause of all other intellects.

He investigates its properties and finally traces the details of its creation of the universe, its activity, and its providence.[74] This last is not long—a much simpler account than that of *The Philosophy of Illumination*—since most of the details of causality on lower levels were covered earlier.

The Properties of the Intellects

In *The Pearly Crown* the intellects are known in the first instance by their effects. In the first part of the fifth book "On the intellects and their effects in the bodily and spiritual

71. *Crown,* 1:4:70–78.
72. *Crown,* 1:5:1–34.
73. *Crown,* 1:5:34–35.
74. *Crown,* 1:5:46–119.

worlds," Quṭb al-Dīn says that intellects are the cause of the souls and their intellection, temporal events, bodies, and the movements of the spheres. With respect to the existence of the soul, for example, he deduces that the cause of the souls is not

1. A necessary existent;
2. A bodily accident;
3. A nonbodily accident;
4. A body;
5. Another soul *qua* soul.[75]

Therefore, the cause of all souls is intellect—that is, a substance with no connection whatever with body. Similarly he shows that the ultimate cause of the soul's intellection has to be an abstract intellectual substance. Likewise, unending movements can be traced to an intellect that perpetually emanates on the soul that causes the movements that in turn are the causes of temporal events. Likewise, bodies cannot be caused by bodies, accidents, souls, or the Necessary Existent. Finally, the movements of the spheres have to be in imitation of an intellect or its accident.

So far then, he deduced from the effects of the intellect that it is a substance, that it has no connection with bodies, that it possesses the intellectual forms, that it can have accidents, and that it can affect and be known by what is below it.

He previously showed that ultimately knowledge is just the occurrence of an image of the thing before the knower (*mudrik*). In other words, "the existence of the known to the knower is the knowability of the known to the knower."[76] This does not imply anything about the process of knowing except that it has

75. *Crown,* 1:5:1–6.
76. *Crown,* 1:5:34.

to end with the subjective confrontation of the known and knower.

First, when the concept of self-consciousness is examined, the only correlate of the notion *I* is life. Obviously, nothing that exists in another can be self-aware. Therefore, nothing material can be self-conscious. On the other hand, since intellect is abstracted from matter and is self-subsistent, it cannot be veiled from its essence and has to be self-conscious. This self-consciousness cannot be anything other than its essence itself.[77]

Second, the intellect's self-knowledge implies its knowledge of another. Just as intellection of another implies intellection of the self, so the reverse is true. If an intelligible were self-subsistent, then it can intellect what intellected it, and there is an intellectual connection between the two.[78] A simpler proof, but one applying only to intellects that actually cause souls, is based on what Suhrawardī calls "the noblest contingency." If knowledge and life are essential perfections of souls acquired from the intellects causing them, then those intellects have to have them in a higher degree, although intuition leads to the conclusion that this applies to all intellects. These three—essence, knowledge, and life—differ only subjectively from each other and in different intellects can differ only in degree.

Finally, the knowledge of the intellects has to be unchangeable—since its change would require a sufficient reason. Therefore, it has to know particulars universally, so that it does not change and does not need a bodily instrument for its knowledge.[79]

It will be noted that all of these arguments and theorems about intellects and intellection are precisely parallel to those

77. *Crown,* 1:5:35.
78. *Crown,* 1:5:35–36.
79. *Crown,* 1:5:38–39.

Suhrawardī made about abstract lights and their life and knowledge in *The Philosophy of Illumination*.[80]

The Horizontal Order of Intellects

The most distinctive and blatently Platonic feature of Suhrawardī's cosmology is the horizontal order of intellects. In Avicenna's system, in accordance with the principle that only one can emanate from one, a first intellect emanated from the Necessary Existent. From the first intellect emanated a second intellect in virtue of the first intellect's knowledge of the essence of the Necessary Existent, the soul of the first heaven in virtue of its knowledge of its necessity by another, and the body of the first heaven by virtue of its knowledge of its own essence as contingent. The process continued until a last intellect, probably the tenth, was generated from which no further intellect could come.[81]

Suhrawardī keeps this series (although with the suspicion that there might actually be more than ten intellects in it) but argues that it is insufficient to explain the observed multiplicity in the universe: multiplicity of species in this world and of celestial movements and stars above us.[82] He argues that a vast multiplicity of other intellects was generated from accidental relations among the intellects in the main "vertical order" of intellects. These other intellects were the lords of terrestial species, and their interrelations were the objects of imitation of the celestial souls.

Quṭb al-Dīn accepts Suhrawardī's basic argument that one or a few intellects are insufficient to explain observed multiplicity without contradiction of the principle of sufficient reason. If

80. See pp. 53 ff. above.
81. Avicenna, *Ilāhīyāt,* 402–9.
82. See pp. 57 ff. above.

there were only one or a small number of intellects accounting for the diversity we see, then those intellects would have to be compound, be described by many real attributes, or have many subjective attributes. The intellect, we know, is not compound—does not have real parts. Unlike the Light of Lights, the intellects can have real attributes. They could also have subjective attributes: relations with other intellects, for example. Nevertheless, sufficient subjective multiplicity is possible only if the lower intellects are assumed to have many real attributes. However, with a small number of intellects—such as the ten of the Peripatetics—even this does not supply enough multiplicity to account for the positions of the stars, the multiplicity of encompassing and nonencompassing spheres in the heavens (a subject that Quṭb al-Dīn had spent much time trying to work out in detail in his studies of planetary motion), and the multiplicity of their movements. Therefore, the intellects have to be many, along with their relations, and this multiplicity of intellects accounts for the multiplicity and complex order of the world.[83]

On the other hand, he was not willing to endorse absolutely the conclusions Suhrawardī drew about the detailed mechanisms by which this multiplicity and order are achieved, although he advances his theory as plausible and mentions no other. For example, in the Avicennan system, intellects differed by nobility (by the intensity of their light, in Illuminationist terms). Suhrawardī held that there can also be intellects of equal nobility differing by accidents. Quṭb al-Dīn says, "It is not unlikely that there exist intellects equal in the way that human souls are equal"[84]—that is, in ontological rank. He then outlines Suhrawardī's theory that species lords are responsible for the maintenance of species and his theory of the operation of plant and animal faculties. Of the argument he used, he says, "You

83. *Crown,* 1:5:40–42.
84. *Crown,* 1:5:43.

might be able to prove this to yourself by"[85]—mentioning Suhrawardī's proof. The implication is that he considers this theory possible, or even probable, but not demonstrated. The proofs he advances in this connection we may assume to have been rhetorical.

Although Quṭb al-Dīn's account of the exact mechanism of the relation between the intellects and the preservation of species is very tentative, the principle of sufficient reason, in which he firmly believed, certainly implies that the basis of the species is in the intellects, although the exact nature of their influence might be unknown.

This is the final answer to the problem of universals that first arose in connection with the discussion of quiddities in first philosophy. The validity of universals is ultimately guaranteed by the intellects that make them active in the universe. The physical world was created in the image of the spiritual world. Its order reflects the rational order of that higher world and even its disorder reflects the incomprehensible complexity of the world of intellect.

The Necessary Existent and the Details of the Emanation of the Intellects

Quṭb al-Dīn offers ten proofs of the existence of the Necessary Existent. All are based on the principle of sufficient reason and in some cases on the impossibility of an actual ordered infinity. All are expressed in terms of the necessary and the contingent.[86] Their dependence on Avicenna and Suhrawardī is clear. This sort of proof, of course, is legitimate from an Illuminationist standpoint. Viewing existents as contingent or necessary does not jeopardize their ontological unity. According to Suhrawardī

85. *Crown*, 1:5:43.
86. *Crown*, 1:5:46–53.

and Quṭb al-Dīn, to say that something is contingent does not mean that it has contingency in it or that at some point existence was added to its quiddity, but only that it had a cause other than itself.

Likewise, the deductions Quṭb al-Dīn makes about the unity, peerlessness, and so on, of the Necessary Existent are expressed in very Avicennan terms. Still this is not such as to imply that the intellectual fictions are real in the Necessary Existent. These proofs show that an existent that is necessary in itself has to be utterly simple. From this follow its unity, peerlessness, immateriality, insubstantiality, and so on.

Quṭb al-Dīn briefly discusses this problem from an Illuminationist viewpoint: "The necessity of that whose existence is necessary does not imply its being compounded from existence and necessity since necessity is its confirmation [*ta'akkud*] and perfection [*kamālīyat*]."[87] On the other hand, if existence were something added in reality—that is, if it were an accident of quiddity—then depending on whether its relation to things is necessary or contingent, all existents are either necessary or contingent. In either case, the Necessary Existent is composite and so cannot be necessary in itself. Thus, the fact that we can say different things about the Necessary Existent should not mislead us into forgetting that it is a simple, unitary thing—infinite, intellecting, and intelligible.

According to Quṭb al-Dīn, the Necessary Existent can have relative or negative attributes but not true attributes, a view that in the *Commentary* he says had been Suhrawardī's discovery.[88] It can be said, for example, to be eternal, but this is only a denial of its temporal beginning. The Necessary Existent as it is in itself, however, can have no name. All names applied to it are said of many and so do not really apply to it. Moreover,

87. *Crown,* 1:5:67.
88. *Commentary,* 314.

the Necessary as it is in its own reality is forever and necessarily unknown to us.

On the other hand, the Necessary Existent can validly be given a number of names insofar as it relates to what is below it. It is the All-knowing, for it is the ultimate cause of everything else and its existence is abstracted from matter. Therefore, its essence would not be veiled from it and it would intellect itself and the correlates of its essence. Its knowledge would include knowledge of particulars since its knowledge does not depend on the acquisition of a form but only on the presence of the existent.[89] In this respect Quṭb al-Dīn follows Illuminationist theory rather than Peripatetic. The Necessary Existent's knowledge also differs from human knowledge in that it is active, not passive.[90] Since everything is strictly dependent on God, the universe is the best of all possible worlds.[91] Finally, since the Necessary intellects itself and others, it is intelligible and is known in varying degrees by the separate intellects, and presumably by enlightened human souls. Thus, it can be called in various respects Knowing, Living, Willing, Wise, Generous, Rich, King, Good, Truth, Beauty, Perfection, Beloved, Lover, and so on.[92]

The task remains to describe the emanation of the cosmos from the Necessary Existent. In this, it will be seen, Quṭb al-Dīn follows Avicenna more closely than Suhrawardī did, but he retains certain essential features of Suhrawardī's system.

The first emanation from the Light of Lights must have been a pure light or intellect since any other type of existent would require the prior existence of another contingent existent. From this first intellect emanated another intellect, the soul of the first

89. *Crown,* 1:5:75–80.
90. *Crown,* 1:5:70.
91. *Crown,* 1:5:100.
92. *Crown,* 1:5:70–74, 78–79.

sphere, and its body by virtue of the differing relations the first intellect had with the Necessary Existent. Although these relations were privative in themselves, as conditions they can serve as parts of the cause.[93] According to both Suhrawardī and Quṭb al-Dīn, in addition to the four causes the complete cause of a thing can include conditions and the absence of hindrances.[94]

Quṭb al-Dīn was well aware of the limitations of this kind of reasoning:

> It is certainly possible that only the second intellect emanates from the first by virtue of these things, and from each intellect only another intellect, until some intellect emanates existents other than an intellect, by virtue of something like these [i.e., the real and subjective multiple aspects in the intellect] by virtue of its comparison with something else or its cooperation with it. These considerations about the first intellect are given merely as a possible example of how the many might emanate from the One without asserting that in reality it could not have been different.[95]

The account of the emanation of intellects from the One, the nature of emanation, the distinction of intellects by perfection and deficiency, the emanation of the horizontal order of intellects from the accidental interaction of other intellects, and the dependence of species on them—all this was closely based on the account in *The Philosophy of Illumination*. Even analogies of light were used occasionally.[96]

It may be assumed, however, that what is true of Quṭb al-Dīn's account of the emanation of the spheres and their souls from the first intellect is true of this as well: that this is but a

93. *Crown*, 1:5:80–84.
94. *Crown*, 1:3:33–34.
95. *Crown*, 1:5:85.
96. *Crown*, 1:5:87, 88.

Figure 3.3 The Ranks of Existents in *The Pearly Crown*

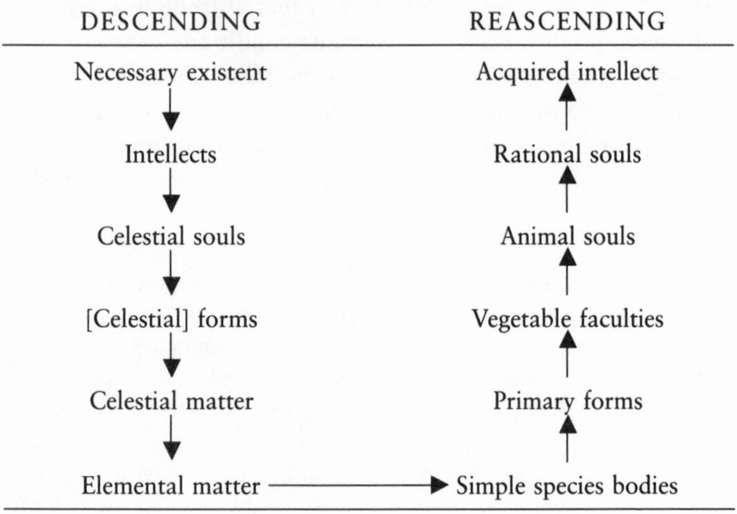

plausible account of how the universe came to be. It is not certain that it happened in precisely this fashion.

Quṭb al-Dīn also gives an interesting summary of the ranks of nobility of existents, descending and ascending[97] (see Figure 3.3).

The acquired intellect, the highest perfection of the human soul, encompasses passively the forms of existents as they are, as the intellects encompass them actively. Thereby, existence returns to resemble what it began from, although the resemblance is weak. This pattern is precisely the opposite of the order of knowing he follows in *The Pearly Crown*.

Quṭb al-Dīn's theology closes with a discussion of providence in which he demonstrates that this is both the best and only

97. *Crown*, 1:5:90–91.

possible world.[98] He concludes with a charming proof that evil is only privative and relative and that good is dominant even in this world, leading him to conclude that most people would fare well in the afterlife.[99]

SUMMARY: THE CHARACTERISTICS OF THE ILLUMINATIONIST PHILOSOPHY

Suhrawardī's *Philosophy of Illumination* is mystical or esoteric in three ways. First, its ideas are to be disclosed only to initiates, those with a sufficient degree of mystical insight to understand the book. Thus Suhrawardī sometimes wrote as though he had founded a mystical order. No such order survived, and there is almost no trace of this aspect of Suhrawardī's thought in Quṭb al-Dīn's works except for a certain discretion in discussing controversial topics. Accordingly, he dropped Suhrawardī's symbolism of light—except in poetic contexts such as prayers—since it no longer served the pedagogical purposes of a community of mystics.

Second, mystical insight[100] was the direct basis for certain of Suhrawardī's philosophical doctrines. In Quṭb al-Dīn's works, *The Philosophy of Illumination* is generally interpreted as a set of philosophical doctrines and arguments subject to rational analysis, rational elaboration, and rational criticism. Although for Quṭb al-Dīn mystical intuition is a fundamental source of philosophical insight, he does not stress it in *The Pearly Crown*. Rational arguments stand on their own—as they had done to a considerable extent even in *The Philosophy of Illumination*.

98. *Crown,* 1:5:99–114.
99. *Crown,* 1:5:114–18.
100. Perhaps the more prosaic term *intuition* might be used instead.

Once brought into systematic relation with the Peripatetic philosophical framework, the Illuminationist philosophy affected three main areas. The first was ontology, the study of the fundamental nature of reality.

Suhrawardī proved and Quṭb al-Dīn accepted that existence is fictitious. The particular things as they are present are what is most real. Deeper analysis of the structure of things tells more about how our minds work than it does about the things themselves. The latter are concrete, particular, discrete, and ontologically indivisible. In holding this Suhrawardī made a clear distinction between the concept and reality of existence. Later philosophers who disagreed with him could maintain their view only by making a further distinction between the ordinary, self-evident concept of existence and the reality of existence as experienced by profound mystics.

Second, when Suhrawardī denied anything but a mental reality to quiddities and the substantial forms of bodies, he weakened the basis of science. If everything but the concrete individual is a mental abstraction, then patterns in the world might be supposed to be arbitrary constructions. All white things could constitute a species just as all dogs do. Quṭb al-Dīn was thus concerned to redefine the basis of order in the universe and to demonstrate the validity of universals. From the Peripatetics he took a more moderate view of the reality of forms, allowing a certain degree of reality to bodily forms. He ultimately placed the basis of this in the horizontal order of abstract intellects. These were the Platonic Forms, as Suhrawardī understood them, angels that maintained species through their solicitude.

The third mystical aspect of *The Philosophy of Illumination* is what might be called the mystical imagination: the realm of visions and dreams, the symbols of light considered in isolation from their philosophical content, and so on. To provide a basis for the reality of this realm of experience, Suhrawardī posited a world of autonomous images. Quṭb al-Dīn considerably refines this conception and uses it not only to validate religious and mystical experience but also to deal with some problems raised by Suhrawardī's presence theory of vision and knowledge. This is discussed in the next chapter.

·FOUR·

The Career of the Soul and the World of Image

INTRODUCTION

A second major area of Illuminationist concern was a group of topics bearing on religion: the nature of time and the preeternity of the world; the preexistence and transmigration of the soul; the ontological status of eschatological events, places, and beings; and the incorporeal images, such as those in mirrors, dreams, and revelation.

The philosophers of Islam inherited from the Greeks a belief that the world had no beginning in time; and despite the bitter opposition of the orthodox, they continued to hold this, largely because of the difficulty of providing a sufficient reason for the world's creation at a particular moment. With this sometimes went a belief in cosmic cycles and even the Eternal Return, in which all events recurred in precisely the same way in each cycle—a doctrine identified with Pythagoras but seriously considered by Plato, Plotinus, and perhaps even Aristotle.[1]

From certain of the Greek philosophers came ideas about the preexistence of human souls and their reincarnation. Finally

1. *The Encyclopedia of Philosophy,* 1967 ed., s.v. "eternal return," by Miliç Çapek.

from Islam, Christianity, and Judaism came a need to explain Revelation and the rewards and punishments of the afterlife. To do this and to provide an alternative explanation for the phenomena supporting a belief in the preexistence and reincarnation of the soul, Suhrawardī posited a world of immaterial images. Quṭb al-Dīn seems to have played a major role in developing the concept philosophically.

TIME

For reasons not entirely clear, the theologians of Judaism, Christianity, and Islam generally concluded that the world was created out of nothing at a particular moment.[2] In general, Islamic philosophers did not accept this, holding that the world had no beginning in time. They argued that it would be contrary to God's goodness to delay the creation of the world and—what for Suhrawardī, at least, amounted to the same thing—that there would be no sufficient reason for God to create the world at one moment rather than another.[3] Moreover, positing a moment before which there was no time implied a before and after and hence a preexistent time.[4] (The same arguments proved that time cannot come to an end.[5]) Although there were also difficulties with this view and ways to get around these arguments, somehow a world without beginning seems to appeal to the scientific imagination. Even today, in the face of what seems to

2. Harry Austryn Wolfson, *The Philosophy of the Kalam* (Cambridge, Mass.: Harvard University Press, 1976), 355–59.
3. *Illumination,* 171–74/391–97; *Crown,* 1:3:32–33, 1:5:91–96. According to Suhrawardī, providence is not God's arbitrary will to do good but the benevolent order resulting from the inevitable relations among the abstract intellects.
4. *Illumination,* 179–81/404–7.
5. *Illumination,* 181/408.

be overwhelming evidence that the universe came into being at a specific moment some billions of years ago, many scientists are attracted to theories that would restore a universe without beginning and, if not stable, then at least cyclical.

Leaving aside the theological implications of the age of the universe, the problem of time is an important philosophical and scientific problem in its own right. For Suhrawardī and Quṭb al-Dīn, time is a measure of change, motion, and succession.[6] Thus, time has to be preeternal since the existence of a first moment of time would imply a moment before that moment. Time as such is most intimately related to the spheres, for in them the Illuminationists found the purest and most uniform motion. The spheres are important also because they are the cause of all change in the sublunar world. In the Illuminationist universe, unlike Aristotle's, there is no chance, and all events on Earth are strictly determined by motions and positions of the celestial bodies. The celestial bodies by their motions and relative positions express serially the timeless interrelations of the immaterial intellects,[7] rather as a phonograph expresses serially the grooves of a record created by a single impression of a master disk.

Still, the number of immaterial lights and rays, although too large for human comprehension, is finite. From this Quṭb al-Dīn concludes that history is cyclical, explaining that this is the Greater (*kubrā*) Resurrection, as opposed to the lesser resurrection of the individual soul after death in the World of Image.[8] This explains the accusation made against Suhrawardī by the *'ulamā'* of Aleppo that he said that God can send a prophet

6. *Illumination,* 179/404–5; *Crown,* 1:3:51, 59, 61.
7. See pp. 90–91 above.
8. *Illumination,* 175–76 and n. 8/399–400.

after Muḥammad.[9] If Quṭb al-Dīn's interpretation is correct, then God not only is able to send a prophet after Muḥammad, but he will certainly send an infinite number of such prophets and even an infinite number of Muḥammads.

Quṭb al-Dīn hints at this in his dedication to the *Commentary*, saying the honor of a philosophical work is greater than that of a religious book in that it can last through various religious dispensations.[10] This must, in fact, have been an unexpressed conclusion of many Islamic philosophers. If time is infinite in the past and future, then Muḥammad can scarcely be the end of prophecy.

Although there have been and will be an infinite number of times with the world exactly as it is now, just as Pythagoras claimed, the Illuminationist notion of the concrete individuality of particulars implies that while there will be an infinite number of Socrates, these will not be the same Socrates, though their circumstances will be the same.

Quṭb al-Dīn does not explicitly work out all the implications of his theory—the elimination of free will, the limited dispensation of Islam, and so on—probably for good reasons.[11] However, it is necessary to understand this theory of the cyclical nature of history and the preeternity of the world to follow his arguments about the career of the human soul.

Another implication of this is that according to Suhrawardī, each creature and its history are engraved in the spheres—a

9. Corbin, *Sohravardī,* 15.
10. *Commentary,* 9.
11. Quṭb al-Dīn explains that there are many mysteries in this matter. They should be contemplated but not disclosed (*Commentary,* 534). The only discussion of this matter in the exoteric *Pearly Crown* is a proof that it is impossible for time and particular things to return (*Crown,* 1:3:8–10). This, however, does not affect the Illuminationist view that events are reenacted.

lower analog of the notion of species lords. This is the basis of the foreknowledge of events, whether by human beings, angels, or God.[12]

THE PREEXISTENCE OF THE SOUL

The doctrines of the preexistence of the soul and reincarnation are found in one form or another in most civilizations, either as a universally accepted religious tenet—such as among the Hindus and Buddhists—or as a minority belief—as among the Greeks, Muslims, and modern Westerners. In the philosophical tradition deriving from Greece, these doctrines were identified preeminently with Plato and Pythagoras, a fact well known to the medieval Islamic world. These two ideas were similar and were normally accepted or rejected together, but their histories were, in fact, rather different, as were the philosophical uses to which they were put. Reincarnation, in its oldest form among the Greeks, involved the Wheel of Birth—souls passing endlessly from one body to another, their lot in one life being determined by their deeds and wisdom in the last. This idea was early combined with the belief that the soul had fallen into this world and would leave it when at last it was purified. The conception of the fallen soul then developed in two directions. On the one hand, its religious side was emphasized when it was added to reincarnation to account for the origin of souls and to allow for the escape of the blessed from the Wheel of Birth. This is found, for instance, in the philosophy of Empedocles. Plato took the fallen soul idea in another direction when he based his theory of learning as recollection on it. Thus, the philosophical treatment of these two ideas has been distinct ever since: the preexistence of the soul has been connected with epistemology

12. *Illumination,* 244/541–42.

and been dealt with in a more philosophical manner, while reincarnation has been connected with morality and eschatology and been dealt with in mythological and religious terms.[13]

The term in Arabic for the preexistence of the soul is *qidam al-nafs,* which implies that the soul existed from the beginning that had no beginning. Its opposite is *ḥudūth al-nafs,* which may be translated as *the temporality* or *createdness of the soul.* This term implies that the soul was created in time at the moment of the creation of the body.

According to Quṭb al-Dīn,

> Plato believed in the pre-existence of souls. It is indeed "the truth which falsehood cannot reach from before or behind,"[14] as evidenced by the Prophet's statement, "The spirits are armies mustered, and those which know each other are united, and those which are ignorant of each other quarrel," and also His statement, "God created the spirits two thousand years before the bodies." He specified two thousand years only to make it easier for the multitudes to understand; the priority of the soul to the body, however, is not limited and defined but is infinite because of the soul's pre-eternity and the body's temporality.[15]

The first philosopher to think deeply on the consequences of the preexistence of the soul in a context other than that of reincarnation was indeed Plato, who believed that the preexistence of the soul followed from the demonstrations of its immortality:

13. *Encyclopedia of Religion and Ethics,* 1958 ed., s.v. "transmigration (Greek and Roman)," by A. C. Pearson. *The Encyclopedia of Philosophy,* s.v. "reincarnation," by Ninian Smart. *Encyclopedia of Religion,* s.v. "reincarnation, by J. Bruce Long, "transmigration," by R. J. Zwi Werblowsky.
14. Qur'ān 41:42.
15. *Commentary,* 449–50.

> Then since it is not destroyed by any evil whatever, either its own or alien, it is evident that it must necessarily exist always, and that if it always exists, it is immortal.
>
> Necessarily, he said.
>
> Let this, then, I said, be assumed to be so. But if it is not so, you will observe that these souls must always be the same. For if none perishes they could not, I suppose, become fewer nor yet more numerous. For if any class of immortal things increased you are aware that its increase would come from the mortal and all things would end by becoming immortal.[16]

The premise was that the supply of souls is finite and constant, nothing coming to be from nothing. From this the preexistence of the soul follows, as does its immortality and reincarnation. This general picture also emerges from the arguments of the *Phaedo* and the various myths of reincarnation.[17] Plato saw the universe as a closed, finite system that remains fundamentally unchanging. In such a world there is no room for a one-way process.[18] If the soul is immortal, then it also has to be preexistent—as, for example, in the *Meno*.

Plato's interest in this matter is not confined to eschatology; for him the preexistence of the soul also has epistemological consequences. He argues that our knowledge of universals does not originate in particulars but is recollected from some previous, nonbodily existence:

> Besides, Socrates, rejoined Cebes, there is that theory which you have often described to us—that what we call learning is really just recollection. If that is true, then surely what we recollect now we must have learned at some time before, which is impossible unless our souls existed somewhere before they entered this human shape. . . .

16. Plato, *Republic,* tr. Paul Shorey, 10.610e–611a.
17. See pp. 142–43 below.
18. Plato, *Phaedo,* tr. Hugh Tredennich, 70c–72e.

> One very good argument . . . is that when people are asked a question, if the question is put in the right way, they can give a perfectly correct answer, which they could not possibly do unless they had some knowledge and a proper grasp of the subject. And then if you confront people with a diagram or anything like that, the way in which they react is an unmistakable proof that the theory is correct.[19]

Although the historical Aristotle had little use for this kind of philosophy, he had the fortune to have attributed to him a collection of excerpts from Plotinus's *Enneads,* which passed into Arabic as *The Theology of Aristotle.* This purported to be the capstone of Aristotle's system in which he at last deals with the lofty matters he never quite seemed to reach in his other books. Historically, there was a certain fitness in this, for the works of Aristotle came to be considered the standard of natural science and as such were incorporated with minor modifications into everyone's philosophy, Neoplatonism included. Muslim philosophers, of course, realized that there was something strange about the *Theology,* and doubts were cast on its authenticity. Nevertheless, it was the most important Neoplatonic text to reach the Arabs and as such was tremendously influential.

In the *Theology* Plato's doctrines receive a cosmological interpretation in which recollection is combined with the fall of the soul to explain the origin of order in the world. In the higher world the pure disembodied intellects are unchanging and motionless, for they are fully actual. If an intellect somehow acquires a desire, it becomes soul and is no longer fully actual, for its desire implies a lack, which can be filled. Its desire is to actualize in material things the forms that it has seen in the intelligible world:

19. *Phaedo,* 72d–73b.

> When the mind receives the desire to go downwards, the soul is informed by it and the soul is then a mind informed with the form of desire, although the soul has sometimes a universal desire and sometimes a particular desire. When she has a universal desire she fashions the universal forms into actuality and governs them intellectually and universally, without departing from her universal world. When she desires the particular things, which are forms of her universal forms, she adorns them and increases them in purity and beauty, and corrects what error has occurred in them, and governs them in a higher and loftier way than their proximate cause, which is the heavenly bodies. When the soul enters the particular things she does not become confined in them: I mean she is not in the body as though confined in it, but is in it and outside it.[20]

This is a combination of the epistemological interests of Plato with the moral interests of the pre-Socratics. The soul is the principle of order in the world, actualizing the forms, while the heavenly bodies are responsible for accidents. At the same time the soul is liable to be ensnared by the delights of the material world and be hindered in its return to the intelligible world.

By a fluke Avicenna's commentary on this work survived the sack of Isfahan in 420/1030. He seems to have considered the *Theology* a visionary book, akin to scripture, for he preferred to interpret away difficulties rather than criticize the work directly, as he did in the corresponding commentary on Aristotle's *De anima*. At any rate, he wasted no time in clearing the ground for an interpretation of the *Theology* consistent with his own views. In his first comment, in reference to the passage cited on the previous page, he says,

20. Plotinus, "The Theology of Aristotle," tr. Geoffrey Lewis, in *Plotini Opera*, ed. Paul Henry and Hans-Rudolf Schwyzer, Museum Lessianum series philosophica, no. 34 (Paris: Desclée de Brouweer et Cie., 1959), 2:219.

> He does not mean that the human soul existed before the body during a period in which it had not taken over and been clothed by a body, only entering it later, for this has been proven absurd in the books, even allowing that the soul does not die. Its meaning is rather that the soul, since it cannot exist disembodied like the disembodied intellects mentioned in metaphysics, has by nature a connection with the body from the very beginning and has an inclination to it.[21]

The proximate cause of Avicenna's denial of the preexistence of the soul was his development of a theory of intellection that, although rather Platonic in spirit, derives from Aristotelian models and has no need of a preexisting soul. This theory, systematically used in his understanding of the *Theology,* attributes intellection to direct contact with the Active Intellect, the intellect of the lowest of the heavenly spheres. Contemplation of particulars is the occasion for the acquisition of the immaterial form from the Active Intellect. Since a completely immaterial form cannot be contained in a material organ such as memory, the form has to be reacquired each time it is used. By repeated intellection of the same form, it becomes progressively easier to acquire it.[22] There is, therefore, no need to assume that the soul had a previous life where it acquired the intelligibles; Meno's slave does not recollect what he already knew of geometry but instead is led by Socrates through contemplation of particulars to a state in which he is prepared for contact with the active intellect. Avicenna thought this theory of intellection actually precludes the preexistence of the soul, as he argues in his commentary on the *Theology*:

21. Avicenna, "Tafsīr Kitāb Uthūlūjiyā," in *Arisṭū 'Ind al-'Arab,* ed. 'Abd al-Raḥmān Badawī (Cairo; al-N̄ahḍat al-Miṣrīya 1947), 37.
22. Avicenna, *Kitāb al-Shifā': al-Ṭabī'īyāt,* vol. 6: *al-Nafs,* ed. Ibrāhīm Madkūr (Cairo: al-Hay'a al-Miṣrīya al-'Āmma li'l-Kitāb, 1975), 247.

> [The reading in the text] "which it has seen in the intellect" is a copyist's error [*taḥrif*], for if the soul had already seen the intelligible world, it would have become perfect, because to see the thing is to receive its form. Rather its desire to see the things in the intellect is general, not detailed, like the desire for sexual intercourse of one who has not known it nor experienced its pleasure.[23]

In other words, if the soul had seen the intelligibles in an earlier life, its intellect would already be fitted to receive them and would know them all perfectly. This is absurd, since it contradicts our experience.

In the beginning of the commentary on the *Theology,* Avicenna alludes to the books in which the preexistence of the soul was refuted. These may include Aristotle's *De anima,* especially in light of the assumption that the *Theology* was Aristotle's ultimate work, but he certainly refers to his own books, especially the *Psychology of the Healing,* where he devotes a chapter to the subject.[24] He approaches the problem here through his favorite logical technique, *reductio ad absurdum,* and from a different point of view.

If we assume that the soul does exist before the body, then what is the manner of its existence? Before they join the body, souls, like everything else, have to be either one or many. They cannot be many, for they are all of one species and quiddity and can therefore differ only in matter and material attachments, which they do not yet have. They cannot, however, be numerically one either, since when two human bodies come into existence, they both acquire souls. These plainly cannot be the same soul in two bodies, so they have to be parts of the original soul. This too is impossible, for the original soul has no dimen-

23. Avicenna, "Tafsīr," 39.
24. Avicenna, *al-Nafs,* 198–201.

sions by which it might be divided. It is plain, therefore, that the soul cannot exist before the body.

Another version of the same argument shows that the individuality of human souls, at least, cannot predate their attachment to the human body, since souls are individuated by material accidents and attachments that do not come to be until the soul's connection with the body. Avicenna was aware that the same argument might be turned against him to deny the individuality of souls after death, but he responded that then the souls would be differentiated by the varying dispositions acquired in association with their former bodies.

The position of Suhrawardī in *The Philosophy of Illumination* is very similar. He advances four arguments against the preexistence of the soul. The first two, stripped of the Illuminationist terminology, are Avicenna's: that the preexistent souls of men can be neither one nor many, and that a soul that existed earlier in the intelligible world would enter this world perfect.

The second pair of arguments, really two halves of one *reductio ad absurdum,* is based on the impossibility of an actual infinity. If we take three premises—the preeternity of the world, the preexistence of souls, and the impossibility of an actual ordered infinity—we can show that they are mutually inconsistent. On the one hand, if the souls are actually existent before the bodies and the world always existed, then given the impossibility of an actual infinity, all available souls would have already been used up. On the other hand, the assumption of a world that has always been and of preexistent souls implies an infinite number of actually existent souls and therefore an infinite number of degrees of illumination corresponding to the human constitutions within a finite range of illumination: that is, between the highest animals and the lowest immaterial intellects. The reason is that if the souls come into being by the occurrence of a suitable body, as in Avicenna, then any infinity is only potential or unordered. On the other hand, if the souls are preexistent, then they would be caused only by celestial factors—that is, indirectly by the Light of Lights. That, according to Suhrawardī's theory, implies that there can be only a finite number of human souls. Otherwise, the infinity would be actual and ordered.[25]

Quṭb al-Dīn holds that these four arguments are only rhetorically convincing (*iqnāʿī*), not demonstrative, since each depends on the unproven assumption that there is no transmigration of souls. Each is, in addition, flawed on other grounds. He was perfectly correct that the arguments rest on the denial of transmigration: Suhrawardī and Avicenna before him assumed that before the soul enters the body, it is not in another body. Quṭb al-Dīn goes through each argument in turn and points out other flaws. The argument that human souls existing before the body would be neither one nor many relies for one of its contradictions on the assertion that two embodied human souls do not have the same knowledge, as they would if they were numerically one. He responds that some knowledge, such as self-consciousness, is actually common to all men. The second argument, from men's lack of perfection, can be attacked by assuming different ranks of beings of different capacities. Some, due to their degree of luminosity, are fit to acquire perfection in the intelligible world; others, less worthy, can seek only their perfection in conjunction with a body. Moreover, the third argument, assuming among other things that a soul that never manages a body is wasted, contradicts the second argument, which assumes that if the soul were to have a glimpse of the intelligible world, it would immediately attain perfection. This contradiction, he remarked, indicates the weakness of both arguments.[26]

Suhrawardī's (and Avicenna's) arguments disposed of, Quṭb

25. *Illumination,* 201–3/441–47.
26. *Commentary,* 447–49.

al-Dīn goes on to argue for the preexistence of the soul, citing Plato as its outstanding exponent. After mentioning certain *ḥadīth* that implicitly supported this view, he gives an argument he attributes to Plato:

> Plato relies for proof on this argument: If the cause of the existence of the soul exists in its totality before the existence of a body suitable for the soul to manage, then the soul will exist before the body because an effect cannot be delayed after its complete cause. If the cause does not exist completely before the body, but is completed by it, then the soul's existence is dependent on the existence of the body, since on this assumption the body is part of the cause or a condition of the soul. But the existence of the soul cannot depend on the body since in that case it would be nullified with the nullification of the body, which is not the case according to the demonstrations proving the immortality of the soul.[27]

This form of the argument clearly incorporates some Peripatetic elements, but the linking of the arguments for immortality and preexistence is certainly characteristic of Plato.[28]

He also cites the argument of a certain unnamed contemporary scholar who asserted the preexistence of the soul on the grounds that a temporal soul has to be a simple substance with a compound cause. This, however, Quṭb al-Dīn rejects on logical grounds, since a simple effect can have a compound cause.[29]

In *The Pearly Crown* he devotes a chapter to proving the immortality of the soul. He begins by showing that the soul is essentially prior to the body. The exact conclusion of the argument is as follows:

27. *Commentary,* 450.
28. See pp. 131–33 above.
29. *Commentary,* 450–51.

> Therefore, the body with its particular dispositions, is not a condition of the existence of the soul with respect to the soul's being an immaterial substance but only with respect to its being the basis of a species form.[30]

Therefore, the soul in itself is imperishable since it can only cease to be if its efficient cause, the immaterial intellect, were to perish. There is, however, no account of the creation of the soul in relation to the body comparable to Avicenna's statement that the soul emanates on the occurrence of a suitable constitution.[31] The body, though, is no part of the cause of the soul, nor is there anything to prevent the soul preexisting the body.

The key passage on the preexistence of the soul in *The Pearly Crown* occurs at the beginning of the discussion of reincarnation. Here Quṭb al-Dīn asserts that if souls are finite in number and the world has no beginning in time, then souls must be reincarnated.[32] The reasoning, as extrapolated from other passages and the *Commentary,* is as follows:

If the soul does not preexist the body, as in Avicenna's system, it has to have emanated in response to the occurrence of a suitable constitution. Over the unending ages the souls would then be infinite in number but in a permissible way—being dependent on the unending motions of the celestial bodies and the eternal emanation of the intellects. If, however, they preexist the body and exist coeternally with their cause—that is, they are eternal temporally but not essentially—then neither the constitution of bodies nor any other temporal events could be their cause. In that case, their causes would have to go back to aspects of the emanating intellects. Since the number of ranks of intellects is finite, so too must be the number of these intellects, their

30. *Crown,* 1:4:121.
31. *Avicenna's Psychology,* tr. Fazlur Rahman (London: Oxford University Press, 1952), 24.
32. *Crown,* 1:4:129.

aspects, and the souls they cause. In that case, human souls, like immaterial intellects and bodily species, would have to be finite. The implications of this will be seen in the discussion of Quṭb al-Dīn's theories about reincarnation.

Here Quṭb al-Dīn repeats the argument for the preexistence of the soul based on its coeternity with its cause, which he attributes to Plato. This, he warns, requires careful thought.[33]

REINCARNATION

Herodotus's claim to the contrary, the Greek believers in reincarnation did not borrow their doctrine from the Egyptians—who did not, in any case, believe in it—but instead drew on a native belief of great antiquity. Reincarnation first attained prominence in Greece as an Orphic belief, but it came to be identified with the name of Pythagoras, who was said to have been able to remember his four previous incarnations:

> None the less the following became universally known: first, that he maintains that the soul is immortal; next, that it changes into other kinds of living things; also that events recur in certain cycles, and that nothing is ever absolutely new; and finally, that all living things should be regarded as akin. Pythagoras seems to have been the first to bring these beliefs into Greece.[34]

This was connected with a belief in universal cycles:

> If one were to believe the Pythagoreans, with the result that the same individual things will recur, then I shall be talking to you again sitting as you are now, with this pointer in my hand,

33. *Crown,* 1:4:130.
34. Porphyry, *Vitae Pythagorae,* 19, in G. S. Kirk and J. E. Raven, *The Pre-Socratic Philosophers* (Cambridge: Cambridge University Press, 1966), 223.

> and everything else will be just as it is now, and it is reasonable to suppose that the time then is the same as now.[35]

This original conception of the Wheel of Birth was eventually combined, as in the thought of Empedocles, with the idea of the fallen soul, cast from heaven and doomed to wander the world until it is once again sufficiently purified to return to its heavenly homeland. The moral aspect seems stronger in Empedocles, who talked about the gradual rise of the souls through the series of births until their final escape from the world.

Plato took over the Pythagorean-Empedoclean ideas about reincarnation and treated them in a more sophisticated manner. In view of his acceptance of the preexistence of the soul and his "steady-state" cosmology, some sort of doctrine of reincarnation was inevitable, and in several of his great myths he told how it might happen. The details varied, but the common pattern was that the soul falls into the world for some sin it committed and enters the succession of births. After death it is punished or rewarded for a time for the life it led on Earth and then was finally reborn as an animal or human being of a character suitable to the morals and wisdom or folly that it acquired in its previous existence. In certain dialogues the soul could become sufficiently purified or so incorrigibly wicked as to leave forever the chain of earthly lives. Philosophy, at any rate, was the key to passing successfully through the valley of death, whether to a good life in the next rebirth or to a happy life among the stars.

It is, however, difficult to know just how seriously Plato took all this, for the disclaimer given after the account of reincarnation in the *Phaedo* is typical:

35. Eudemus, in Kirk and Raven, 223.

> Of course, no reasonable man ought to insist that the facts are exactly as I have described them. But either this or something very like it is a true account of our souls and their future habitations—since we have clear evidence that the soul is immortal—this, I think, is both a reasonable contention and a belief worth risking, for the risk is a noble one. We should use such accounts to inspire ourselves with confidence.[36]

Belief in reincarnation was never very common among Muslims, but it was notorious that the doctrine was widespread in various other nations. Shahrastānī, for instance, reports,

> Every nation has a firm tendency towards reincarnation, but each has its own views about how it occurs. The reincarnationists of India are the firmest believers in it.[37]

He goes on to mention that they believed that eventually the heavens would return to their original positions and everything would begin again just as it had at the beginning of the previous cycle. Shahrastānī attributes many such Indian beliefs when found in Islam (although not specifically this one) to the influence of a student of Pythagoras who had gone to India to teach. Occasional Islamic sects believed in reincarnation, especially more radical Shīʿite groups. To support their views they could call on various Qur'anic verses and *ḥadīth,* especially those that mentioned men being turned into animals or being resurrected in their forms.[38] Perhaps the most important supporters of reincarnation in Islam were the Brethren of Purity.[39]

More important for Islamic philosophers was the knowledge

36. Plato, *Phaedo,* 114d.
37. al-Shahrastānī, *Kitāb al-Milal wa'l-Niḥal,* ed. Muḥammad b. Fatḥ Allāh Badrān (Cairo: Maṭbaʿat al-Azhar, 1910), 2:1279.
38. *Encyclopedia of Islam,* 1936 ed., s.v. B. Carra de Vaux, "tanāsukh."
39. At least according to Quṭb al-Dīn, *Commentary,* 477–78.

that belief in reincarnation was widespread among the ancient sages. Quṭb al-Dīn surveys the situation in the introduction to the chapter on reincarnation in his commentary on *The Philosophy of Illumination.* Reincarnation interested him, it seems, for moral and religious reasons, for he defines it as "the transfer of the souls of the wicked to animal bodies corresponding to them in morals and deeds."[40] To this should be compared his more philosophical treatment of the preexistence of the soul. A few of the ancients, he tells us—those known as the "Reincarnationists"—held that the soul was bodily and was transferred eternally among human and subhuman bodies, but most agreed that the blessed and perfected could attain the intelligible world and enjoy its unimaginable joys and delights. They differed, however, about the fate of lesser souls in the Afterlife. Those who denied reincarnation, like Aristotle and his followers, believed that even after the soul was completely freed from the body, it would remain tormented in the darkness of its ignorance and wickedness.

The third group of philosophers,

> the believers in reincarnation like Hermes, Agathadaemon, Empedocles, Pythagoras, Socrates, Plato, and others among the sages of Greece, Egypt, Persia, Babylon, India, and China, thought that their souls were not completely detached from matter but were transferred to the management of another body. They differed, however, about the direction of transfer.[41]

From a Neoplatonic point of view, the idea of the reincarnation of the wicked in bodies suitable to their moral traits was not entirely fanciful. It was accepted by everyone that a body received a soul suitable for it. It was, therefore, not implausible

40. *Commentary,* 476. cf. Hirawī, *Anwārīyya,* 148–66, for another discussion of reincarnation.
41. *Commentary,* 477.

that the soul of a human being who had developed his animal side at the expense of his human side, acquiring in the process too great an attachment to the body to be released from it completely, should become attached to the body of an animal of corresponding disposition. Other accounts could, of course, be given.

Even concerning Aristotle, that great skeptic, Quṭb al-Dīn said,

> it is reported that he gave up his view denying reincarnation and returned to the opinion of his teacher Plato, continuing, however, to reject reincarnation in his books out of prudence. It is also possible that he accepted reincarnation after he had formerly denied it.[42]

In summary, it is quite clear that reincarnation tended to be viewed from a religious and mythological perspective, rather than a philosophical one. Certainly, the colorful details so often given must have been considered to belong to the realm of the plausible or probable, not the demonstrative.

For Avicenna the rejection of reincarnation is a corollary of his views on the temporal origin of the soul.[43] If every suitable body necessitates the emanation of a new soul, reincarnation would mean that some bodies would have two souls. This is not possible, however, since one or the other of the souls would not really belong to that body. It is impossible, moreover, that only bodies for which there are no reincarnated souls available receive newly emanated souls, for all the bodies of a species are alike in essence and the distinction cannot simply be by chance.

Suhrawardī's approach, on the other hand, is quite different, since he was very interested in the opinions of the ancient sages

42. *Commentary,* 493.
43. Avicenna, *al-Nafs,* 207.

and was not eager to disagree with them. Since he did not feel on very strong philosophical grounds regarding reincarnation, he tried to have things both ways.[44] His explanation began with a statement in Illuminationist terms of his theory of the temporal origin of the soul, a theory that does not differ significantly from Avicenna's except that it denies the emanation of animal and plant souls. He then calls forth a certain Būdhāsaf[45] as spokesman for the Oriental sages who believed in reincarnation. Būdhāsaf's theory, which Suhrawardī lukewarmly endorsed, was that the human body was the gate of gates for the entry of lights into the world—that is, that only human bodies receive an emanated soul directly. Blessed human souls might escape back into the World of Lights directly at death, but the imperfect would be reincarnated in the bodies of animals suitable to their characters. Therefore, all animals had human souls.

> No creature is there crawling on the earth, no bird flying with its wings, but they are nations like unto yourselves. We have neglected nothing in the Book; then to their Lord shall they be mustered.[46]

From human bodies the lights (souls) descended into lower and lower animals until all the evil traits were eventually extinguished and, we may hope, the souls rejoined the ranks of the blessed, from whom they parted company at the first stop, in the World of Lights. This neatly sidestepped Avicenna's objections to reincarnation without serious violence to his system. A human body would not have two souls, for reincarnated souls could only go down the phylogenetic ladder. Although they might go directly from one member of a lower species to an-

44. *Illumination,* 216–23/478–96.
45. We may suppose him to have been Buddha, although no one at the time was very sure who he was or how to spell his name.
46. Qur'ān 6:38, tr. A. J. Arberry.

other, animals did not receive their lights directly from the triumphal light. They might even go back up to higher animals to begin the extinction of a second undesirable trait, as in the case of a soul both greedy and cruel.

Suhrawardī also manages to avoid two Peripatetic objections to reincarnation. First, the difficulty of reconciling the small number of humans with the very large number of animals, insects, and so forth, can be dismissed by considering the large number of people who died in the past. And, indeed, if we accept a world in which there was never a beginning and in which the human race always existed, then this is perfectly reasonable although a soul would obviously have to spend a very long time in its purification. The second difficulty concerns the implausibility of an animal being born just at the moment another animal or human being died. Of this he remarks loftily that matters are presumably subject to a celestial regulation hidden from us, so that the death of one body is the life of another, just as one man's loss of wealth is another's gain.[47]

Suhrawardī alludes to various groups of sages and their opinions on reincarnation, but he assures us that most accepted it. There is some question about whether he himself believed in reincarnation. Quṭb al-Dīn tells us that he did but that he may have had doubts.[48] Suhrawardī says,

> It makes no difference whether reincarnation is true or false [in this case]—for the arguments on both sides are weak—when the souls are freed from the barrier fortresses [the terrestrial bodies], they will have shadows of the suspended forms in accordance with their morals.[49]

47. Perhaps this is better philosophy than economics.
48. *Commentary,* 478.
49. *Illumination,* 230/511.

In his *Four Journeys* Mullā Ṣadrā accuses Quṭb al-Dīn of believing in reincarnation.[50] This is only partly true. He considered reincarnation in the physical world—at least in the way Suhrawardī described it, where human souls passed down the phylogenetic ladder—to be possible but not proven.[51] In *The Pearly Crown* he argues that physical reincarnation is implied by the preexistence of the soul and the preeternity of the world.[52] If human souls are preexistent, as we saw above,[53] they are finite in number. Since the number of individual bodies in the unending ages would be infinite, then the souls would have to be reincarnated.

There is a flaw in this argument that Quṭb al-Dīn does not mention and that he may not have noticed. If the supply of souls is finite and some souls escape forever from the Wheel of Birth, then the supply of human souls must already have been exhausted.

To judge by the argument he presented and his various disclaimers, he most likely held that

1. The preeternity of the world was demonstrated;
2. The soul was probably preexistent;
3. Reincarnation in physical bodies was possible or probable.

Certainly he thought that if reincarnation did occur, it was most probably as Suhrawardī had described it. This theory, it should be noted, is logically contrary to the preexistence of the human soul in other bodies since it presumes a new soul for each human conception and provides no way for a soul to pass from a human or animal body into another human body. While

50. Mullā Ṣadrā, *al-Ḥikma al-Muta'āliya fī al-Asfār al-'Aqlīya al-Arba'a* ([Tehran]: Shirkat Dār al-Ma'ārif al-Islāmīya, 1378), 8:372.
51. See p. 157–58 below.
52. *Crown,* 1:4:129.
53. See p. 137–38 above.

it is not clear how many of the difficulties he knew about, he was well aware of the thorniness of the problem and the tentativeness of any solutions he might have advanced. "There may be aspects of the problem of which we do not yet know."[54]

THE HISTORY OF THE CONCEPT OF THE WORLD OF IMAGE

Avicenna was apparently the first Islamic philosopher to try to use the imagination to solve the problems associated with justifying the religious theory of reward and punishment in the afterlife.[55] Suhrawardī takes a major step by positing in addition to the world of body, soul, and intellect a fourth world of autonomous images.[56] Suhrawardī uses the concept mainly as a metaphysical basis for the objective validity of visions without working out all the philosophical implications. The most famous text of Ibn 'Arabī on the subject is so mythological in character as to render its interpretation difficult.[57] Quṭb al-Dīn, on the other hand, seems to have made a determined effort to work out the philosophical implications of the concept.

According to most Islamic philosophers, the existence or knowledge of a particular requires matter. A nonmaterial thing, such as an immaterial intellect, cannot know material accidents.

54. *Crown,* 1:4:129.
55. See Rahman, "Dream, Imagination, and 'Ālam al-Mithāl," for an account of the precursors of Suhrawardī's theory of the World of Image.
56. Translations of and commentary on some of the important texts on the subject are found in Henry Corbin, *Spiritual Body and Celestial Earth,* tr. Nancy Pearson, Bollingen Series no. 91:2 (Princeton: Princeton University Press, 1977).
57. Ibn 'Arabi, *al-Futūḥāt al-Makkīya* (Beirut: Dār al-Ṣādir, n.d.), 1:126–31; partly translated in Corbin, *Spiritual Body,* 135–43. Quṭb al-Dīn quotes a less familiar passage. See pp. 209–11 ff. below.

The intellect alone, for example, cannot tell left from right or know a particular human being without the aid of a material organ.[58] Likewise, matter is necessary for there to be individuals within one species. This is the basis of the famous scholastic proof that each angel is of a different species, an angel being form without matter. However, certain phenomena cannot be explained satisfactorily within that framework: forms that can be seen but that do not themselves have matter, such as those seen in a mirror or memory, and the reward and punishment of the individual soul after death. Quṭb al-Dīn argues that these phenomena can be explained only by the World of Image.

He does not develop a clear ontological basis for that world. It is not obvious where it is. Sometimes it seems that it is coextensive with our world—as when we see its manifestations in miracles or the like. Other times he speaks of the souls of the dead being manifested in one of the spheres of the planets. When he discusses the afterlife, the World of Image seems to be wrapped around our world, with its ground being our heaven.

The World of Image has an attic-like quality, stuffed full of phenomena that do not fit elsewhere: the forms in mirrors, visions, and dreams; the conjurings of prophets and magicians; the contents of our individual imaginations; as well as vast cities and lands with their inhabitants living autonomously of us.

The most important source for our knowledge of Quṭb al-Dīn's ideas on the World of Image is a small essay written in reply to the questions of an unnamed scholar—"*Risāla fī Taḥqīq 'Ālam al-Mithāl wa-Ajwibat As'ilat Ba'ḍ al-Fuḍalā*'"—"An Epistle ascertaining the Reality of the World of Image and Answers to the Questions of a Certain Scholar."[59] To under-

58. Avicenna, *Psychology,* 41–45.
59. For the text, translation, and a discussion on the textual problems, see App. F below.

stand the place of this essay among his works, several considerations should be kept in mind. First, it deals with matters discussed in the *Commentary on "The Philosophy of Illumination"* but not in *The Pearly Crown.* These two works—his major philosophical works—differ considerably in scope and approach while overlapping in certain respects. *The Pearly Crown* was a popular textbook, dealing with matters well known and well established—exoteric philosophy. The *Commentary,* on the other hand, concerns problems of esoteric metaphysics. In the beginning of the *Epistle* he explains that the matters with which it deals are but imperfectly known.[60] Since this work is by and large an expansion of discussions in the *Commentary,* it is clear that this applies to the analyses of the World of Image in *The Philosophy of Illumination* and its commentary.

Unlike the *Epistle,* the *Commentary* was written as a non-Islamic book in the sense that it does not assume the doctrines and terminology of Islam. Quṭb al-Dīn says as much in the introduction by writing to his patron that such a work would endure through other religious dispensations.[61] The doxology does not mention Allāh, only the Absolute and the Light of Lights, and Muḥammad is mentioned only incidentally.[62] The *Epistle,* on the other hand, is specifically Islamic. Islamic terms and examples are used throughout, sometimes substituting for neutral terms in passages that are otherwise exact quotations from the *Commentary.* It is Islamic in intent, as well, attempting to use the concept of the World of Image, developed in the *Commentary,* to reconcile apparent contradictions between well-known philosophical doctrines and certain Islamic beliefs about the Afterlife.

60. See pp. 201, 206 below.
61. *Commentary,* 9.
62. *Commentary,* 2–3.

Quṭb al-Dīn divides the sciences into the philosophical (*ḥikamī*) and the religious, the distinction being whether or not they are in principle the same at all times and places.[63] There is some overlap since the science of the principles of religion (*uṣūl-i dīn*) concerns those matters that can be supported by rational proof, whether or not they could also be supported by revelation.[64] The difference presumably is that the subjects dealt with in the science of the principles of religion are determined by revelation, whereas philosophy treats subjects without regard to their relevance to religion and the science of the branches of religion treats only those matters that can be proven from revelation. Thus, in the *Commentary,* a work specifically intended to transcend any specific religious community, Quṭb al-Dīn avoids terms like *Allāh* that were specifically associated with Islam. In general, he does the same thing in the philosophical portions of *The Pearly Crown.*[65] Thus, the *Epistle* should perhaps be considered part of the science of principles of religion rather than of philosophy proper since its occasion was the justification of certain religious doctrines and since traditional as well as rational proofs were used.

Because the *Epistle* quotes the *Commentary*—passages toward the end of the book, at that—and even quotes it with embedded chunks of *The Philosophy of Illumination,* it must have been written later—that is, in the last two decades of the author's life. As such, it was effectively contemporary with both the *Commentary* and *The Pearly Crown.*

The *Epistle* was written in reply to an unidentified scholar, evidently with both Ṣūfī and philosophical background, who had written raising questions on these topics. His letter is quoted

63. *Crown,* 1:1:71.
64. *Crown* 1:1:85.
65. For example, *Crown,* 1:5:114, where he identifies the Necessary Existent as *al-Ilāh, ta'ālā,* a self-consciously non-Islamic usage.

in full in the treatise.[66] His questions, he says, were the result of certain doubts that arose in the course of his search. Those he submitted are those most important in the quest for happiness.

The Philosophical Assumptions behind the Questions

To judge by his questions and his explanations of them, the scholar made the following specifically philosophical assumptions:

1. The soul is a self-subsistent substance.
2. At death the soul is separated from the body, but the individual soul is immortal.
3. Conception of the particular requires a material organ.
4. Only human beings have substantial souls.

These, of course, were commonplaces of Islamic philosophy, and in this form date from Avicenna. All except the last are asserted in *The Pearly Crown.*

On the other hand, Islam makes certain definite statements about what happens to the individual after death, and these had to be taken as fact.

The Questions

The scholar asked first how the disembodied spirit can conceive and imagine—that is, experience—the conditions of the Barrier (*al-Barzakh*)[67] and the embodiment of deeds that Islamic belief held takes place after death. In this life matter is a precondition for conceiving the particular. Since this conception cannot take

66. See pp. 201–206 below.
67. The use of *barzakh* to mean *interworld* is not to be confused with Suhrawardī's use of it to mean *body.* The Barrier in this case is the state of limbo between death and resurrection referred to in Qur'ān 23:100.

place in the immaterial spirit as such or in the—now dead—earthly body, it has to take place by the spirit's connection with some other body, but it was not at all clear how this could happen. In any event, he asked in another question, why should conception and imagination take place in the disembodied spirit anyway? Here these take place only at the instance of the material body; after death there would be no reason for them. Moreover, why should the human spirit be a substance? Why could it not be an accident arising from the proper mixture of the four elements? The animal spirit was commonly held to be material in this sense. On the other hand, animals seemed to possess universals in a primitive way: they could generalize from their experience. Since the knowledge of universals was one of the principal arguments for the existence of the human substantial soul, how could the spirits of animals perish? Finally, given that animals differ in their degrees of perfection, how could it be compatible with the Divine Generosity for them to be prevented from reaching perfection?

Quṭb al-Dīn's Reply

The second and third parts of the *Epistle* are a discussion of the World of Image and detailed answers to the scholar's questions. The reply begins with a geography of the World of Image.[68] There are, we are told, four worlds. The highest is that of the immaterial intellects. Below that is the World of Souls, both of the spheres and of bodies in our world. The lowest is the World of Bodies. The World of Image falls between the Worlds of Bodies and Souls, being more immaterial than one and less so than the other.

The World of Image contains the images that are not forms in material bodies. It corresponds with our world in its structure

68. See pp. 206–209 below.

and its finite number of species, but the number of individuals in each species can be infinite. This is because different species result from the interactions of the emanations of God. Since there are not an infinite number of levels between the Light of Lights and the material and imaginal worlds, the number of such combinations, and hence the number of different species of things, is finite though very large.[69] On the other hand, since the world had no beginning in time and since the individuals in the World of Image have no material bodies, there can be an infinite number of individuals present together within each of these finite number of species.

Since the forms in this world are suspended—immaterial, not dependent on material bodies—this is obviously the location of the miracles and promises of eschatology and the source of the wonders of magicians and sorcerers.

The existence of this world is known both by reason and authority. It was mentioned, for example, in the Qur'ān and the Ḥadīth. The Saints spoke of it. Quṭb al-Dīn quotes a long passage from *The Meccan Revelations* in which Ibn 'Arabī expounds the paradoxes of the forms seen in mirrors, explaining that the Barrier between this world and the next in which these forms subsist is also the location of visions, dreams, and the experiences of the dead. The ancient sages also spoke of a spatial world other than this world in which the illumined and dark images of the imagination are suspended. These are not to be confused with the Platonic Forms, for those were luminous and in the World of Intellects.

The rational proof for the existence of the World of Image is based on Suhrawardī's explanation of vision as the presence of a lighted object before a sound eye. This—along with his denial that the forms in mirrors, visions, imagination, and dreams are material—is based on the denial of the possibility of the form

69. See p. 207 below.

of a large thing being contained in something smaller than it—although, to be sure, the retina, the imagination, and the mirror were the locii and conditions of their manifestation. If we perceive something, it must be really present to us, not just represented to us in our minds by some sort of model in the brain. The forms of mirrors, although conditioned on the matter of the mirror, cannot be said to be in the mirror. Therefore, they have to have a real existence somewhere else, which is the World of Image.[70] The same argument applies to dreams, visions, phantasies of the imagination, and certain sorts of miracles like the projection of an astral body, illusions, ghosts, and so on. These have to have an autonomous existence in the World of Image, intermediate in abstraction from matter relative to the Worlds of Sensation and Intellect. Although they are immaterial, they are self-subsistent apparitions and simple substances, even the accidents among them, like tastes and odors.[71]

Finally, although the World of Image is spatial, it is not somewhere else. It is neither separated from our world by any certain distance nor is it in some particular direction from us (although Quṭb al-Dīn did sometimes speak as though it surrounds our universe).[72]

The final section of his description of the World of Image concerns the afterlife, which by and large takes place there.[73] It was notorious that al-Fārābī, the first Muslim philosopher to study the relation between Islamic doctrine and classical philosophy, had been unable to establish the survival of the individual soul after death, much less provide a metaphysical basis for the delights of Paradise and the torments of Hell so graphically described in the Qur'ān. Doubts persisted despite Avicen-

70. *Commentary,* 99–103/267–74, 211–16/470–76.
71. See pp. 214–15 below.
72. See pp. 215–16, 218–19 below.
73. See p. 217 below.

na's attempt to justify the religious view by arguing that although imagination and comprehension of the particular were made possible in this life by the material body, the immaterial soul was tinged during earthly life by its material body to such an extent that after death it retained its individuality and suffered such blissful or painful imaginings as were appropriate to its moral condition. Such reasonings did not inspire much confidence apparently, for later philosophers found it necessary to posit a realm of autonomous images instead.

Although those few perfected both in theoretical and practical philosophy would pass directly to the realm of Lights—the World of the Intellect—less developed souls would need to be purified in the World of Image. Quṭb al-Dīn thought that it would be contrary to the mercy of God for underdeveloped souls not to develop in the afterlife. In fact, the souls intermediate in practical or theoretical philosophy or both would ascend by stages through the various levels of the World of Images, being manifested in one of the celestial spheres, as the testimony of the Prophet about His Night Journey made clear. Eventually, they too would pass to the World of Lights. Incidentally, Quṭb al-Dīn explains in the *Commentary* that the good far outnumber the wicked in this world.[74]

The lowest class of souls, those deficient in both practical and theoretical wisdom, suffer torment in accordance with their particular dispositions.[75] (It is not their lack of wisdom, as such, that condemns them, nor its presence in the higher classes that saves them, but the conduct that springs from wisdom.) Here he admits the possibility of metempsychosis, although he says that the arguments on both sides are indecisive. Therefore, it is possible that the souls of the vicious pass at death into the bodies of animals befitting their character, dying from one an-

74. *Illumination,* 235/519–23.
75. See pp. 219–23 below.

imal to another until their vices are extinguished. In any case, the souls of the wicked pass eventually into the apparitional bodies of animals in the World of Image. Once their wicked traits are eliminated there by passing through the bodies of successively smaller animals corresponding to each of their vices, they can eventually rise to the World of Pure Light. Their reincarnation in animal bodies was attested by verses of the Qur'ān, by Traditions of the Prophet, and by the testimony of some of the ancient sages.

Once the existence and nature of the World of Image were established, the answers to the scholar's questions were obvious.[76] Quṭb al-Dīn deals with them briefly, doing little more than referring to his earlier discussions and pointing out errors of logic. The work ends with a brief avowal of his own limitations.

Obviously, Quṭb al-Dīn intended these speculations to be taken with a grain of salt, especially in details. While he presumably thought the existence of the World of Image was demonstrated, he made no claim to know all details perfectly. Such details were a combination of allegorical interpretations of scripture, visions of mystics, and practical speculation.

The problems of reincarnation and the preexistence of the soul were inherited from classical Platonism. Suhrawardī introduced them, not without reluctance, because he knew they were generally accepted by the ancient and Oriental philosophers whom he claimed to follow. Quṭb al-Dīn held these views with more enthusiasm than his master, but he seems to have been the last in Islam to do so.

The doctrine of the World of Image that Quṭb al-Dīn uses to support his notions about reincarnation played a different role in the long run. While the Illuminationist epistemology, ontology, and cosmology took mystical insight as evidence for par-

76. See pp. 223–29 below.

ticular philosophical doctrines, the World of Image provided a philosophical justification for the unloosing of the mystical imagination. It provided both a rational basis for the reality of the mystics' visions and freed these visions from the constraints of rationality.

The doctrine of the World of Image was, of course, elaborated by later philosophers. Dāwūd Qayṣarī, commenting on Ibn 'Arabī, identifies the substratum of the World of Image as the imagination of the Universal Soul, in which our individual imaginations could participate[77]—something like Avicenna's theory of intellection. Lāhījī, commenting on Shabistarī, said that it contained the archetypes of existing things and the other souls of the dead.[78] Shaykh Aḥmad Aḥsā'ī, the founder of the Shaykhī school, developed an elaborate metaphysics of the imagination in which the human body existed simultaneously on four levels of the material and imaginal worlds. By systematically relegating the events of the afterlife and the Resurrection to the World of Image, he prepared the way for the symbolic resurrection of the Bābīs. I do not know, however, of any Muslim philosopher who followed Quṭb al-Dīn's ideas on metempsychosis.

77. Dāwūd Qayṣarī, *Sharḥ Fuṣūṣ al-Ḥikam* (Bombay, 1299/1881), 30 ff., and (Bombay, 1300/1882), 25 ff., tr. in Corbin, *Spiritual Body,* 144–47.

78. *Gawhar-i Murād* (Tehran, 1313/1895), pp. 287–89, tr. in Corbin, *Spiritual Body,* 171–75.

·FIVE·

Conclusion

I have based this work on the assumption that Suhrawardī was the most important influence on Quṭb al-Dīn. His best-known philosophical work, after all, was a commentary on *The Philosophy of Illumination;* and the influences of Suhrawardī on *The Pearly Crown* are plain. Moreover, while Avicenna's philosophy has been studied in the West for eight hundred years, Suhrawardī was little known outside the Islamic world until thirty years ago and his philosophy is still widely misunderstood. It is more interesting, given the current state of the art, to identify Illuminative influences in Quṭb al-Dīn's thought than to trace there the continuation of Avicenna's ideas.

There remains, however, other work to do before we can understand completely Quṭb al-Dīn's place in the matrix of Islamic philosophy. Among Suhrawardī's works are books in the Peripatetic style, notably *The Book of Paths and Havens.*[1] I have confined myself to interpreting Suhrawardī in the light of *The Philosophy of Illumination*, the work with which Quṭb al-Dīn was directly concerned. However, Hossein Ziai has argued—correctly, I think—that it and Suhrawardī's Peripatetic works form a philosophical unity and that the former cannot be considered in isolation. Based on my very unsystematic in-

1. *Kitāb al-Mashāri' wa'l-Muṭāriaāt.* The metaphysics is published in Suhrawardī, *Œuvres,* 1:194–506.

vestigation of *The Book of Paths and Havens,* I suspect that *The Pearly Crown*'s relation to Suhrawardī's thought would be much clearer in its light.

The second area that deserves further study is Quṭb al-Dīn's relation to the thirteenth-century revival of Avicennism, especially the commentaries on Avicenna's *Book of Hints and Allusions*. Fakhr al-Dīn Rāzī, the anti-Peripatetic theologian, and Naṣīr al-Dīn Ṭūsī, Quṭb al-Dīn's teacher, both wrote commentaries on it. Several manuscripts in Turkish libraries purport to be commentaries by Quṭb al-Dīn on this work. Whether or not they are (and if they are genuine, I suspect they are juvenalia), we do know that Quṭb al-Dīn urged one of his students, Quṭb al-Dīn Taḥtānī, to write a work evaluating the arguments of Rāzī and Ṭūsī.[2] I have not studied these commentaries, but I have seen at least one passage in which Ṭūsī was clearly responding to Suhrawardī's criticisms of Avicenna.[3] This literature deserves examination.

There is also a literature of particular controversies. A series of articles exists, for example, written by Quṭb al-Dīn's two main philosophy teachers, Ṭūsī and Kātibī, debating the problem of proving the existence of a necessary existent.[4] The problem of conception and assent in logic was another popular topic. It is reasonable to suppose that such articles were concerned with the most controversial topics of the time.

Very few of the principal philosophical works of Quṭb al-Dīn's contemporaries have been studied. I do not know of any good study of Ṭūsī's philosophy, for example. Quṭb al-Dīn's other teacher, Kātibī, wrote a philosophical textbook entitled

2. See p. 25 above. Taḥtānī's *Muḥākamāt* (Brockelmann, S2: 816.20) was printed in Istanbul in 1290. It is quite rare. See App. B, no. 2, below.
3. See pp. 147–48, 84 above.
4. Published as *Muṭāraḥāt Falsafīyah*. An article by Quṭb al-Dīn on the same subject also exists. See App. C, no. 7.

Ḥikmat al-ʿAyn.[5] This, along with a companion work on logic, was a popular textbook for centuries, but it has no modern study, so far as I know.

Probably the most tantalizing area for investigation concerns Quṭb al-Dīn's relation with Ibn ʿArabī and his student Ṣadr al-Dīn al-Qūnawī. Ibn ʿArabī is known to modern students mainly through his *Bezels of Wisdom* (*Fuṣūṣ al-Ḥikam*). Whether or not Ibn ʿArabī ever dealt seriously with the problems of Peripatetic philosophy, we know that his student Qūnawī did. There is an unpublished correspondence between him and Ṭūsī. Perhaps when Chittick's studies of Qūnawī are complete, Quṭb al-Dīn's position in all this will be clearer.[6]

Another set of problems that I did not pursue relates to the originality of Quṭb al-Dīn's *Commentary on the "Philosophy of Illumination."* I am aware that this work consists in part of verbatim quotations from the earlier commentary of Shahrazūrī. Presumably some of the ideas I have attributed to Quṭb al-Dīn are originally Shahrazūrī's. There cannot be much doubt that comparing Quṭb al-Dīn's commentary with Shahrazūrī's would shed light on the nature of Quṭb al-Dīn's distinctive views.[7]

As I pursued this study, it became clearer to me just how difficult it is to evaluate an Islamic philosopher in isolation and how necessary it is to take seriously his methodology and its expression in his works as a whole. To make any sense at all of Quṭb al-Dīn's works, I found I had to understand the central

5. Brockelmann, G1:466, S1:847, where the entries for this work—manuscripts, commentaries, glosses, and so on—cover almost three pages.
6. See Appendix D below.
7. Another puzzle to be analyzed is the relation of the anonymous *al-Muthul al-ʿAqlīya al-Aflāṭūnīya,* ed. ʿAbd al-Raḥmān Badawī (Cairo: Dār al-Kutub al-Miṣrīya, 1947). This work, probably written a few decades after Quṭb al-Dīn's death, shares some text with both the *Commentary* and the little essay on the World of Image.

ideas of Suhrawardī's *Philosophy of Illumination*. Most modern studies, however, I found to be almost exclusively concerned with mythical aspects. For my purposes, I found I had to work out from the beginning the logical and conceptual structure of the work in the light of the canons of scientific method as expounded in the Islamic tradition of logic. Having done this, I was rewarded by the discovery that the work has a clear and logical structure, that Suhrawardī had something very precise and reasonable in mind when he said that his book was based on mystical intuition, and that the principles of *The Philosophy of Illumination* have a clear and specific relation to other Islamic philosophy. This understanding supports the interpretation of Suhrawardī held by later Islamic philosophers against that of Henry Corbin and his school.

Thus I found I could generally accept Quṭb al-Dīn's assertion that in his commentary he simply clarified Suhrawardī's meaning without altering it to fit his own ideas.[8] When Quṭb al-Dīn actually says he is expressing his own opinions, he is to be taken seriously.

Moreover, this understanding of Suhrawardī also serves to show that *The Pearly Crown* is in fundamental ways an Illuminative book, again validating the view of later Islamic philosophers that the key feature of *The Philosophy of Illumination* is not the mythology but the doctrine of the primacy of quiddity. Later exponents of the primacy of existence only bypassed Suhrawardī by positing a deeper level of being, "the reality of existence," that Suhrawardī had not reached.

While I am reasonably confident of the correctness of my interpretation of Illuminationist metaphysics as expressed in Suhrawardī's *Philosophy of Illumination* and Quṭb al-Dīn's *The Pearly Crown*, I have less confidence in my interpretation of Quṭb al-Dīn's views on the afterlife and reincarnation. It is

8. *Commentary*, 7.

possible that the logical inconsistencies that I attribute to him are due to the limitations of medieval thought in dealing with infinities. However, it is certainly the case that Quṭb al-Dīn is not putting all his cards on the table when he deals with this issue, especially in *The Pearly Crown*. If, for example, Quṭb al-Dīn actually did believe in reincarnation—as Mullā Ṣadrā thought he did—then he would not have wished to advertise the fact. Thus, although I am confident that I have identified the relevant philosophical issues and premises, it is quite possible that I have not drawn the correct inferences from them. Perhaps clearer analysis or additional sources will make the matter clear.

THE VALUE OF THIS PHILOSOPHY

Within the tradition of Islamic philosophy, Suhrawardī is obviously a pivotal figure to be ranked with such men as Fārābī, Avicenna, Averroes, Mullā Ṣadrā, and a few others. Quṭb al-Dīn is a philosopher of the second rank. His light is borrowed from Suhrawardī, his position akin to that of Porphyry to Plotinus, Wolff to Leibniz, or Feuerbach to Hegel. In the context of the study of Islamic philosophy, my work finds its justification in its attempt to isolate what was essential in Suhrawardī's Illuminative philosophy. It will have served its purpose if it identifies characteristic doctrines of *The Philosophy of Illumination* and allows us to recognize them elsewhere.

The larger question of the contemporary value of this sort of philosophy is more complex. The fact that this tradition of philosophy has continued to live up to the present gives it at least historical and even a certain political relevance.

The most important philosophical limitation of these works is their reliance on an outdated science. The transformations of astronomy, physics, and biology have destroyed the basis of the cosmology and physics of Quṭb al-Dīn and his contemporaries. To be sure, as a practicing scientist he was well aware just how tentative and uncertain his knowledge was. Virtually his whole cosmology was advanced only as a plausible explanation.[9]

On the other hand, Suhrawardī and Quṭb al-Dīn's criticism of mechanistic theories of perception and knowledge applies to modern discussions of artificial intelligence and brain research even more than to medieval theories of sensation and knowledge. The basic questions of the origin of the world and the nature of consciousness remain unanswered. Indeed, the medieval philosophers had a good deal more to say about traditional philosophical questions than some schools of modern philosophy.

Perhaps, though, the most important reason for reading the works of thinkers long dead is more human and has nothing to do with the hope of solving what may really be insoluble philosophical problems—that by seeing their attempts to reach knowledge and wisdom, however unsuccessful they may have proven to have been, we may find inspiration and courage to pursue goodness and excellence in our own lives.

9. *Crown,* 1:5:43, 85; pp. 117–18, 121 above.

Appendixes

·APPENDIX A·

Quṭb al-Dīn's Life: Sources

ANCIENT SOURCES

There are two preeminent biographical sources for Quṭb al-Dīn al-Shīrāzī. The first is the autobiography he includes in the introduction to his commentary on Avicenna's *Canon of Medicine.*[1] This is the only account of his family background, childhood, and early education. It is limited in that it is mainly concerned with his medical education and research and that it goes up to only 682/1283 when he was forty-seven. Some of the early biographers used this material.[2] The second source is Ibn al-Fuwaṭī, the librarian of the Marāgha observatory, who knew Quṭb al-Dīn for more than half a century. He wrote his biography in his *Majma‘ al-Ādāb fī Mu‘jam al-Alqāb,* a very large biographical dictionary of his contemporaries. Only Ibn al-Fuwaṭī's own abridged version of this work now survives. Portions of the original version are preserved in Ibn Rāfi‘ al-Sallāmī, probably via al-Dhahabī, who seems to have known the original version. Other original material is included in biographies by Abū 'l-Fidā', al-Asnawī, Ibn al-Wardī, al-Sallāmī, al-

1. See p. 7, n. 12.
2. For instance, Ibn Ḥajar, al-Sallāmī, and al-Suyūṭī.

Subkī, and Ibn Ḥajar, the last apparently based on an unpublished work by al-Dhahabī.[3]

A good deal of colorful material of uncertain provenance is to be found in the biography by Kāzarūnī, preserved by the fourteenth-century historian Khwānsārī. Mishkāt insists that Kāzarūnī's material is thoroughly unreliable and refutes it point by point.[4]

The other class of primary sources is manuscript colophons, book dedications, and incidental references in sources not mainly concerned with Quṭb al-Dīn. All of the above need to be coordinated with the general historical sources for the period.[5]

MODERN BIOGRAPHIES

In the nineteenth and early twentieth centuries, a number of short accounts of Quṭb al-Dīn's life and works were published, the most outstanding of which were E. Wiedemann's article in the first edition of *The Encyclopedia of Islam* (reprinted unchanged in the second edition) and the section on Quṭb al-Dīn in the second volume of Sarton's *Introduction to the History of Science*. These were superseded by Sayyid Muḥammad Mishkāt's biographical introduction to his edition of the philosophical books of Quṭb al-Dīn's *The Pearly Crown*. Mishkāt's work has been the basis for all later research on Quṭb al-Dīn's life. A number of articles were later published on Quṭb al-Dīn in Iran,

3. These and other sources mentioned below are found in the first part of the bibliography.
4. *Crown,* 1:1:ṣ–gh.
5. There are also two sources which I missed while doing this research: the biography presumably to be found in an unpublished volume of Dhahabī's *Tārīkh al-Islām* and an *ijāza* written by Quṭb al-Dīn and described in App. C, no. 54.

the most important being that of Mīnawī, who examined a number of manuscripts of his works and quotes at length from the introductions to several.

In the mid-1970s Muḥammad-Taqī Mīr, a professor of surgery at Pahlavi University in Shīrāz who had been doing research on the history of medicine in Iran, collected all the previous research on Quṭb al-Dīn's life, added some additional primary material, and published it in a useful but uncritical work entitled *Sharḥ-i Ḥāl wa-Āthār-i Quṭb al-Dīn . . . Shīrāzī*.

·APPENDIX B·

Quṭb al-Dīn's Students

The following individuals are known to have been Quṭb al-Dīn's students:

1. *Tāj al-Dīn 'Alī b. 'Abd Allāh al-Ardabīlī al-Shāfi'ī al-Tabrīzī* (c. 670/1271 to 746/1345–46), who studied part of Ibn al-Athīr's *Jāmi' al-Uṣūl* with him.[1]
2. Quṭb al-Dīn Muḥammad b. Muḥammad al-Rāzī al-Buwayhī, known as *Quṭb al-Dīn al-Taḥtānī* (d. 766/1364–65). He was also a student of al-'Allāmah al-Ḥillī and the teacher of Shams al-Dīn al-Shahīd al-Awwal. He was the author of several commentaries on philosophical works in addition to his *Muḥākamāt,* in which he analyzed the commentaries of al-Rāzī and al-Ṭūsī on Avicenna's *Book of Hints,* a project he undertook at Quṭb al-Dīn's suggestion.[2]
3. *Niẓām al-Dīn al-A'raj al-Nīshābūrī,* who wrote on grammar, the Qur'ān, and astronomy. Quṭb al-Dīn corrected his glosses on Ṭūsī's epitome of the *Almagest* in 704/1305. [3]

1. *Crown,* 1:1:f; Subkī, 6:146; Suyūṭī, 339–40; Ibn Ḥajar; Brockelmann, S1:53546.
2. *Crown,* 1:1:f–q; Subkī, 6:31; Suyūṭī, p. 389; Ibn Ḥajar 4:339; Khwānsārī, s.v. "Quṭb al-Dīn;" Brockelmann, G2:271; S2:293–94. Muḥsin Amīn, *A'yān al-Shī'a* (Beirut: Dār al-Ta'āruf, 1986) 9:413. The *Muḥākamāt* was published in Istanbul in 1290.
3. *Crown,* 1:1:q; Khwānsārī, 225; Majlis, 1:87–88; Brockelmann, G2:200; S1:930,*39*,b, 931,*40*,b; S2:273.

4. *Kamāl al-Dīn Abū al-Ḥasan b. 'Alī al-Fārisī* (665/1266–67 to 718/1318–19), Quṭb al-Dīn's most famous student and author, at his suggestion, of *Tanqīḥ al-Manāẓir,* a revision of Ibn al-Haytham's *Optics.* Quṭb al-Dīn mentioned him favorably in one of his late astronomical works.[4]
5. *Shaykh Zayn al-Dīn Ṭāhir b. Muẓaffar al-Baghnawī al-Shīrāzī,* author of works on mystical and religious topics, another of those who studied the *Jāmi' al-Uṣūl* with him.[5]
6. *Najm al-Dīn 'Abd al-Raḥim b. al-Shaḥḥām al-Mawṣilī.* Quṭb al-Dīn gave him a general license to teach his books in Rabī' II 708/September–October 1308.[6]
7. *Sharaf al-Dīn Khwārizmī,* who copied a manuscript of *The Commentary on "The Philosophy of Illumination"*[7] and wrote one of the reviews of Rashīd al-Dīn's works.[8]
8. *Tāj al-Dīn Maḥmūd al-Sharīf al-Kirmānī.* A copy of a license to teach one of Quṭb al-Dīn's books, dated 696/1296–97, is preserved in Konya.[9]
9. *Abū 'Abd Allāh Maḥmūd b. 'Umar al-Najātī al-Nīshāpūrī.* Quṭb al-Dīn urged him to complete a commentary on *al-Kitāb al-Yamīnī fī Tārīkh Yamīn al-Dawlah,* a history of the Khwārizmids by Abū al-Naṣr al-'Utbī (d. 427/1036).[10]
10. *Shams al-Dīn Iṣfahānī.* When Quṭb al-Dīn was on his death bed, he gave this man from under his pillow about fifty sheets of notes on the *Uṣūl al-Īmān* of Fakhr al-Islām 'Alī b. Muḥammad al-Ḥanafī (d. 482/1089–90) and asked him to try

4. Brockelmann, S2:295; Mīnawī, 197; *Dictionary of Scientific Biography,* s.v. "Kamāl al-Dīn."
5. Mīr, 57; Raḥmat Allāh Mihrāz, *Buzurgān-i Shīrāz,* Silsilah-yi Intishārāt (Tehran: Anjuman-i Āthār-i Millī, 1348), 215.
6. Mīnawī, 199–200. See App. C, no. 54, below.
7. Konya: Yūsuf Agha, no. 6624.
8. Mīnawī, 191–92.
9. Mīnawī, 192.
10. Ḥājjī Khalīfah, 6:514–15; Brockelmann, G1:314, S1:548, S2:257.

to complete a commentary on the work. Shams al-Dīn worked on it for some time but finally gave up.[11]

11. *Muhadhdhib al-Dīn Shīrāzī.* A student of his in Sivas.[12]
12. *Mawlānā Sa'īd Multānī.*[13]
13. *Abū-Bakr Muhammad b. Muhammad al-Tabrīzī,* for whom Quṭb al-Dīn wrote an *ijāza* in 701/1301–2.[14]

In an early manuscript of Quṭb al-Dīn's *Key to the Key* written by Humām al-Dīn Tabrīzī[14] there is a collection of poems written in Quṭb al-Dīn's honor. The authors—presumably students and associates of Quṭb al-Dīn—were:

Humām al-Dīn himself.

Qāḍī Majd al-Dīn Ismā'īl b. Yaḥyā al-'Umarī al-Shīrāzī (670–756/1271–1355), the long-time Qāḍī al-Quḍāt of Fārs and a Ṣūfī.

Najm al-Dīn al-Turk.

Hindūshāh b. Sanjar b. 'Abd Allāh al-Ṣāḥibī.

Ṣadr al-Dīn 'Alī b. al-Muṣliḥ al-Simnānī.

Kamāl al-Dīn al-Fārisī.

Ibn al-Fuwaṭī.

Mawlānā Shams al-Dīn Shīrāzī, the maternal uncle of Qāḍī Majd al-Dīn.

Qāḍī Najm al-Dīn Shīrāzī.

11. Ḥājjī Khalīfah, 1:336–37.
12. See p. 20 above.
13. Mīnawī, 179.
14. The text is published in 'Īsā Ṣiddīq, *Tārīkh-i Farhang-i Īrān* (4th ed; Tehran: Tehran University, n.d.).
15. Br. Mus. nos. 7449–50. See Mīr, 58–67, for a description of the MS and a transcription of some of the poems. On Humām, see E12, s.v. "Humām al-Dīn b. 'Alā' Tabrīzī," by G. M. Meredith-Owens.

·APPENDIX C·

Quṭb al-Dīn's Works

More than fifty works are attributed to Quṭb al-Dīn in various sources, ranging from well-known treatises of hundreds or thousands of pages to fragments of a page or two. Some are misattributions, variant titles, or phantoms. For the dissertation on which this book is based, I prepared a comprehensive list of these works based on ancient bibliographies, manuscript catalogs, and secondary literature published through about 1980. It is far from perfect, but I was able to sort out many confusions that existed in the previous lists of Quṭb al-Dīn's works.

In this appendix that list is presented in an abbreviated form—without the lists of manuscripts, references to secondary literature, and first and last lines of works. Since I have not updated this bibliography and since the details are of rather limited interest, it did not make sense to publish it in its long form. Those who need the details are referred to my dissertation. The list in its present form is intended to show the nature of Quṭb al-Dīn's interests.

The philosophical works, being relevant here, are discussed in the most detail.

PHILOSOPHICAL WORKS

1. *Durrat al-Tāj li-Ghurrat al-Dubāj* [*The pearly crown for Dubāj's brow*]—Persian

A very large philosophical encyclopedia. (It would run to about 2500 printed pages.) It was later known as *Unmūdhāj al-ʻUlūm* [*The pattern of the sciences*] and *Anbān* or *Himyān-i Mullā Quṭb* [*The purse of Mullā Quṭb al-Dīn*]. Under the last two titles it passed into popular Persian as a proverbial, all-inclusive book.

The arrangement is as follows:

Fātiḥa: knowledge;

Jumla I: logic;

Jumla II: first philosophy;

Jumla III: physics;

Jumla IV: mathematics;

Jumla V: rational theology;

Khātima: dogmatic theology, religious law, practical philosophy, and mysticism.

According to the introduction, this was intended as a popular work, which was the reason it was written in Persian. Several chapters are translations of classic works in their fields. The geometry and astronomy are abridged translations of Euclid and Ptolemy. The "principles of religion" (*uṣūl-i dīn*) is a translation of Fakhr al-Dīn Rāzī's *Book of Forty Chapters.* The practical philosophy contains a translation of Fārābī's *Aphorisms of the Statesman.*

The sections that are genuinely Quṭb al-Dīn's were popular in that they avoided the more arcane areas of mystical philosophy. (See p. 81 above.) Other important sources include Avicenna's *Book of Healing,* Suhrawardī's *Paths and Havens* and *Philosophy of Illumination,* and Shahrazūrī's *Divine Tree* for the philosophical sections; Fārābī, Avicenna, and ʻAbd al-Mu'min al-Urmawī for the music; Avicenna's *Reform of Morals* in the practical philosophy; and Saʻīd al-Dīn Farghānī's *Paths of the Righteous* in the mysticism. The overall arrangement of the work is largely based on Avicenna's *Division of the Sciences.*

Dubāj was the Isḥāqid amīr of a small independent principality around the cities of Fūmān and Safīd-Rūd in Gīlān. He was deposed by the Mongols in 706/1306–7. ('Abbās Iqbāl Āshtiyānī claims Dubāj was actually a princess. The text of Quṭb al-Dīn's introduction does not, alas, support this.) Quṭb al-Dīn probably came to Gīlān in 704/1305 (if the date given below for this work is correct) when he fell from favor at the Mongol court after Rashīd al-Dīn became vizier. (See pp. 19, 22–23 above.) Quṭb al-Dīn made a pointed reference in the introduction to the generosity of Dubāj's vizier.

The natural reading of the colophon of the oldest known manuscript indicates the work was finished 12 Rajab 705/ 18 January 1306, a date that fits well with what is known of this period of Quṭb al-Dīn's life. Two other existing manuscripts were made for unidentified princes in 705 and 706. Thus *The Pearly Crown* was probably begun in the late 690s/1290s or very early 700s/1300s, soon after the completion of *The Commentary on "The Philosophy of Illumination."* Internal evidence indicates that the *khātima* on religion and practical philosophy was written last, at the suggestion of the patron, and was not part of the original plan of the work.

The Pearly Crown was well thought of by later scholars though its size and the fact that it was in Persian militated against its wide use as a text of philosophy and presumably explain why few commentaries were written on it. Mullā Ṣadrā cited it several times in his *Four Journeys*. Its extensive mathematical chapters seem to have been especially popular and were sometimes copied separately. The chapters on religion were a novel feature in such a work and also exist in separate manuscripts.

The Pearly Crown was partially published in Tehran in the 1930s in two volumes. The first volume (*bakhsh*), edited by Muḥammad Mishkāt, contains the philosophical books, i.e., the *fātiḥa* on knowledge and *jumlas* 1, 2, 3, and 5. The second volume, edited by Sayyid Ḥasan Mishkān Ṭabasī, contains the mathematics with the exception of the rather long summary of Euclid's elements. The published volumes contain about 45 percent of the whole, the geometry 15 percent, and the *khātima* on religion 40 percent. The edition seems sound and is made from a number of manuscripts, one very ancient—Majlis 4720, which has been my authority for the unpublished portions of the work.

Mishkāt states that a gloss on *The Pearly Crown* was written by a Muḥammad-Riḍā b. 'Abd al-Muṭṭalib al-Tabrīzī (d. 1108/1762–63).

Durrat al-Tāj li-Ghurrat al-Dubāj. 8 vols. in 2. Vol. 1, edited by Sayyid Muḥammad Mishkāt; vol. 2, edited by Sayyid Ḥasan Mishkān Ṭabasī. Tehran: Majlis, 1317–24, 1938–45.

2. *Sharḥ Ḥikmat al-Ishrāq* [*Commentary on "The Philosophy of Illumination"*]—Arabic

A word-by-word commentary on the celebrated philosophical treatise by Shihāb al-Dīn Yaḥyā Suhrawardī (see pp. 22, 27–28 above), completed in Rajab 694/April 1295. Two variant titles listed in some bibliographies—*Sharaf al-Ishrāq* and *Sharḥ Kitāb al-Asrār*—are misreadings. According to the preface, Quṭb al-Dīn undertook this work because *The Philosophy of Illumination,* despite its importance, had no satisfactory commentaries. (He was not altogether candid about his debt to Shahrazūrī's works.) He dedicated it to Jamāl al-Dīn 'Alī b. Muḥammad al-Dastjirdānī, the grand vizier of the moment who was executed a few months later.

This book was lithographed in 1896 along with a famous gloss on it by Mullā Ṣadrā. Ḥājjī Khalīfa mentions another gloss written in Persian around 900/1495 by a Mawlānā ʻAbd al-Karīm. A Persian commentary by Muḥammad-Sharīf b. Harawī entitled *Anwarīya* has been published by Hossein Ziai.

Sharḥ Ḥikmat al-Ishrāq. Edited by Asad Allāh Harātī. [Tehran], 1313–15/1896–98. 565 pp.

3. *Ḥawāshī ʻalā Ḥikmat al-ʻAyn* [*Glosses on Qazwīnī's "Ḥikmat al-ʻAyn"*]—Arabic

   Short comments on the celebrated philosophical textbook written by Quṭb al-Dīn's teacher, Najm al-Dīn Dabīrān al-Kātibī al-Qazwīnī (d. 675/1276–77), the first to be written on this book and incorporated totally in Mīrak al-Bukhārā'ī's widely used commentary. So far as I know, they survive only in this form.

   Mīrak al-Bukhārā'ī, Shams al-Dīn Muḥammad b. Mubārakshāh. *Sharḥ Ḥikmat al-ʻAyn*. 2 vols. Kazan, 1904.

4. *Sharḥ al-Ishārāt* [*Commentary on Avicenna's "Book of Hints and Allusions"*]—Arabic

   Not mentioned in any ancient bibliography.

5. *Ḥawāshī ʻalā al-Ishārāt* [*Glosses on Avicenna's "Book of Hints and Allusions"*]—Arabic

   Also unknown in the early bibliographies. It may be the same as the previous work.

6. *Risāla fī Taḥqīq 'Ālam al-Mithāl wa-Ajwibat As'ilat Ba'ḍ al-Fuḍalā'* [A treatise ascertaining the reality of the World of Image and Answers to the questions of a certain scholar]—Arabic

   See App. F below. A short work dependent on *The Commentary on "The Philosophy of Illumination"* and so dating after 694/1295. It is certainly authentic.

7. *Risāla fī Ithbāt al-Wājib* [A treatise on proving the existence of the Necessary Being]—Arabic

   There was a famous written debate on this subject between Quṭb al-Dīn's two teachers, Ṭūsī and Qazwīnī. Brockelmann mentions that there are glosses on it by Ibrāhīm b. Muḥammad 'Arabshāh al-Isfarā'īnī. The one known manuscript has ten folios.

8. *'Ishq-Nāma* [*The book of love*]—Persian

   On mystical knowledge (*'irfān*), with an introduction, three chapters, and a conclusion, in twenty folios. It may be something comparable to Avicenna's philosophical *Treatise on Love.*

9. *Risāla fī al-Taṣawwur wa'l-Taṣdīq* [*Treatise on Conception and Assent*]—Arabic

   Probably a work of Quṭb al-Dīn Rāzī incorrectly attributed.

10. [*A Note on Philosophy*]—Arabic

11. *Sharḥ al-Najāt* [*A Commentary on Avicenna's "Book of Salvation"*]—Arabic

12. [*Commentary on Ṭūsī's "Rawḍāt al-Nāẓir" ("Garden of the Spectator")*]—Persian

A commentary on a work on truth and actuality.

13. [*A Book on Ethics*]—Persian

Attributed to Quṭb al-Dīn by Mīnawī and supposedly written for 'Izz al-Dīn al-Ṭībī, "the king of Shīrāz." No manuscript is known.

ASTRONOMICAL WORKS

14. *Nihāyat al-Idrāk fī Dirāyat al-Aflāk* [*The Highest Attainment in the Knowledge of the Spheres*]—Arabic

Quṭb al-Dīn's first and largest astronomical work, completed on the eve of 15 Sha'bān 680/28 November 1281 in Sivas (assuming that "Shīrāz" is a misreading) and dedicated to Shams al-Dīn Juwaynī (killed 683/1284), the grand vizier and an eminent patron of scholars. (Mishkāt and Mīr, probably accepting that it was written in Shīrāz, say that it was dedicated to Bahā al-Dīn Juwaynī, the bloody-minded governor of Isfahan—who was, however, already dead.) It was composed partly at the suggestion of a friend, Ashraf al-Dīn Muḥammad b. 'Umar Badakhshānī. It is likely that most of Quṭb al-Dīn's other astronomical works are based on this one. In the slightly later and shorter (though still quite long) *King's Offering,* Quṭb al-Dīn remarks that he did not intend to mention the views of other scholars; those who were interested could find them in *The Highest Attainment.* It was based on the work of Ṭūsī, especially his *Tadhkira,* but it is much more elaborate and has distinctive features of its own. Aside from astronomy, it contains information on geography, meteorology, mechanics, and optics. At the end of the work he cites a number of his sources. A detailed table of contents is given in the Berlin catalog, no. 5682.

The book was quite popular in the Middle Ages and is known in more than thirty manuscripts, including several written during the author's lifetime. Except for short quotations, this work has never been edited or published.

Ḥājjī Khalīfa says there was a gloss by a certain Sinān Pāshā.

15. *Al-Tuḥfa al-Shāhīya fī al-Hay'a* [*The King's Offering, on Astronomy*]—Arabic

Similar to the previous work but mentioning only the author's own views and containing some additional material. Quṭb al-Dīn finished it in Jumādā I 684/July–August 1285 while he was busy serving as a judge in Sivas and Malatya. He dedicated it to the vizier Amīr Shāh Muḥammad b. Tāj al-Dīn Mu'tazz b. Ṭāhir, the Saljūq prince who evidently suggested the project.

Its general arrangement is similar to that of the *Attainment*.

Several early and authoritative manuscripts exist. There is an incomplete word-by-word commentary as well as incomplete notes (*ta'līqāt*) by 'Alā' al-Dīn 'Alī al-Qūshjī (d. 879/1474), an astronomer from Samarqand who eventually became a professor at Aya Sofia. There were also glosses by al-Sharīf al-Jurjānī (d. 816/1413).

According to Mīr, a Shams al-Dīn Khafrī wrote another commentary in 901/1495–96 entitled *Muntahā al-Idrāk fī Dirāyat al-Aflāk*, though the title sounds to me like a commentary on the *Highest Attainment*.

16. *Ikhtiyārāt-i Muẓaffarī* [*Selections for Muẓaffar al-Dīn*]—Persian

Apparently a translation of selections from *The Highest Attainment* giving Quṭb al-Dīn's distinctive opinions on astronomy and refuting the views of others. It seems to be about two-thirds the size of the two previous works and has almost the same arrangement. It was dedicated to Muẓaffar al-Dīn Yūlaq (or Būlaq) Arslān (d. 704/1304–5), the Chūpānid ruler of the small emirate of Kastamonu on the Byzantine frontier near the Black Sea. Thus it was probably composed toward the end of Quṭb al-Dīn's stay in Anatolia, perhaps in the late 680s/1280s. It could conceivably also date from the period in the 1300s when Quṭb al-Dīn was out of favor at the Mongol court, although there is no other evidence of his having gone to Anatolia at this time. Its style is well spoken of by Iranian critics.

17. *Kitāb "Fa'altu fa-lā talum" fī al-Hay'a* [*The book of "I Tried, So Don't Blame Me" on Astronomy*]—Arabic

Also known as *Sharḥ al-Tadhkira al-Naṣīrīya* [*Commentary on the "Reminder" of Naṣīr al-Dīn Ṭūsī*]. It is a gloss dedicated to Ṭūsī's son Aṣīl al-Dīn on the commentary by Muḥammad b. 'Alī al-Ḥumādhī entitled *Bayān* (or *Tibyān*) *Maqāṣid al-Tadhkira* [*Explanation of the intentions of the "Reminder"*], in which Quṭb al-Dīn's *al-Tuḥfa al-Shāhīya* was severely criticized and plagiarized. He also wished to criticize a work called *Tarkīb al-Aflāk* by Abū 'Ubayd al-Jūzajānī, a student of Ṭūsī. The book was completed in Tabrīz in 704/1304–5. According to Mīnawī, its purpose was to refute the errors that certain individuals had attributed to Quṭb al-Dīn.

The work's two titles have caused some confusion. Ḥājjī Khalīfa said he had heard that Quṭb al-Dīn had commented on the *Tadhkira* but had not seen it. That the two titles represent one book is proven by the opening lines quoted in various catalogs under both titles. I have not seen an explanation for its peculiar title.

'Alī Qūshjī, who commented on *The King's Offering,* also commented on this work.

18. *Al-Tabṣira fī 'l-Hay'a* [*Enlightenment in Astronomy*]—Arabic

    According to Mīnawī, who examined the manuscript, this is a work of Bahā' al-Dīn Kharaqī (d. 527/1132) erroneously attributed to Quṭb al-Dīn.

19. A Revision of *Al-Zīj al-Jadīd al-Riḍwāni* [*The New Astronomical Tables of Riḍwān*]—Arabic

    Perhaps these are some notes Quṭb al-Dīn took on an earlier set of tables. I can find no record of the original work.

20. *Al-Zīj al-Sulṭānī* [*The Sultan's Astronomical Tables*]—Persian

    Also attributed to Shams al-Dīn Mīrak al-Bukhārā'ī, the author of *Commentary on "Ḥikmat al-'Ayn"*. The only copy I know of is defective and has 243 folios. I think that if this were actually Quṭb al-Dīn's work and not just notes or something of the sort, some further record would have survived.

21. *Kharīdat al-'Ajā'ib* [*The Wondrous Pearl*]—Arabic

    There is no evidence to support its attribution to Quṭb al-Dīn.

22. Extract from Jābir b. Aflaḥ's *Iṣlāḥ al-Majistī* [Correction of Ptolemy's *Almagest*]—Arabic

    Jābir b. Aflaḥ was a twelfth-century Spanish astronomer who criticized Ptolemy. These are presumably Quṭb al-Dīn's notes on the work.

23. *Ḥill Mushkilāt al-Majistī* [*Solution of the Difficulties of Ptolemy's "Almagest"*]—Arabic

    Possibly identical with the previous work. If it is not and is not a variant title for one of the other works, it would seem to be lost.

24. *Jahān-Dānish* [*Geography*]—Persian

    Actually written by Muḥammad b. Mas'ūd Ghaznawī (d. 550/1155).

MATHEMATICAL WORKS

25. *Tarjuma-i Taḥrīr-i Uṣūl-i Uqlīdis* [*Translation of the Recension of Euclid's "Elements"*]—Persian

    A translation in fifteen parts of Ṭūsī's recension of the *Elements*. It was completed in Sha'bān 681/November–December 1282 and dedicated to the Amīr Shāh Tāj al-Dīn, to whom *The King's Offering* was also dedicated.

26. *Risāla dar Tawḍīḥ-i Qaḍāyā-i Uqlīdis* [*Treatise in Explanation of the Theorems of Euclid*]—Persian

    Also called *Uṣūl-i Mawḍu'a-i Uqlīdis* [*The Principles Laid Down by Euclid*]. It deals with six theorems and is very short, only about five folios.

27. *Taḥrīr Uqlīdis* [*Recension of Euclid*]—Arabic

    A very short introduction to geometry. The only known manuscript has eight folios and was written in 1054/1644–45.

28. *Fī Ḥarakat al-Daḥraja wa'l-Nisba Bayn al-Mustawī wa'l-Munḥanī* [*On Rolling Motion and the Relation between the Straight and the Curved*]—Arabic

A commentary on an anonymous treatise examining the paradox of whether the straight line is actually shorter than the arc. Quṭb al-Dīn's commentary is also known as *Risāla fī al-Handasa* [*Treatise on Geometry*].

MEDICAL WORKS

29. *Al-Tuḥfa al-Sa'dīya fī 'l-Ṭibb* [*The Offering to Sa'd al-Dīn, on Medicine*]—Arabic.

A careful and detailed commentary on the first book of Avicenna's *Canon of Medicine,* the so-called *Kullīyāt* or *Principles of Medicine.* It is also called *Sharḥ Kullīyāt al-Qānūn* [*The commentary on "The Principles" of the "Canon"*]. Quṭb al-Dīn apparently considered this his major work. It is quite large, complete copies having up to five volumes. He undertook the work as a very young man, although he was unable to get far until he came on several additional commentaries on the *Canon* when he visited Egypt in 681/1282. The first edition was finished in 682/1283, the second in 694/1294–95, and the third on the eve of the first of Rajab, 1310/23 November 1310, two and a half months before his death.

The title comes from its dedication to Sa'd al-Dīn Muḥammad Sāwujī, appointed Ṣāḥib-Dīwān by Ghāzān. Thus this title presumably was only adopted in the third edition with the two previous editions known as *Sharḥ Kullīyāt al-Qānūn.* It is not known how the three editions differ and how the surviving manuscripts relate to them.

30. *Sharḥ al-Qānūn* [*Commentary on Avicenna's "Canon"*]—Arabic

    Mīnawī claims a commentary on the complete *Canon* exists. I doubt that is the case.

31. *Risāla fī Bayān al-Ḥāja ilā al-Ṭibb wa-Ādāb al-Aṭibbā' wa-Waṣāyāhum* [*A Treatise in Explanation of the Need for Medicine and the Etiquette and Testaments of Physicians*]—Arabic

    Evidently a small work, in three chapters. The only known manuscript is bound with a copy of the commentary on the *Canon,* along with two treatises by other authors, all written in 913/1507–8.

32. *Risāla fī 'l-Baraṣ* [*Treatise on Leprosy*]—Arabic

    A short work of four folios.

33. *Sharḥ al-Urjūza* [*Commentary on the "Canticle"*]—Arabic?

    Probably a misreading of the Latin *Canon*—i.e., the *Offering*—as *Canticum.*

34. *Fī Amrāḍ al-'Ayn* [*On the Diseases of the Eye*]—Arabic

    A misattribution to Quṭb al-Dīn of a work by 'Alī b. 'Īsā.

35. *Fī al-Nār al-Fārisī* [*On the Persian Fire*]—Arabic

    A small work. Since it is bound with a treatise on fevers, it is presumably about anthrax, not Zoroastrianism.

36. *al-Īḍāḥ fī Asrār al-Nikāḥ* [*In Explanation of the Mysteries of Sex*]—Arabic

    Presumably a misattribution of the work by Shayzarī.

THE "ARAB SCIENCES" AND RELIGION

37. *Fatḥ al-Mannān fī Tafsīr al-Qur'ān* [*The Triumph of the All-Bounteous in Commentary on the Qur'ān*]—Arabic

Also known as *al-Tafsīr al-'Allāmī.* According to Mishkāt it followed strictly traditional principles. Ḥājjī Khalīfa said it had forty volumes. The Esad Efendi manuscript has twenty-nine volumes, including at least one duplicate. Probably half a dozen volumes are missing. The Cairo and Princeton manuscripts contain only small portions.

38. *Fī Mushkilāt al-Tafāsīr* [*On Difficulties in Interpretations*]—Arabic

A single volume presumably dealing with apparently contradictory verses in the Qur'ān. The work is not famous, but it is attested by Ḥājjī Khalīfa. Brockelmann and sources following him give the title as *Mushkilāt al-Qur'ān,* but this is not correct.

39. *Mushkil al-I'rāb* [*Difficulties in Vocalization*]—Arabic.

Presumably about odd vocalizations in the Qur'ān. It might also be an alternate title for the preceding work.

40. *Sharḥ al-Kashshāf* [*Commentary on "The Unveiler"*]—Arabic

Glosses in two volumes on Zamakhsharī's (d. 538/1176–77) well known Qur'ān commentary, *Unveiler of the Realities of Revelation*—to be distinguished from a similar work by Quṭb al-Dīn Rāzī. It is a fairly late work, being incomplete as of 701/1302. Its title is also given as *al-Intiṣāf fī Sharḥ al-Kashshāf* [*Doing Justice to Commentary on*

"The Unveiler"]. In popular Persian "to say a *Commentary on the Kashshāf*" came to mean "to speak in great detail."

41. *Sharḥ al-Mukhtaṣar* [*Commentary on the "Abridgement"*]—Arabic

A commentary on the abridged version of Ibn Ḥājib's (d. 646/1249) *Muntahā al-Su'āl wa'l-Amal fī 'Ilmay al-Uṣūl wa'l-Jadal* [*All That Can Be Asked or Hoped Concerning the Twin Sciences of the Principles of the Law and Dialectics*], a famous epitome of Mālikī law (though Quṭb al-Dīn was himself a Shāfi'ī). It was written before 701/1301 and before 683/1284, if Mīnawī is right in claiming it was dedicated to Juwaynī.

42. *Intikhāb-i Sulaymānīya* [*Solomon's Choice*]—Persian

An abridged translation of Ghazālī's *Revival of the Religious Sciences* made for Maḥmūd Bey, the son of the Amīr Muẓaffar al-Dīn, for whom *Selections for Muẓaffar al-Dīn* was written.

43. *Miftāḥ al-Miftāḥ* [*The Key to "The Key"*]—Arabic

The earliest commentary on the rhetoric (*ma'ānī wa-bayān*) of the popular textbook of Arabic grammar and style, *Miftāḥ al-'Ulūm* [*The Key to the Sciences*], of Sirāj al-Dīn al-Sakkākī (d. 626/1228–29). Quṭb al-Dīn composed it for the poet Humām al-Dīn Tabrīzī (d. 714/1314–15), another student of Ṭūsī and the man responsible for collecting the book of panegyrics presented to Quṭb al-Dīn a few years before his death. The commentary was completed in Rajab 701/March 1302. It is a large book of some 32,000 lines (*abyāt*).

44. *Sharḥ Talkhīṣ al-Miftāḥ* [*Commentary on Qazwīnī's Abridgement of Sakkākī's "The Key to the Sciences"*]—Arabic.

Probably composed after the previous work around 705/1305, since it is dedicated to the same Amīr Dubāj for whom the previous work was written. Quṭb al-Dīn wrote it to deal with certain difficulties remaining in Qazwīnī's Abridgement and commentary. It is possible that some of the manuscripts attributed to the previous work are in fact of this one. Mīnawī, who discovered this work, was unable to compare the two commentaries.

45. *'Ahd-Nāma* [*Covenant Book*]—Persian

Also called *Shajarat al-Īmān* [*The Tree of Faith*]. Eighty-five folios on supererogatory religious observances. The manuscript is late and defective, and the authorship far from certain.

46. *A Note on the Treatment of Heretics and Infidels*—Arabic

Transcribed from an original written by Quṭb al-Dīn in Rabī' II 685/June 1286 at Konya.

47. *Risāla fī Taḥqīq al-Jabr wa'l-Qadar* [*An Epistle Ascertaining the Reality of Fate and Predestination*]—Arabic

One and a half folios found in an early ninth/fifteenth century compilation of sixteen short works on religion and mysticism.

48. *Lawāmi' al-Asrār fī Sharḥ Ṭawāli' al-Anwār* [*The Shining Mysteries in Commentary on Bayḍāwī's "Ascendant Lights"*]—Arabic

A commentary on a treatise on dogmatic theology. It is probably a work of Dawwānī incorrectly attributed.

MISCELLANEOUS

49. [*Two Treatises on Various Subjects*]

50. [*In Answer to 'Imād al-Dīn Kāshī*]

    A mathematician, fl. 744/1363?

51. [*Two Reviews of the Works of Rashīd al-Dīn Faḍl Allāh*]

52. [*Text of a Debate between Quṭb al-Dīn and Rashīd al-Dīn Faḍl Allāh*]

53. *Dīwān* [*Collected Poems*]—Arabic and Persian

    Quṭb al-Dīn wrote poems occasionally in both Arabic and Persian, usually occasional pieces or mnemonics. Much of what survives is to be found in his biographies, but, so far as I know, there was never a collected edition.

54. [*An Ijāza* for Najm al-Dīn Mawṣilī]

    Three and a half folios. An autograph *ijāza* written in 708/1308 in Tabrīz authorizing the recipient to teach all Quṭb al-Dīn's works and the works he himself had studied.

55. [An *Ijāza* for Abū-Bakr Tabrīzī]

    Another authorization to a student to teach his works. See p. 174 above.

·APPENDIX D·

Quṭb al-Dīn and Ibn 'Arabī

Quṭb al-Dīn's period of study with Ṣadr al-Dīn Qūnawī suggests the possibility that the works of Ibn 'Arabī influenced him. The historical evidence of the extent of Quṭb al-Dīn's knowledge of Ibn 'Arabī's thought is ambiguous. He mentions in *The Pearly Crown* that he read Ibn al-Athīr's harmony of the authoritative *ḥadīth* collections with Qūnawī, along with "the sciences of the Law, the Path, and the Truth."[1] There is no specific mention of Ibn 'Arabī's works.

We do not know when Quṭb al-Dīn went to Konya or how much of this time he spent with Qūnawī. From what we know of his early life, he could not have been there too long. The period does not loom large in his biographies.

There are at least two direct citations of Ibn 'Arabī's *Meccan Revelations* his works.[2] In both cases he is adduced as support for doctrines derived in Ibn 'Arabī's characteristic terminology. I do not know of any citations of Qūnawī's works.

According to Affifi, Quṭb al-Dīn was one of those who wrote in defense of Ibn 'Arabī's orthodoxy when this was being hotly

1. *Crown,* "khātima," quṭb 4, pt. 2, ch. 2. See p. 14 above. Chittick points out that Qūnawī was a renowned teacher of such subjects as *ḥadīth* and had a great many students, most of whom certainly did not study Ibn 'Arabī.

2. *Commentary,* 520; pp. 209–11.

debated in the Muslim intellectual world.[3] I do not know the source of this report.

The more subtle question of an influence of Ibn 'Arabī's ideas unaccompanied by citations or characteristic terms is exceedingly difficult. To begin with, our knowledge of Ibn 'Arabī's ideas is superficial, except insofar as they are embodied in *The Bezels of Wisdom.* How the teachings of *The Meccan Revelations* might be interpreted in Peripatetic terminology in the context of a systematic philosophical work is not at all clear, especially in the absence of good studies of Qūnawī's philosophy. To add to this problem, Quṭb al-Dīn was noticeably reticent about discussing higher questions of mystical thought.

There is, though, a *prima facia* case that any influence on Quṭb al-Dīn by Ibn 'Arabī would be at best secondary. It is clear that Quṭb al-Dīn's system is primarily derived from that of Suhrawardī, who was the preeminent exponent of what came to be called the primacy of quiddity. Ibn 'Arabī, on the other hand, developed the idea of the unity of existence, what came to be called the primacy of existence. Suhrawardī's view, I have argued, was based on an intuition of the concrete specificity of things. Insofar as Ibn 'Arabī's view implied the continuity of the substance of things, it contradicted Suhrawardī and thus Quṭb al-Dīn. While some have argued that on a deeper level, these two views are closer than is generally thought, this is nonetheless unproven. It is not, therefore, justifiable in the light of current knowledge to claim Quṭb al-Dīn as a link between Ibn 'Arabī and the later Islamic philosophical tradition.[4]

3. A. E. Affifi, "Ibn 'Arabī," in M. M. Sharif, *A History of Muslim Philosophy* (Wiesbaden: Otto Harrassowitz, 1963–66), 2:406.
4. I am working on a paper on Quṭb al-Dīn's mystical views, based on the chapter on mysticism in *The Pearly Crown.* It may be that my reexamination of this text in the light of recent studies of Ibn 'Arabī by such scholars as Chittick will shed more light on this question.

·APPENDIX E·

Illuminationist Terms and Their Peripatetic Equivalents

The following is a list of some Illuminationist terms found in *The Philosophy of Illumination* and their equivalents in the standard Arabic philosophical terminology. This is not a complete glossary of the work but only a set of examples of attested equivalences (*ay*, *wa-huwa*, etc.) of Illuminationist and Peripatetic terms. It could be greatly lengthened without much trouble. In most cases, the source of the equivalent is Quṭb al-Dīn's *Commentary;* in the case of entries marked with an asterisk the source is Suhrawardī himself. The numbers in parentheses refer to Corbin's text of *The Philosophy of Illumination* and Quṭb al-Dīn's *Commentary.*

Anwār mudabbira li'l-barāzikh [lights managing the barriers]: *al-nufūs al-nāṭiqa falakīya aw insānīya* [the rational souls, whether celestial or human] (145/352, 167/385, 168/386).

al-Barāzikh al-qawābis [the kindled barriers]: *al-'anāṣir wa-mā yatawallad min-hā* [the elements and what is generated from them] (187/418–19), *al-'unṣurīyāt* [the elementals] (188/420).

**Barzakh* [barrier]: *falak* [sphere] (138/342), *jism* [body] (193/428).

al-Barzakh al-mushtarik [the common barrier]: *kurrat al-thawābit* [the sphere of fixed stars] (146/353).

Barzakhī [of barriers]: *jism, jismānī* [body, bodily] (208/466).

Faqr [need]: *imkān* [contingency] (108/284).

Ghinā [independence]: *wujūb* [necessity] (108/284).

Hay'a [mode]: *'araḍ* [accident] (61/171).

Jism fārid [single body]: *basīṭa* [simple substance] (187/418).

Jism muzdawij [double body]: *jism murakkab* [composite body] (187/418).

Muḥīṭa [comprehensive proposition]: *kullīya* [universal proposition] (25/71).

Mustaghriq [full]: *kullī* [universal] (35/105–6).

al-Nūr al-aqrab [the proximate light]: *al-'aql al-awwal* [the first intellect] (138/342).

al-Nūr al-isfahbad [the commanding light]: *al-nafs al-nāṭiqa al-mudabbira* [the managing rational soul] (147/354).

al-Nūr al-qāhir [the triumphal light]: *al-'aql* [the intellect] (154/368).

Nūr 'āriḍ [accidental light]: *nūr maḥsūs* [sensible light] (108/286–87).

Nūr mujarrad [immaterial light]: *'aql* [intellect] (138/342, 167/385).

Nūrī [luminous]: *'aqlī* [intellectual] (183/412).

al-Qawābis [the kindled ones]: *al-'anāṣir al-thalātha* [the three elements] (198/436).

Ṣayṣīya [fortress]: *badan* [body] (212/470), *al-badan al-musta'idd li-nuzūl al-nafs* [the body prepared for the descent of the soul] (216/478).

Shākhiṣa [individual]: *juz'īya* [particular] (17/49).

**Siyāq* [course]: *shikl al-qiyās* [form of the syllogism].

al-Siyāq al-atamm [the most perfect course]: *al-shikl al-awwal* [the first figure] (35/105).

·APPENDIX F·

An Epistle of the 'Allāma al-Shīrāzī Ascertaining the Reality of the World of Image and Answers to the Questions of a Certain Scholar

THE MANUSCRIPTS AND AUTHORITIES

Although the *Epistle Ascertaining the Reality of the World of Image* [*Risāla fī Taḥqīq 'Ālam al-Mithāl wa-Ajwibat As'ilat Ba'ḍ al-Fuḍalā'*] is not mentioned in any ancient list of Quṭb al-Dīn's works, it is certainly authentic. Since its text is based in part on that of *The Commentary on "The Philosophy of Illumination,"* he must have written it between 694/1295 and his death in 710/1311.

There are two surviving manuscripts: a sixteenth-century manuscript in the library of the shrine of the Imām Riḍā in Mashhad,[1] and a seventeenth-century manuscript in the Millī Library in Tehran.[2]

The Mashhad manuscript was written in 906/1503 by one 'Abdu'l-Awwal Maḥmūd b. Maḥmūd al-'Abbāsī in a legible *nasta'līq* script. There are some corrections in the same hand.

1. Mashhad, vol. 4, no. 313.
2. Millī 3:347, no. 1384F.11.

The Tehran copy is the eleventh article in a collection of short works on philosophy and related topics copied by a certain ʿAbd al-Qādir al-Urdūbādī in Shīrāz in 1022/1613. The manuscript is clearly written but almost entirely unpointed except for a few difficult words. There are some subject heads in the margin written by the scribe, and on the first two pages a few difficult words are defined in Persian by a different writer. Paragraphing is sometimes indicated by overlining, and there are some simple abbreviations. There are some copying errors. There is no indication from where the manuscript was copied.

The readings of these two manuscripts can be supplemented from several sources:

1. *The Commentary on "The Philosophy of Illumination"* is in large part the basis of the work, although the material has been reworked by selection, abridgement, and the change from Illuminationist to Peripatetic terminology. These passages and their contexts do greatly clarify the philosophical meaning of the *Epistle*.
2. Insofar as the text incorporates passages of *The Philosophy of Illumination* itself, Suhrawardī's text may also be used—cautiously—as a control.
3. Ibn ʿArabī's *Meccan Revelations* is quoted in the text with some differences from the published edition.
4. The Qur'ān is quoted frequently, sometimes with minor differences from the accepted version. These are noted.
5. There are some *ḥadīth* quoted.

Nothing is really known about the work other than what can be inferred from internal evidence. Even the title I have given is attested only in the later and inferior manuscript. Also the identity of the recipient is unknown.

The contents of the work are discussed in detail in Chapter Four above.

PRINCIPLES OF THE EDITION AND TRANSLATION

1. It is obvious that the Tehran manuscript was not copied from the earlier Mashhad manuscript, since it includes some passages omitted in the Mashhad text. There is no way to tell whether their common source was Quṭb al-Dīn's original or some later copy.
2. I assume that neither manuscript (nor the manuscripts they were copied from) were corrected from the *Commentary* or the other sources quoted in the text. This seems most likely since both manuscripts omit material quoted in the other from the *Commentary.*
3. Therefore, when either of the manuscripts agrees with the *Commentary* or one of the other sources against the other manuscript I follow that reading, on the assumption that a copying error is unlikely to duplicate the reading of the *Commentary.*
4. When both manuscripts agree against the *Commentary,* I follow the manuscripts, although if the *Commentary* reading is illuminating or obviously better, I put it in the notes.
5. The Mashhad manuscript is superior since it includes many words, sentences, and even paragraphs omitted in the Tehran manuscript. Moreover, when the two manuscripts disagree, the *Commentary* usually supports the Mashhad manuscript.
6. Therefore, when the two manuscripts disagree without further evidence, I follow the Mashhad manuscript.
7. All variants are in the notes to the Arabic text.
8. Where one or the other manuscript is clear and the other illegible, I tacitly follow the legible reading.
9. Orthography and pious epithets tacitly follow the Mashhad manuscript.
10. Classical names follow the spellings of the Mashhad manuscript. The Tehran readings are noted at their first occurrence.

11. I generally follow the paragraphing (indicated by overlining) and the chapter numbers of the Tehran manuscript.
12. I have not corrected misquotes of the Qur'ān, but the standard reading is in the notes.
13. I have not assumed that bad grammar indicated bad copying since both author and scribe were Persian.
14. Pointing and punctuation, of course, rests on my judgment.

SYMBOLS AND SIGNS

Material in brackets with no further explanation is included in the Mashhad manuscript and omitted in the Tehran manuscript. Omissions in the Mashhad manuscript supplied from elsewhere are in brackets with the source indicated. The symbols used are explained on p. 270 of the edition.

TRANSLATION

The translation is based on my edited text and does not include references to the variants. These are easily available in the Arabic notes to those who would care. The translation is relatively literal.

An Epistle of the 'Allāma al-Shīrāzī Ascertaining the Reality of the World of Image and Answers to the Questions of a Certain Scholar [Translation]

In the Name of God, the Merciful, the Compassionate!

My Lord, give bounty and increase!

The most learned[1] master, that model and accomplished philosopher, the point to which turn the profound scholars, the pole of truth, religion, and faith,[2] Maḥmūd b. Mas'ūd b. Muṣliḥ al-Shīrāzī—may God make his resting place more fragrant than the breezes of dawn and gardens of sweet grapes—said:

Praise be to God the Exalted for His favors outspread in His Earth and Heaven. Blessèd be Muḥammad—the Seal of His Prophets—and peace be upon His sons.[3]

1. *'Allāma*: "most learned," the title by which Quṭb al-Dīn al-Shīrāzī was commonly known.
2. *quṭb al-ḥaqq wa'l-milla wa'l-dīn,* playing on his title Quṭb al-Dīn.
3. Ṭ gives the text to this point slightly differently.

[AUTHOR'S INTRODUCTION]

"A noble book hath been given unto me from one wise and knowing,"[4] wherein are questions of which the one questioned knows no more than the questioner. But since it is proverbial that "what is not wholly apprehended ought not to be wholly forsaken," I saw fit to mention what I knew concerning these questions, quoting his words and then examining them with care.

The author of the letter said:

[THE WORDS OF THE SCHOLAR]

In the name of God, the Merciful, the Compassionate!

"Praise be to God, and may His peace be upon those of His servants whom He hath chosen."[5]

In the course of his search every seeker must needs be pulled this way and that by doubts he endeavors to dispel, though he be in the utmost purity of faith, for thus is the nature of mankind. Otherwise, the Friend of God[6]—Upon Him be peace!—could not have said: "Show me how Thou wilt resurrect the dead!"[7] In such a state the seeker requires by necessity one to strip away the confusions of his difficulties and to illumine the dark places of his dilemmas, lest his thought remain distracted from his goal. So in this condition it seems to him that the devil of doubt beguiles him, seeking to distract him from the object of his desire. But because of his zeal for faith, the seeker disputes

4. Cf. Qur'ān 27:6.
5. Qur'ān 25:59.
6. Abraham.
7. Qur'ān 2:260.

with his Rival in every way he can. He seeks refuge sometimes with the Absolute, and sometimes with one whom the Absolute has taught. Sometimes he resists that Satan, expelling him from his mind—each seeker in accordance with his condition.

Many questions of this sort have disturbed me; but seeing that to list all of them would lead to prolixity, I have confined myself to those among them most important in seeking happiness. God it is Who giveth aid in seeking truth and attaining of one's heart's desire!

The True Law hath promised and threatened us with the states of the Barrier and the incarnation of deeds.[8] Might it be the spiritual substance,[9] now released from the attachments of the body, that conceives these forms? But how can this determinate conception arise from something like this, which is immaterial?[10]

Is the seat of its imagining the body? But it is well known that the seat of the imagination is the brain, which is so disordered by the slightest illness that conception, memory, recall, and thought are all corrupted. What then will be the result of death, which is total corruption?

Is the seat of the imagination another body—a sphere or something else? Then it must be by a relation occurring between them at death, for it is well known that the connection of a spiritual substance is due to a relation between the bodily and the spiritual. This relation must necessitate the particular connection of the spiritual substance to that thing, alone among the rest of the separate substances, and to it alone to the exclu-

8. Events experienced by the soul between death and resurrection.
9. The soul, separate from the body after death.
10. A particular can be thought only with the aid of a material organ. Immaterial substances, like the heavenly intellects and the disembodied souls, thus can conceive only universals. If this is so, then how are the torments and pleasures of the afterlife possible?

sion of all other bodies—indeed, to the exclusion of all other instances of that species of body.[11]

Then, if the imagining of this spiritual substance was completed by the mediacy of the body, all the separate substances would be conjoined with the bodies in the world. Thus those substances would be finite in number or the bodies infinite. Either alternative requires demonstration. Or else, it may in the end escape its connection to attain felicity. This implies that after death it will ascend again.[12] This would require full explanation. If misery is real, then the soul must descend. This, however, is contrary to what we hope for from the Divine mercy. If it goes neither to bliss nor to misery, a suspension will occur. Its going to both together will combine two opposites.

If, as some people claim, everyone has two existences—concrete, which is the external, and mental—then after death the connection of the spiritual substance transmigrates to the inner body, its mental existence existent in the knowledge of God, and its actions are incarnated for it there. Thus, its inner aspect will become external there, and this its worldly exterior will become internal, even if its exterior is superior. But this is rhetorical and not demonstration. Nevertheless, just as the body has two existences, so too will the spirit. Therefore, when the spirit transmigrates in its existence from its concrete existence to its existence in a mental body, the state of its mental existence will differ by its transmigration, for it was first existent with a concrete body and is now existent with a mental body. This

11. There would have to be some special affinity between the soul and that particular celestial body, just as there is between the soul and the earthly body.
12. One of the standard arguments against reincarnation was that the number of bodies is finite but the number of potential souls in a world without beginning is infinite. Therefore, souls must eventually pass out of this world forever, presumably to the World of Intellect.

implies the conjoining of the mental existence of the spirit and the concrete existence with the mental existence of the body.

Even allowing all this, how could deeds be incarnated there? The knowledge of God would be the seat of temporal events.

Chapter [1]

It has been claimed that the human essence is a self-subsistent substance. However, why should it not be the case that the composition of the human body from the elements simply necessitates the existence of a fifth thing[13]—just as combining vitriol, gall, and water causes blackness? This would be what causes the human states. Or this fifth thing could be a capacity occurring by the mixture of the elements. At each moment this mixture would cause a state necessitating a particular human state, in accordance with the changing states caused by the influences of the celestial bodies.

Thus you see that a newborn infant is almost without perception. It does not have most faculties, despite its efforts, except for desire and anger in a weak way. The rest of its internal and external senses are not perceptive. But after some time passes, you will notice that it hears the sound when someone speaks near it, and it sees whomever is close before it. Then, as it becomes stronger in the actions of the vegetative faculties, it will take something given to it, but it will not be disturbed by the thing's being taken away again. However, after a little while more, it is distressed when the thing is taken away. And so it is, stage upon stage, degree after degree, until the end of life.

Why then might not all of these be properties emanated upon it through the influences of the celestial bodies in accordance with the capacity of its constitution? At decomposition all that

13. In addition to the four elements.

would cease. Or if the variation of conditions were due to an emanation reaching it from the Giver of Forms in accordance with the variation of capacities, the receptivity would vary in accordance with the variation in states of capacity. All those would be accidents perishing with decomposition.

Chapter [2]

How should someone be answered who claims that these conceptions and imaginings arise in the human spirit only through its connection with the body, the body needing this from the spirit by the nature of its control of the body? At the separation of the spirit from the body, all that would cease because there would no longer be a need for it. Thus, the spirit's concern with the interests of the body would be due to its connection to it. When it ceased, the concern would cease because the desire of the spirit for the body is not essential to it. Otherwise, it would not cease. Therefore, it is accidental, occurring at the body's summons, so that when there was no longer any summons, it would cease.

Chapter [3]

What is the fate of the animal spirits? Do they perish with their bodies? If so, they are not immaterial substances; and, therefore, they do not understand universals. But sometimes we see that if one of them is struck with a stick and then after a while another stick is raised against it, it will flee from it. If there were not a universal meaning remaining in its mind corresponding to every variety of that species, it would not have fled. This is not because it perceives the particular meaning, for it is impossible for the previous blow to be exactly repeated, only for something similar to recur.

Moreover, we can see that while these animals are alike in being animals, they differ in nearness to and distance from the human plane. Certain animals, like the ape, are extremely near, for they have some of the practical faculty though little of the scientific. Man knows intuitively that this kind of animal must progress toward perfection; but if it does progress, how can this be? For it not to progress, however, is unworthy of the Divine Generosity, since what is capable of perfection would be kept from its perfection. Far exalted is God above that!

In hope of attaining certitude through the wondrous grace of God,

Aḥmad.[14]

REPLY [OF THE PROFOUND '*ALLĀMAH*]

Those were the words of the scholar. Now first we will mention what we know about these questions and then, second, we will return to his text and see what may be advanced against his arguments. We say, but it is God who grants success:

[The Four Worlds]

There are four worlds: the world of the intellects, which have absolutely no connection with bodies; the world of the souls, which are attached to celestial and human bodies; the world of the bodies, comprising the spheres, the elements, and what is in them; and the world of image and imagination, which the students of the Sacred Law call "the Barrier" and the practitioners of the rational sciences call "the world of immaterial apparitions."

The Ancients alluded to this world:

> There is in existence an extended world other than the sensible world but corresponding to the sensible world in its spheres and

14. I presume this is the name of the scholar who wrote this letter.

> elements, in all the planets and composites in them—mineral, vegetable, animal, and human—and in the perpetual movements of its imaginal spheres, and in the receptivity of its elements and composites to the influences of the movements of its spheres and the illuminations of the intellectual worlds.[15]

The species of suspended forms arise infinitely there in levels differing in subtlety and coarseness, for the individuals in each level are infinite though the levels are finite. That is because, on the one hand, the imaginal world is finite insofar as it results from the creative first emanation—finite in its spheres, in its planets and their souls, and in its elements in their mineral, vegetable, and animal primary imaginal compounds, for these need causes and aspects of the intellects. These aspects are finite, as is known from the demonstration showing that the finitude of intellectual ordered things implies that their imaginal effects are finite.

On the other hand, the immaterial apparitions that result from the second emanation in accordance with the capacities occurring in the unending ages are infinite. These apparitions can be infinite since they lack order and arrangement.[16]

That world is in levels, each level having species found in this world of ours, though infinitely.[17] Some are inhabited by a folk of angels and virtuous humans. Some are inhabited by a people

15. It is not clear how far this quotation goes.
16. Suhrawardī, discussing the emanation of the many from the One, explains that the difference of species in the world is due to the different interrelations of the Light of Lights, the Immaterial Lights emanated from it, and their illuminations. Since the number of levels of reality and the number of these interrelations are finite, Suhrawardī held that the number of different kinds of things in the universe must also be finite. The number of individuals of each kind, however, may be infinite, at least over an infinite period of time since they do not exist simultaneously or in any sort of order of rank.
17. I.e., there are an infinite number of individuals in each species.

of angels, *jinn,* and devils. None save the Creator can reckon the number of levels nor what is in them. The higher a level one reaches, the more refined it is, the fairer its prospect, the more intense its spirituality, and the greater its pleasure in comparison to what was before it. The last level, which is the most exalted of them, is adjacent to the intelligible lights and is the degree of that which is like unto them.

None know the wonders of that world save God Exalted. As they desire and will, the wayfarers[18] therein manifest wonders and miracles: the manifestation of their imaginal bodies in various places at one or more times; summoning such food, drink, and clothing as they desire; and the like. Likewise, thence it is that the master sorcerers and soothsayers behold and manifest wonders.

The resurrection of the body takes place in that world, in accordance with what is recorded in the Sacred Laws. It is also there that the lordly apparitions appear—the comely and gracious apparitions and those mighty and terrifying—in which the First Cause appears—as well as the apparitions that occur therein in connection with the manifestation of the First Intellect and its apparitions, for each of the intellects has many apparitions in various forms appropriate for its manifestation. The lordly apparitions may have manifestations in this world. While they are thus manifest, they would be perceptible by sight—as when Moses, son of ʿImrān, saw the Creator appear on the Mount and the like, as is attested in the Torah. Likewise, the Prophet and His Companions—Upon them be peace!—saw Gabriel when He was manifest in the form of Diḥya al-Kalbī.

It may be that the entire World of Image consists of manifestations of the Light of Lights and other immaterial lights, each of which would appear in a particular form at a specific time in accordance with the capacity of the recipient and agent. The

18. Ṭ: "the inhabitants therein."

Light of Lights, the intellects, the celestial souls, and the separated and embodied souls of perfect men would at times appear in forms varying in beauty and ugliness, in subtlety and coarseness, and in other such attributes, in accordance with the capacity of the agent and recipient.

Also through that world are realized all the promises of prophecy: the bliss of the folk of Paradise and the torment of the denizens of the Fires, with all the species of pleasures and kinds of bodily agonies. The imaginal body which the soul controls there exactly corresponds to the sensible body in that it has all the external and internal senses and in that the rational soul is the entity that perceives in it. But in this world it perceives with bodily organs, and in the World of Image with spectral organs.

The existence of that world—i.e., the World of Image—is attested by the testimony of the Prophets, saints, and divine sages. Among the Prophets, the Messenger of God tells, for example, of the Barrier and the incarnation of deeds there. Among the saints, the great and inspired Shaykh Muḥyi al-Dīn Ibn al-'Arabī, for example, spoke of it—mentioning the reality of the Barrier in the sixty-third book of *The Meccan Revelations:* "On the knowledge of men's abiding in the Barrier between this world and the Resurrection." He said:[19]

[Ibn 'Arabī's Discussion of the Barrier]

It is an intelligible bar between two adjacent things—not exactly the same as either one of them,[20] but having the potentiality of each one of them . . . like the line separating shadow and sun. . . . It is only imagination . . . as when the man who sees his

19. Ibn 'Arabī, al-Futūḥāt al-Makkīyah (Būlāq, n.d.), 1:304 ff.
20. Ibid., 304: The original text reads: "That intelligible dividing line is the Barrier, for if it is perceived by sight, it is one of the two things—not the Barrier. If two things are adjacent, together they require a barrier that is neither one of them."

form in the mirror knows definitely that he perceives his form in one sense and that he does not perceive his form, since he sees it as very small due to the small size of the mirror's body or as large due to its great size.[21] He will not be able to deny that he saw his form, yet he will know that his form is not in the mirror and that it is not between him and the mirror. Therefore, it is neither true nor false to say that he saw his form and did not see his form.

What then is that visible form? Where is its locus?[22] What is its character? It is denied yet affirmed, existent yet nonexistent, known yet unknown. God the Exalted has manifested this reality to His servant as a token that he might know and be certain of this: that since he is baffled and bewildered before this thing, though it is of the world, and is unable to acquire knowledge of its reality, how much more must he be baffled by, ignorant of, and bewildered by its Creator! Man is apprised of this when he beholds that the self-manifestations to him of the Absolute are finer and subtler in meaning than this thing before which the intellects are baffled and whose reality they are so unable to fathom that they are even led to say: "Does this have a quiddity, or has it no quiddity at all?" After all, the intellects could not classify it as pure nonbeing, since vision perceives something, nor as pure existence since they know there is nothing there, nor as pure possibility.

It is to this kind of reality that the sleeping and the dead betake themselves, seeing therein accidents as self-subsistent forms that speak to them and to which they speak as bodies without doubt possessing spirits. And the visionary sees while awake what the sleeping see while asleep and the dead after death, as when in the afterlife he sees the forms of deeds being weighed—though

21. *Futuḥat:* "due to the fineness he sees in it if the body of the mirror is small, for he knows that his form is larger, though they are not dissimilar. If the body of the mirror is large, he sees his form as very large, though he knows definitely that his form is smaller than what he sees."

22. *maḥall:* "locus," lit. "place." Material forms are embodied in some matter as opposed to imaginal (*mithālī*) forms, which are not.

they are accidents—and sees death as a piebald ram—though death is a relation of separation after conjunction.

Some men perceive this imaginal subject with the eye of sense, and some perceive it with the eye of imagination—I mean, while in a state of wakefulness. However, in sleep it is definitely with the eye of imagination.[23]

[The Rest of Ibn 'Arabī's Discussion]

After mentioning the Last Trump and the Clarion and describing the forms in the Luminous Horn,[24] Ibn al-'Arabī continues:[25]

> After we have established this, let it be known that when God seizes the spirits from these natural bodies, wherever they be, and from the elemental bodies, He deposits them in bodily forms throughout this Luminous Horn. Therefore, everything perceptible that men perceive after death in the Barrier is perceived with the eye of that form which they have in the Horn and by its light. . . .

He says at the end of the chapter:[26]

> In the Barrier each man is in pawn for what he has earned and imprisoned in the forms of his deeds until he is brought forth on the Day of Resurrection as a new creation. God speaks the Truth and guides the way!

[The words of the Sages:]

Among the sages, Plato, Socrates, Pythagoras, Empedocles, and other divine ancients[27] spoke of illumined and darkened forms

23. In this chapter Ibn 'Arabī expounds a distinction between what is seen with the eye of sense and what is seen with the eye of imagination.
24. Ibn 'Arabī associates these eschatological objects with the Barrier.
25. Ibid., 307.
26. Ibid.
27. *Commentary,* 511: "just as they propounded the doctrine of luminous Platonic forms, so also they spoke."

of imagination suspended without locii. They held that these were immaterial substances, separate from matter and fixed in the soul's thought and imagination—that is, as manifestations of these suspended images existent among concrete objects but not in a locus. They also held that the world is two worlds: the ideal world,[28] divided into the world of lordship and the world of intellects and souls; and the world of forms, divided into the sensible forms that comprise the world of the spheres and elements with what is in them, and the spectral forms that make up the world of suspended images.

From this it may be known that the suspended forms are not the forms of Plato, for just as those great sages spoke of these forms, so also did they speak of the Platonic Forms.[29] The difference between the two is that the Platonic Forms are luminous, intelligible, and fixed in the world of intelligible lights, whereas these are images suspended in the world of immaterial apparitions. Some, those by which the wretched are tormented, are dark. These are blue and black, ugly and repulsive, painful for the soul to behold. Others, those in which the blessed find delight, are luminous—fair and splendid forms, like youths bright and smooth-cheeked, like unto hidden pearls.

In the same way, all the wayfarers of the diverse nations affirm this world. What we have mentioned is sufficient to establish the agreement of the learned and the visionaries about the existence of this world.

28. *'Ālam al-ma'nā;* Ṭ.: "The World of Intellect."

29. The same word *mithāl,* pl. *muthul,* is used for the Platonic Forms and for the immaterial images of the imagination and the world of image, though the later are usually distinguished as *muthul mu'allaqa,* "suspended"—i.e., immaterial—"images." My translation eliminates this ambiguity by replacing it with another—between Platonic forms (*muthul aflāṭūnīya*) and material form (*ṣūra*).

[An Intellectual Proof Thereof]

The rational proof of this is as we explained in *The Commentary on "The Philosophy of Illumination"*:[30] Vision does not occur by imprinting of the object's form in the eye, as was the opinion of the First Teacher[31] and those who followed his theory of imprinting. Nor does it occur by the emmission of rays from the eye to the object seen, as is the view of those practitioners of the mathematical sciences who assert this—particularly the authorities on the science of perspectives. Thus vision occurs by the illumined thing being opposite a sound eye—nothing more. An illumination of presence thereby occurs in the soul of the lighted object, and so the soul sees it.[32]

Also in that book we see that the forms in mirrors are not in the mirrors. Neither are they in the air, for things like the sky that are larger than the air are perceived in the air. Nor are they in the eye since it is impossible to imprint the large in the small. Nor, as some have imagined, do you see your form or the form of the thing itself with the rays being reflected from the mirror to your face, everything being reversed in the direction of the mirror, for we have shown the falsity of vision being by rays, let alone by their reflection!

We have explained that the form is not in the mirror, nor in any body, and that the relation of the retina to the objects seen

30. *Commentary,* 336.

31. I.e., Aristotle.

32. Quṭb al-Dīn accepts Suhrawardī's theory of vision by "presential illumination" (*ishrāq huḍūrī*) as correct. However, in the discussion of vision in *The Pearly Crown* (1:4:89 ff.), he explains that the imprinting and visual ray theories of vision are adequate models under most conditions for use in mathematics and optics though they cannot be considered literally true. This has caused some confusion to students of Quṭb al-Dīn's scientific works.

is like the relation of the mirror to the form manifested from it. This is because the retina is also a mirror, a mirror for the soul by which it perceives the forms of things and their apparitions occurring when the things are opposite the retina. Thus the form that some people posit to be in the retina is similar to the form in the mirror. Just as the form in the mirror is not within it, so too the forms by means of which the soul perceives things are not in the retina; rather they occur when the thing and the eye are opposite each other, as we have mentioned. Thereupon a presential illumination falls from the soul upon that lighted thing—if the thing has an external reality—and it sees it. If it is a sheer apparition, it needs another locus of manifestation, such as a mirror. If the retina happens to be opposite the mirror in which the forms of the things opposite appear, a presential illumination occurs in the soul so that it will see those things by means of the mirror of the retina and the external mirror—though only if the necessary conditions exist and hindrances are removed.

This is so in the world of sense and in wakefulness. Now we will discuss what happens in sleep or between sleep and wakefulness. Just as forms cannot be imprinted in the eye, they cannot be imprinted anywhere in the brain. Therefore, the forms of the imagination do not exist in minds because the large cannot be imprinted in the small. Nor can they be in concrete things since in that case everyone with sound perception would be able to see them. Nevertheless, they are not sheer nonbeing since in that case they could not be conceived nor distinguished one from another nor be defined by differing determinants.

Since they are existent and are neither in minds nor in concrete things nor in the world of intellects—because they are bodily, not intelligible, forms—necessarily they must exist in another region, which is the world of image and imagination. That world is intermediate between the worlds of intellect and sense, being higher in rank than the world of sense and lower than the world of intellect since it is more immaterial than sensation and less immaterial than intellect.

Therein are all the shapes, forms, magnitudes, and bodies, and the movements, rests, positions, modes, and so forth associated with them, all self-subsistent and suspended without place or locus. Thus the places of manifestation for the forms of the mirror and the imagination are the mirror and the imagination, but they are suspended without place or locus. It is the same for everything the sleeper sees in dreams—mountains, seas, lands, loud sounds, and individual men, animals, plants, minerals, elements, spheres, planets, and so on. All are self-subsistent images, neither in a locus nor in a place. Likewise, odors and other accidents like colors, savors, and so on are also self-subsistent images, neither in a locus nor in matter in that world. Though with us they subsist only in matter, there is no matter there. If there were matter there, and were the accidents imprinted in it, these would be bodies possessing matter, forms, and accidents. If that were the case, they would be spatial in this world, and anyone with sound vision could see them.

The forms and accidents witnessed in sleep or wakefulness in the imaginal world are sheer apparitions. The pleasure we take during sleep from foods and drinks having taste, color, and odor is not due to the imprinting of these accidents in those apparitions but through their having forms by means of the imagination. All the things in this imaginal world are simple substances, for they are self-subsistent and immaterial. They do not interfere with each other, nor do they keep each other from a locus or place.

When one who is asleep or imagining or between sleep and wakefulness is awakened from sleep or is turned aside from the contemplation of what he imagines or what he sees between sleep and wakefulness, he leaves the imaginal world without any movement requiring the traversal of a distance, and nor does he find that world to be in any particular direction from him. So likewise one who dies from this world will behold the world of light and be in it without making any movement. If he is one of the perfect, he will behold the world of pure light, but if he is one of the intermediate, he will behold the world of imaginal light. If he is one of the deficient, he will behold what suits his condition. We will indicate what this will be.

[The Conditions of Human Souls after Separation][33]

Now that you have understood that, let us briefly indicate the conditions of human souls after separation [from the body.] After that we will occupy ourselves with answers to the questions.

There are no less than five classes, for the soul is either perfect in theoretical and practical wisdom or intermediate in each or perfect in practical but not theoretical wisdom or in theoretical but not practical wisdom or deficient in them both. The first are perfect in happiness and are "those who excell and are nigh unto God."[34] The second, third, and fourth classes are the intermediate in happiness and among "the companions of the right hand." The fifth are the perfect in misery, "the companions of the left hand," dwelling in "the infernal chasm, and what shall tell you what is the Blazing Fire?"[35]

As for the first class, if the soul is adorned with knowledge of the realities of existents through theoretical wisdom and frees itself from wicked habits through practical wisdom, it will love the Source of Light. It will desire the luminous world more than the dark world, for that which would hinder its purification from the ignorance and vices arousing desire for the dark and separating it from the light will have vanished, and it will have

33. Margin.
34. Qur'ān 56.
35. Qur'ān 101:9–11

that which will cause it to be adorned with the knowledge and virtues that lead to the light and dispel the darkness. Moreover, light by nature yearns for its source,[36] so when the soul witnesses the world of pure light after the death of the body, it will be entirely freed from the body to go to that world because of the fulfillment of its potentiality and the intensity of its attraction to it, to the exclusion of the shadowy world. For the soul will have no desire for this world nor will it be enraptured by it: it will have mastered the darkness, not the darkness it. When the soul is joined to that world, "it sees what no eye hath seen, nor ear heard, nor hath entered the heart of any man."[37]

The second, third, and fourth classes—the intermediate in happiness—escape to the world of the suspended images, whose locus of manifestation is one of the celestial spheres. However, their locii of manifestation vary in accordance with the different conditions of their souls; for the nobler and more splendid the soul, the purer and loftier its locus of manifestation. In the Ascension of the Prophet there is an indication of this, for He beheld and spoke face to face with the imaginal forms that the Prophets possess in the Heavens. Therein is a mystery that has been told and whose answer is contained in hints—if you are able.

The second and third classes—the intermediate in knowledge and practice and the perfect in practice—can and do bring into existence suspended spiritual forms that have no locus. They can summon pleasurable viands, delightful forms, fine music, and other things such as delicate drinks and noble clothing—things that souls desire and eyes take pleasure in. Those forms are more perfect than these forms in our world, for the locii of manifestation and bearers of these forms are deficient, being the common matter of the world of generation and corruption—

36. I.e., the World of Lights.
37. Bukhārī, *Ṣaḥīḥ*, "Bad' al-Khalq" 8:5. A *ḥadīth* alluding to Paradise.

always changing from one state to another, doffing one form and donning another. The locii of manifestation of that world are perfect—the celestial bodies, never generated nor corrupted.

The Ancients differed as to whether souls dwelt forever in those bodies, or only a very long time, after which they escaped to the World of Pure Light. The earliest sages held that those intermediate in knowledge and practice and those perfect in practice but without knowledge would both abide forever in some sphere, for they would not have the capacity to escape to the World of Pure Light nor to ascend to a sphere higher than the one they were attached to. However, the one perfect in knowledge but not in practice would not abide there forever; rather would he ascend from the lower to the higher until he reached the encompassing sphere and would escape to the World of Light, if he had the capacity to escape to it.

Plato held that they would not remain in the heavenly bodies below the encompassing sphere but would pass from one to another. Thus, the souls whose locus of manifestation was the lowest sphere, that of the moon—like Ismāʿīl, whom the truthful Prophet tells of seeing in the First Heaven during His Night Journey—only abide there a shorter or longer time until some of their traits vanish. Then they ascend to the sphere of Mercury where they likewise abide for a time. The souls continue to ascend step by step in order from lower to higher spheres, abiding a long or short time in each sphere in accordance with their praiseworthy or blameworthy traits, until they reach the encompassing sphere. If they have the capacity to ascend to the World of Pure Intellect, they do so and do not remain forever in the encompassing sphere.

Some hold they must inevitably pass through the spheres and from there find deliverance to the World of Pure Light. The Brethren of Purity incline to this view.

The truth is that when the souls have ascended to the highest sphere and remained there a time suitable for them, their connection to this world transmigrates to the World of Luminous Images that adjoins it. There they ascend from degree to degree until they reach the highest sphere of the World of Image. Thence they pass to the World of Pure Light that is adjacent to it.

However, most of the souls capable of reaching the World of Intellect ascend in the sensible and imaginal worlds in order from one degree to the next above it until they reach the World of Intellect. There they then remain forever and changeless. This is because these worlds are way stations and caravansaries on the way to God the Exalted, and it would be absurd to reach Him without passing through all of them, or to reach the World of Light without passing through the World of Image because of the absurdity of reaching a goal while there remain stages between you and it that you have not traversed. This is the custom of God in Earth and heaven "and in the custom of God you will find no alteration."[38]

The fifth class are those deficient in knowledge and practice—the wretched folk "kneeling in Gehenna"[39] "whom morning found fallen prostrate in their abode"[40]—that is, those inclined toward animality. When they are delivered from the bodies of animals, if metempsychosis is true, or from human bodies, if it is false (for the proofs of both extremes of the contradiction are weak), these souls have imaginal shadows, forms of the imagination suspended without locus in accordance with their traits corresponding to them. These souls, unlike the souls of the perfect, cannot be delivered from their citadels[41] to reach

38. Qur'ān 17:77.
39. Ibid., 19:68.
40. Ibid., 7:91.
41. *Ṣayāṣī*, an old Persian word used by Suhrawardī in *The Philosophy of Illumination* to mean the body. Usually, Quṭb al-Dīn changed these terms to their Peripatetic equivalents in this essay.

the World of Light. And, unlike the intermediate,[42] their souls cannot be manifested in the spheres. The evil traits in them make them seek refuge in their connection, and so they are connected to imaginal forms appropriate to them. For to each of the blameworthy moral qualities and wicked traits established in the soul correspond bodies of species peculiarly characterized by that moral quality. Arrogance and rashness, for example, correspond to the bodies of lions and the like; malice and cunning to the bodies of foxes; mockery and derision to the bodies of apes and their likes; pillage and robbery to the bodies of wolves and such; vanity to peacocks; greed to pigs; and so on.

Each body has a portion of the moral quality that is connected to that body and has it in its measure. For example, for greed there are bodies like swine and ants. Because the greed of ants is not like the greed of swine, each such body has a specific measure of greed in accordance with its species. Neither is the greed of a particular individual of either species like the greed of the rest, but each individual among them has a specific greed that it does not share with any other. The reason for this is that the connection of souls described by a particular moral quality differs in accordance with the intensity and weakness of each blameworthy moral trait in the soul and with the rest of the praiseworthy and blameworthy moral traits connected with it, strong and weak, in their many combinations, whose number none save God may reckon. For example, the greed of one species of animal, and not another, and likewise the greed of one individual of that species, and not the rest, may describe a soul. Thus, any moral quality—viciousness,[43] for example—has

42. I.e., the second, third, and fourth classes.

43. *Sharr.* M and Ṭ agree on this reading against the corresponding passages of the *Commentary,* which always reads *sharah* (*greed*). The latter is a more plausible reading, but it is not supported by the MSS.

a particular limit of intensity and weakness. If a soul reaches that limit, it is attached to a body of a species of animal corresponding to viciousness, like the dog and so forth. Moreover, its connection to the bodies of individual dogs varies in accordance with the intensity and weakness of the viciousness and what is associated with it, as we mentioned: individual dogs strong or weak in viciousness, wretched like the dogs of the market or happy like hunting dogs.

Because people differ in praiseworthy and blameworthy moral qualities and in their intensity, weakness, and differing combinations, so too differ the imaginal shadows that are suspended without locus. A person having vile traits will be connected after separation from the body with the largest animal corresponding to the strongest of those traits. Then he will descend therein in order from the largest to the intermediate and from that to the smallest such animal until that vile trait is gone. Thereupon he will form an attachment to the largest body corresponding to the trait which follows the first trait in strength, descending step by step until all those traits are gone, at which time he will reach the World of the Intellects. For example, greedy, vicious people in whom greed is stronger are first transmigrated to bodies of numerous species having the trait of greed in adjacent degrees of largeness and smallness—the levels and descending steps of Hell—for example, swine and ants. This procedes step by step in order until the transmigration finally ends in the bodies of ants or even something smaller than that, if these possess the trait of greed. When they have reached the smallest greedy animals, and that vile trait has entirely perished from the soul, they transmigrate in the way mentioned through other bodies in species having the trait of viciousness. Thus, it first resorts to tigers and wolves, then to dogs, and then to what is still less vicious and smaller in body until that vile trait is also entirely effaced from the soul. The same thing happens for other vile traits, if they exist. Then finally, it is separated from the World of Suspended Images,[44] entering the world of the spheres thereof, if it has the capacity to ascend to them.

The verse "Whenever their skins scorch, once more we give them new skins"[45] indicates the substitution of skins in the way mentioned. Likewise, the verse: "Whenever they desire to go forth from there, they are brought back therein"[46]—that is, into the various fires that are the depths of Gehenna—refers to the imaginal bodies of animals that they are brought back into: that is, into those fires that are also the bodies. Likewise, it is written: "Our Lord, bring us forth from there, then if we relapse, we will be wicked doers."[47] Likewise, it is written of the damned: "Our Lord, Thou hast twice brought us death, and Thou hast twice brought us back to life. We have acknowledged our sins, so is there any path to come forth?"[48]—that is, any path from the bodies of animals so that we will not die another time or other times. Concerning the Blessed it is written: "They shall taste no death therein save the first death, and He shall guard them from the torment of Hell,"[49] for it is absurd that their souls transmigrate to animal images because of the dominance of virtuous moral qualities and pleasing attributes. Thus, if they are not reincarnated in them, they will only taste the first death. Likewise, it is written: "We shall gather them on the Day of Resurrection upon their faces"[50] in the forms of animals with bowed heads.

Many are the Traditions received attesting to men's resurrec-

44. *Commentary,* 488: "World of Generation and Corruption."
45. Qur'ān 4:56.
46. Qur'ān 32:20.
47. Ibid., 40:11.
48. Ibid., 23:107.
49. Ibid., 44:56.
50. Ibid., 19:97. "Blind, deaf, and dumb" the verse continues.

tion in forms varying with their moral qualities, as when the Prophet said, "Men will be gathered on the Day of Resurrection with diverse faces" and "As they live, so shall they die and be raised again." Thus did He say that whoever fails to follow the actions of the leader in prayer will be resurrected with the head of an ass. If he lives in that contrariness that is stupidity and asininity itself, it will become fixed in him, and he will be resurrected in the form of an ass due to the predominance of doltishness in him. There are more, but to mention them would lead to prolixity.

Pythagoras said, "Know that thou shalt be confronted with thy thoughts, thy words, and thy deeds. Spiritual or bodily forms will appear from every movement of thought, word, and deed. If the movement is of anger or desire, it will become matter for a devil to harm thee in this life and to veil thee from meeting the Light after thy death. If the movement is mental and intellectual, thou wilt take pleasure in its friendship in this world, and by its light thou wilt be guided in the next nigh unto God and His favor."

Similar statements indicating the incarnation of deeds are frequent in the words of the earliest sages. This is only an example, but it is better to be brief and to avoid the excessive prolixity that leads to weariness. Now that all this has been set forth, let us return to the object, which is to examine the scholar's words and ponder his arguments.

[Answers to the Questions][51]

We say:

He said—May God prolong his erudition and multiply his peers among the learned:

51. Margin.

> The . . . Lawgiver hath promised and threatened us with the states of the Barrier and the incarnation of deeds. Might it be the spiritual substance, now released from the attachments of the body, that conceives these forms? But how can this determinate conception arise from something like this, which is immaterial?[52]

If by its release from the attachments of the body, he means all bodies, sensible and imaginal, then this is not so; for even though it is released from the sensible, it is not released from the imaginal, as has already been established. If he means only some bodies—the sensible, but not the imaginal—then this is, of course, so, but there is nothing far-fetched about it, according to what was explained before.

> Is the seat of its imagining the body . . . ?[53]

If he means by its *body* its sensible body, it would, of course, decompose at death; but if he means its imaginal body, it would not, for it is not corrupted by death.

> Is the seat of the imagination another body—a sphere or something else?[54]

He says this because the seat of imagination of the particular for the intermediate soul is the body of the sphere. We have already explained to you that the intermediate are connected to it and not to other imaginal bodies due to their having ascended from the World of Image without reaching the World of Lights because of their imperfection. Necessarily they are connected to one of the bodies of the spheres—to a higher sphere, if they are purer, or else to a lower sphere.

52. See p. 202 above.
53. See p. 202 above.
54. See p. 202 above.

> Or something else.[55]

He may mean some body in this world other than the sphere. This appears to be his meaning when he says,

> Then it must be by a relation occurring between them at death.[56]

But this is not the intention, and there is no need to explain a relationship between the two. If he does mean one of the bodies of the World of Image and this is actually what he intends, then he needs to explain the relationship between them. I have explained that it is a relationship established between them before death by reason of the dominance of habits in it corresponding to that imaginal body. It could only be said to be "a relationship occurring between them at death" if it was established after death.

> Then, if the imagining of this spiritual substance imagines were completed by the mediacy of the body, all the separate substances would be conjoined with the bodies in the world. Thus those substances would be finite in number or the bodies infinite. Either alternative requires demonstration.[57]

Because we do not assert the necessary connection of all the separated souls with the bodies of the world, it does not matter whether he means by this the bodies of the spheres or the bodies of the World of Image. Now, the separated souls have no connection with anything but these two. Some of them—some of the separated souls—are connected with the spheres, and some with the bodies of the World of Image. Two separated souls cannot be conjoined with one imaginal body. Although it is

55. See p. 202 above.
56. See p. 202 above.
57. See p. 202 above.

possible for separated souls to be conjoined in the body of one sphere as we know from the Prophet's report that Jesus and John were in the Fourth Heaven, this does not imply the conjunction of an infinity of separated souls in one sphere. Even if this were admitted, it would not necessarily be absurd, since the imaginal forms do not exclude each other from a locus because they are not in a locus. Thus, such forms might be witnessed in a sphere, just as any number and any kind of forms may be witnessed in a mirror without their interfering with each other and without absurdity. Therefore, neither the finitude of those substances nor the infinity of the bodies is implied.

> Either alternative requires demonstration.[58]

This statement does not conform to the context; it would have been more correct for him to have said: "Both alternatives are absurd" or "false" or the like.

> Or else, it may in the end escape its connection to attain felicity. This implies that after death it will ascend again. This would require full explanation.[59]

We have explained how the Ancients disagreed about this ascent and what the truth about it is.[60]

> If misery is real, then the soul must descend. This, however, is contrary to what we hope for from the Divine Mercy.[61]

It would only contradict it if its matter were receptive to that, which is not the case. Thus, what is hoped from the Divine

58. See p. 203 above.
59. See p. 203 above.
60. See pp. 218–19 above.
61. See p. 203 above.

Mercy is unchangeable, since there is no miserliness in the Agent. If there is deficiency, it is in the recipient.

> If it goes neither to bliss nor to misery, a suspension will occur. Its going to both together will combine two opposites.[62]

Man's being happy in one respect and in misery in another only implies the conjunction of two opposites in speech, not in reality.

> If, as some people claim, everyone has two existences—concrete, which is the external, and mental . . . existent in the knowledge of God.[63]

If by "his mental existence existent in the knowledge of God" they express metaphorically its imaginal existence existent in the World of Image, this is the truth as was set forth before. If it is meant literally, it is false because God's knowledge is exalted above the possibility of its being a locus for temporal events, as was mentioned—not because of the conjunction of the spirit's mental existence and its concrete existence with the mental existence of the body, for there is no absurdity in this.

In the first chapter he states,

> All those would be accidents perishing with decomposition.[64]

If by their "perishing with decomposition" he means the cessation of their effects on the soul, this is impossible; for such effects[65] may become so fixed in the soul that they can only be

62. See p. 203 above.
63. See p. 203 above.
64. See pp. 204–5 above.
65. I.e., the individual human characteristics caused by the influences of the celestial bodies. If they do not survive at death, then the individual human personality cannot be said to be immortal.

removed by transmigration through the imaginal forms. If he means their cessation in the sensible body, this is agreed and not improbable.

In the second chapter he states,

> Therefore, it is accidental, occurring at the body's summons, so that when there was no longer any summons, it would cease.[66]

The fact that it desires the body and is concerned with its well-being as an accident occurring at the body's summons does not imply that it will cease entirely when there is no longer a summons. That would follow from that accidental thing only if nothing became fixed in the soul necessitating the desire for the body and the concern with its well-being that in turn necessitates the conceptions and imaginings.[67]

To his question in the third chapter as to whether or not the animal spirits are destroyed with the extinction of their bodies,[68] we reply that we explained in the *Commentary on the Philosophy of Illumination*[69] that whatever is aware of itself is an immaterial light. There is no doubt that animals, like men, are aware of themselves. Whoever perversely denies that the animal is aware of itself is like the one who denies its perception of the universal. Anyone who wishes to peruse the demonstrations on this topic should consult that commentary.

66. See p. 205 above.
67. The point is that if the qualities, such as virtues and vices, that come to exist in the soul through its connection with the body are an accident occurring through that relation, then they will cease to exist at death. Quṭb al-Dīn replies that the soul itself is changed through this interaction and that this explains the possibility of happiness and misery after death resulting from things that happened before death.
68. See p. 205 above.
69. *Commentary,* 290 ff.

> Man knows intuitively that this kind of animal must progress toward perfection; but if it does progress, how can this be? For it not to progress, however, is unworthy of the Divine Generosity, since what is capable of perfection would be kept from its perfection.[70]

The fact that man by intuition perceives some practical faculties in the ape does not imply that it will ascend toward perfection, if what he means by that is the perfection connected with the afterlife. If he means thereby the perfection that is connected to certain of the practical faculties, this is a logical consequence and intelligible and is seen in apes, inasmuch as some of them have greater intuition and are subtler in practice than others. Indeed, in the single ape the practical faculties may be perfected with the passage of time, its practicing actions, its application to movements and rests, and the like. In this way, each one of them eventually reaches its perfection in accordance with its condition. No one of them is held back from the perfection it is capable of in this world nor is it hindered therefrom in the World of Image, if it has the capacity. If it has no capacity for it there, it will not ascend, but this does not imply that this is unworthy of the Divine Generosity because it does not imply that what is capable of perfection is kept from its perfection.

So this is what has occurred to this defective consciousness and what this feeble mind has been permitted to reach in his haste. If it conforms with the truth, I have realized my object. If not, let me be excused, for I have presented my apology. I only hope that one whose decision is worthy and who models his conduct on the Forebearing will, if I should chance to be careless of something, shield me with the hem of tolerance and

70. See p. 206 above.

pardon, for my sins I do acknowledge, and of shortcomings and incapacity am I guilty.

May God increase your awareness and ours of our incapacity, for "the inability to achieve attainment is attainment."

This is the end of the reply, but it is God who knows best the truth.

[Colophon of the Mashhad MS]

By the hand of
a humble pauper, conscious of his deficiency,
'Abd al-Awwal b. Maḥmud b. Maḥmud al-'Abbāsī,
—May God make him to know the realities
of things as they are—
through the holiness of
the Lord of Knowers and the most perfect in deeds,
Muḥammad, the Chosen and Trustworthy.
Amen, O Lord of the Worlds.
On the 28th day of holy Ramaḍān
in the year 908.[71]

71. 27 March 1503.

[Colophon of the Tehran MS]

The End of
An epistle in answer to the questions of a certain scholar
on determining the reality of the World of Image
and on other matters
by the 'Allāmah al-Shīrāzī
—May God have mercy upon him!
Completed on the fifth day of the month of Rabī'-I
of the year 1022[72]
in the Abode of Grace, Shīrāz.
Thus is completed the noble epistle
by the hand of the least of God's creation,
'Abd al-Qādir al-Urdūbādī.

72. 25 April 1613.

|١٦٩ط|

|ط: رسالة
للعلامة الشيرازي
في تحقيق عالم المثال
وأجوبة أسئلة بعض الفضلاء

|١م|

بسم الله الرّحمٰن الرّحيم

|ربّ ، أنعمت فزد .

قال الأستاذ العلاّمة قدوة الحكماء الواصلين قبلة العلماء الكاملين قطب الحقّ الملّة والدّين محمود بن مسعود بن مصلح (كذا) الشيرازي--جعل الله ثراه أطيب من نسيم الأسحار وروائح الرّياض <و> عنب القطار .

<مقدمة المؤلف>

أمّا بعد حمد الله [ط : تعالىٰ] علىٰ آلائه المبثعوثة في أرضه وسمائه ، والصّلوٰة علىٰ محمّد خاتم أنبيائه |سلام على أبنائه|١ :

|ف|إنّي ألقِيَ إليّ كتاب |كريم| من لدن حكيم عليم٢ مشتملاً علىٰ مسائلٍ ليس المسؤل عنها بأعلم من السّائل،٣ لكنْ لمّا كان من القضايا المتعارفة أن ما لا يُدرَك كلّه لا يُترَك كلّه ، رأيتُ أن أذكر عليها ما عندي فيها وأن أسرد كلامه |أوّلاً| سردًا٤ ثمّ أنقده نقدًا ، فأقول٥ :

---

١ م : «وآله ، فإنّ المولىٰ الأكمل العلاّمة أفضل المتأخّرين وأكمل المتبحّرين قطب الحقّ والدّين محمود بن مسعود بن المصلح الشّيرازيّ--قدّس الله روحه وكثّر في محافلٍ فتوحَه--قال .»

٢ سورة النمل ٦ ، ٢٩ .

٣ ط : المسائل .

٤ ه : «سرد كارى پيوسته كردن وپى در پى كردن وسخن نيكو ومسلسل گفتن كر .»

٥ ط : «فنقول .»

قال صاحب الكتاب:

<كلام الفاضل>

بسم الله الرّحمٰن الرّحيم

الحمد لله وسلامه على عباده الّذين اصطفى[١].

لا بدّ لكلّ طالب من أن تجاذبه في طريق طلبه شبَه يحاول حلّها وإن كان على غاية صفاء الإيمان، فإنّ طبيعة البشر تقتضي ذلك، ولو لا ذلك ما صدر عن الخليل--عليه الصّلوٰة والسّلام--قوله: «أرِنِي كَيْفَ تُحْيِي الْمَوْتىٰ[٢]،» وفي مثل هٰذه الحالة يحتاج ضرورةً إلى من يكشف عنه شبه مشكلاته ويجلو له ظُلَم معضلاته كيلا يبقى فكره في ذلك شاغلاً عن مقصده، فكأنّه في هٰده الحالة يصوّر له شيطان الشّبهة[٣] .يروم[٤] شغله عمّا يريده، فناظَره[٥] خصمه لغيرته على الإيمان بكلّ[٦] ما يقدر عليه، ويلجأ تارةً إلى جناب الحقّ وتارةً إلى جناب من عرّفه الحقّ، وتارةً يدافع ذلك إخراجًا له من باله، كلّ طالب على قدر حاله.

وقد عَنَتْ[٧] لي أسؤلة كثيرة من هٰذا القبيل، ورأيت تعيين جميعها يؤدّي إلىٰ التّطويل، فاقتصرتُ من الجميع علىٰ ما هو الأهمّ في طلب السّعادة، والله الموفّق لطلب الحقّ ونيل الإرادة.

---

١ سورة النمل ٥٩.
٢ سورة البقرة ٢٦٠.
٣ ط: «البشريّة.»
٤ ه: «رَوْم جُستن كر.»
٥ط: «فناظره.»
٦ ط: «لكلّ.»
٧ ه: «عَنَتْ در كارى افتادن كه از آن بيرون نتوان آمد ودشخوار شدن وسحتى شدن كر.»

--٢٧/

وقد وَعَدَنا الشّرعُ[١] الصّادق فتوعذنا بأحوال البرزخ وتجسّد الأعمال، فهذه الصّور إن كان يتصوّرها[٢] الجوهر الرّوحانيّ مجرّدًا عن علائق الأجسام، فكيف يحصل من[٣] مثله هٰذا التّصوّر المحدود مع[٤] كونه مجرّدًا؟ وإن كان موضوع تخيّله جسمه فمعلوم أنّ موضوع التّخيّل هو الدّماغ وهو بأدنى مرض يختلّ حتّى يفسد التّصوّر والحفظ والذّكر والفكر، فكيف بحالة الموت التي هي فساد بالكلّيّة؟ وإن كان موضوع التّخيّل جسمًا آخر من فلك أو[٥] غيره، فمعلوم أنّ علاقة الجوهر الرّوحانيّ بنسبة[٦] الجسمانيّ والرّوحانيّ، فإنّه بنسبةٍ[٧] حدثت بالموت بينهما حتّىٰ أوجبت [١٧٠ط] اختصاصه به وانجذابه [من] بين سائر الجواهر المفارقة لا بدّ أنّها إليه دون غيره من الأجسام، بل إلىٰ غيره دون بقيّة الأحياز من نوع ذٰلك الجسم.

ثمّ هٰذا الجوهر الرّوحانيّ إن تمّ علىٰ ما هو عليه من التّخيّل بواسطة الجسم لزم اجتماع المفارقات كلّها علىٰ أجسام العالم فتجب نهاية تلك الجواهر أو عدم نهاية الأجسام، فكلّ واحد من القسمين يحتاج إلىٰ برهان، أو يتخلّص في[٨] آخر الأمر من علاقته إلىٰ السّعادة، فيلزم أن يكون له بعد الموت ترقٍّ آخر، [٢م] فيتعيّن بيانه، وإن [التحقيق[٩]] بالشّقاوة لزم انحطاطه[١٠]، ولعلّ هٰذا الحال منافٍ لِما يُرجىٰ من الجود الإلهيّ، أو لا إلىٰ سعادة ولا إلىٰ شقاوة، فيلزم التّعطيل[١١]، أو إليهما معًا[١٢]، فيكون جمعًا بين الضّدّين.

---

١ ه: «الشّارع.»
٢ ص 262 ؛ م: «كانت تتصوّرها»؛ ط: «كان يتصوّر.»
٣ م، ص262؛ ط: «منه.»
٤ م، ص262؛ ط: «ومع.»
٥ ط، ص263؛ م: «و.»
٦ ط: «لنسبة بين.»
٧ ط: «لنسبة.»
٨ م، ص 264 ؛ ط: «من.»
٩ م، ص 265
١٠ ه: «انحطاط افتادن وشتابيدن وفرو آمدن نرخ كر.»

وإن كان كما زعم قوم أنّ لكلّ واحد وجودَيْن: عينيٌّ هو[١] الظّاهر، وذهنيٌّ[٢]، بعد الموت تنتقل علاقة الجوهر الرّوحانيّ إلىٰ باطن جسمه، وهو وجوده الذهنيّ الموجود في علم الله تعالىٰ، ويتجسّد له الأعمال هنالك[٣]، فيصير باطنه [هناك] ظاهرًا وظاهره هٰذا الدّنياويّ باطنًا [وهٰذا] وإن راق[٤] ظاهره، فهو خطابيّ لا برهان عليه، ومع ذٰلك فكما أنّ للجسم وجودَيْن فكذٰلك[٥] الرّوح له أيضًا كذٰلك ، فعند انتقال الرّوح بوجوده [٦] من وجوده العينيّ إلىٰ وجود[٧] جسمه الذّهنيّ. فلا بدّ إن[٨] يختلف حال وجوده الذهنيّ بانتقاله فإنّه[٩] كان أوّلًا موجودًا مع الجسم العينيّ، ولآن فهو موجود مع الجسم الذّهنيّ، ويلزم منه اجتماع الوجود الذّهنيّ للرّوح والوجود العينيّ علىٰ الوجود الذّهنيّ من الجسم.

ومع هٰذا كلّه فكيف[١٠] يتجسّد الأعمال هناك وعلم الله تعالىٰ إن يكون موضوعًا[١١] للحوادث؟

فصـل [١] قدادّعي أنّ اللّطيفة الإنسانيّة [هو] جوهر قائم بنفسه، فما المانع من أن يكون تركيب الجسم الإنسانيّ من العناصر يقتضي وجود شيء خامس

---

١١ م، ص 265 .ط : «التّعطّل .»
١٢ ص 265 : «معانٍ .»
١ ط : «عينيًا وهو .»
٢ ط : «وأنّ ذهنيًّا»؛ ص ... : «وذهنيًّا .»
٣ ط : «هناك .»
٤ ط : «زاد .»
٥ ط : «فذٰلك .»
٦ ط : «من وجوده .»
٧ ط : «وجوده .»
٨ ط : «وإن .»
٩ ط : «فإنْ .»
١٠ ط : «كيف .»
١١ ط : «موضوعات .»

كاقتضاء |اجتماع| الزّاج والعفص والماء وجود السّواد ، ويكون ذلك موجبًا للأحوال الإنسانيّة؟ |أو يكون|١ هٰذا الشّيء الخامس استعدادًا يحصل بامتزاج الأركان يقتضي في كلّ وقت بتغيُّر٢ الأحوال من تأثيرات الأجرام العلويّة حالاً يوجب حالاً من الأحوال الإنسانيّة، كما ترىٰ أنّ المولود عند ولادته عارٍ عن الإدراكات أكثرها ليس معه مع قصده غير٣ الشّهوة والغضب علىٰ ضعف |فيهما| ، وبقيّة حواسّه الظّاهرة والباطنة فغير درّاكة، فإذا مضت عليه مدّة فتراه ويسمع صوت من يصوت له ويرىٰ من يتقابله٤ أدنىٰ رؤية، ثمّ |١٧١ط| إذا اشتدّ قليلاً بأفعال القوىٰ النّباتيّة، فأعطي شيئًا أخذه لكن لا يتألّم باسترجاعه منه، وبعد قليل |يشعر بألم|٥ الاسترجاع،٦ وهٰكذا درجة فوق درجة وطورًا فوق طور إلى آخر العمر.

فلِمَ لا يجوز أن يكون هٰذه كلّها خاصّيّات فائضة عليه من تأثيرات الأجرام بحسب |استعداد تركيبه|٧ ، وعند الانحلال يبطل٨ جميع ذلك، أو يكون اختلاف الأحوال لفيض يصل إليه باختلاف الاستعدادات من واهب |الصّوَر| ، فيختلف٩ قبوله١٠ (كذا) لاختلاف أحوال استعداده١١ ، ويكون جميع ذلك أعراضًا تبطل بالانحلال.

---

١ ط : «ويكون.»
٢ ط : «بتغيير.»
٣ ط : «عند.»
٤ ط : «يقابله.»
٥ ط : «الشّعربالأم.»
٦ كذا في الأصل.
٧ ط : «أشعّة إدراكه.»
٨ ط : «بطل.»
٩ ط : «يتخلّف».
١٠ ط : «قبول.»
١١ ط : «استعداد.»

فصل [٢] ما جواب القائل إنّ هٰذه التصوّرات والتخيّلات إنّما ينشأ للرّوح الإنسانيّ من اتّصاله بالبدن لمطالبة[١] البدن من الرّوح بطبيعة تدبّره، وعند مفارقته إيّاه يبطل جميع ذلك لعدم المطالبة؟ فيكون اهتمامه بمصالح[٢] الجسم للعلاقة، فإذا بطلت يبطل[٣] الاهتمام، إذ ليس نزوعه للجسم[٤] ذاتيًّا له، وإلاّ لم يزل كذلك[٥]، |٣م| فإذن هو عرضيّ يعرض بمطالبة الجسم، فعند عدم المطالبة يبطل ذلك كلّه.

فصل [٣] الأرواح الحيوانيّة مآلها إلىٰ ماذا؟ أهَل[٦] هي فانية بفناء أجسامها؟ وحينئذٍ لا تكون جواهر مجرّدة، ويلزم[٧] أنّ لا يفهم الأمور الكلّيّة، وقد نرىٰ أنّه إذا ضُرب واحد منها بخشبة ثمّ بعد حين جُرّدت له خشبة يهرب |منه|، ولو لا أنّه بقي في ذهنه معنىً كلّيّ مطابق لكلّ ضرب من ذلك النّوع لم يهرب، وليس إدراكه بالمعنى الجزئيّ، فإنّ إعادة |ط: عين| الضّرب الماضي ممتنع إنّما[٨] العائد مثله.

ثمّ قد نرىٰ هٰذه الحيوانات مشتركة في الحيوانيّة مختلفة في قربها إلىٰ العالم الإنسانيّ وبعدها حتّىٰ أنّ بعضها في غاية القرب كالقرد، فإنّ فيه بعضًا من القوّة العمليّة وأقلّ |فيه| من العلميّة[٩]، فقد تحدّس الإنسان من مثل هٰذا الحيوان ترقيه إلىٰ جهة الكمال، فإن كان له ارتقاء فكيف ذلك؟ وإن لم يكن |له|[١٠] فهو غير لائق بالجود الإلٰهيّ

---

١ ط: «بمطالبة.»
٢ ط: «لمصالح.»
٣ ط: «بطل.»
٤ ط: «إلىٰ الجسم.»
٥ ط: «ذلك»
٦ ط: «هل.»
٧ ط: «فيلزم.»
٨ ط: «ممتنعة أنّها.»
٩ ط: «العمليّة.»
١٠ م؛ ص 267

أن يمنع المستعدّ للكمال من كماله--تعالىٰ الله عن ذلك علوًّا كبيرًا .

الرّاجي بالظّفر١ باليقين ابجميل لطف]٢ الله تعالى، أحمد .

---

١ ط : «للطف .»
٢ ط : «للطف .»

|ه : الجواب للعلامة النحرير|
|ط : جــواب|

هٰذا كلام الفاضل، ونحن نذكر ما عندنا في هٰذه المسائل أوّلاً، ثمّ نعود الىٰ تتبّع ألفاظه وما يرد علىٰ أقواله ثانيًا، فنقول، وبالله التّوفيق:

|ه : العــوالــم الأربعــة|

إنّ العالم[١] أربعة: عالم العقول الّتي لا تعلّق لها بالأجسام[٢] البتّة، وعالم النّفوس المتعلّقة بالأجسام الفلكيّة والأبدان الأنسانيّة، وعالم الأجسام الّتي هي الأفلاك والعناصر وما فيها[٣]، وعالم المثال والخيال الّذي سمّاه المتشرّعون |١٧٢ط| البرزخ، و|ط: أرباب علوم| المعقول عالم الأشباح المجرّدة، |وهو| الّذي أشار إليه الأقدمون:

> أنّ في الوجود عالمًا مقداريًّا غير العالم الحسّيّ |يحذو حَذْوَ|[٤] العالم الحسّيّ في[٥] الأفلاك والعناصر بجميع ما فيهما من الكواكب والمركّبات من المعادن والنّبات والحيوان |والإنسان|، وفي دوام حركة أفلاكه |المثاليّة وقبول عناصره ومركّباته آثار حركة أفلاكه| وإشراقات العوالم العقليّة.

ويحصل منه[٦] أنواع الصّوَر المعلّقة إلىٰ غير نهاية علىٰ طبقات مختلفة

---

١ ط: «العوالم.»
٢ ط: «بأجسام.»
٣ ط: «فيهما.»
٤ م، ش٥١٥؛ ط: «حَذْوًا.»
٥ ط: «من.»
٦ ط: «فيه.»

باللّطافة والكثافة كلّ طبقة لا يتناهي أشخاصها وإن تناهت الطّبقات.

وذلك لأنّ العالم المثاليّ وإن تناهىٰ من جهة الفيض الأوّل الإبداعيّ من الأفلاك والكواكب ونفوسها والعناصر مركّباتها المثاليّة الأصليّة من المعادن والنّبات والحيوان[١] لاحتياجها إلىٰ علل وجهات عقليّة، ولتناهى تلك الجهات للبرهان القائم علىٰ نهاية المترتّبات العقليّة يتناهي معلولاتها المثاليّة، إلاّ أنّ الحاصل من الأشباح المجرّدة بالفيض الثاني علىٰ حسب الاستعدادات الحاصلة في الأدوار الغير المتناهية لا يتناهي، لكن لعدم ترتّب تلك الأشباح وعدم تركّب بعد غير متناهٍ منها جاز كونها غير متناهية.

وهٰذا العالم علىٰ طبقات، كلّ طبقة فيها أنواع ممّا في عالمنا هٰذا لكنّها لا |٤م| تتناهي، وبعضها يسكنها قوم من الملائكة |والأخيار من الإنس، وبعضها يسكنها قوم من الملائكة| والجنّ والشّياطين، و لا يحصىٰ عدد الطّبقات و|لا ما| فيها إلاّ الباري[٢] تعالىٰ، وكلّ من وصل إلىٰ طبقة أعلىٰ وجدها ألطف مرأىً وأحسن منظرًا وأشدّ روحانيّة وأعظم لذّة ممّا قبلها، وآخر الطّبقات وهو أعلاها متاخم الأنوار العقليّة، وهي مرتبة الشّبه بها[٣].

وعجائب هٰذا العالم لا يعلمها إلاّ الله تعالىٰ، وللسّالكين[٤] فيها مآرب وأغراض من إظهار العجائب وخوارق العادات كإظهار أبدانهم المثاليّة في مواضع مختلفة في وقت واحد وفي أوقات وإحضار ما يريدون من المطاعم[٥] والمشارب والملابس إلىٰ غير ذلك، وكذا المبرّزون من السّحرة والكهنة |يشاهدونه ويظهرون|[٦] منه العجائب.

١ ش ٥١٥ : «والإنسان.»
٢ ط : «الله.»
٣ ط : «لها.»
٤ ط : «للسّاكنين.»
٥ ط : «المطعم.»
٦ م، ش ٥١٧ ؛ ط : «ويظهرون.»

وبهٰذا العالم يتحقّق بعث الأجساد علىٰ ما ورد في الشّرائع الإلهيّة وكذا الأشباح الرّبّانيّة، أعني الأشباح المليحة الفاضلة والعظيمة الهائلة، ١ التي٢ تظهر فيها العلّة الأولىٰ والأشباح التي |تليق|٣ بظهور العقل الأوّل٤ وأشباحه فيها، إذ لكلّ من العقول أشباح كثيرة علىٰ صُوَر مختلفة تليق بظهوره فيها٥ وقد يكون للأشباح٦ الرّبّانيّة مظاهر في هٰذا العالم |١٧٣ط| إذا ظهرت فيها أمكن إدراكها بالبصر، كما أدرك موسىٰ بن عمران البارئ تعالى لمّا ظهر في الطّور وغيره علىٰ ما هو مذكور في التّوراة، وكما أدرك النّبيّ--صلّى الله عليه وسلّم--وصحابة--٧رضي الله عنهم--جبريل--عليه السّلام--|لمّا ظهر٨| في صورة دحية الكلبيّ--رضي الله عنه.

ويجوز أن يكون جميع عالم المثال مظاهر لنور الأنوار ولغيره من الأنوار المجرّدة يظهر كلّ منها في صورة معيّنة في زمان معيّن بحسب استعداد القابل والفاعل، فنور الأنوار والعقول والنّفوس الفلكيّة والإنسانيّة من المفارقة وغير المفارقة من الكاملين إنّما٩ ظهروا في صُوَر مختلفة |من الحسن والقبح والكثافة واللّطافة|١٠ إلىٰ غير ذٰلك من الصّفات علىٰ حسب استعداد |الفاعل والقابل|١١.

وبهٰذا العالم |أيضًا يتحقّق|١٢ جميع مواعيد النّبوّة من نعيم١٣ أهل الجنان

---

١ ش ٥١٨: «الأشباح العظيمة الفاضلة المليحة أو الهائلة القبيحة.»
٢ ط: «أعني.»
٣ م، ش ٥١٨.
٤ م، ش ٥١٨؛ ط: «الأولىٰ.»
٥ م، ش٥١٨؛ ط: «بظهورها.»
٦ م، ش ٥١٨؛ ط: «الأشباح.»
٧ م، ش ٥١٨؛ ط: «وأصحابه.»
٨ م، ش ٥١٨.
٩ ط: «ربّما.»
١٠ ط: «بالحسن والقبح واللّطافة والكثافة.»
١١ ط: «القابل والفاعل.»

وتعذّب أهل النّيران بجميع أنواع اللّذّات وأصناف الآلام الجسمانيّة ، إذ البدن المثاليّ الّذي يتصرّف النّفس فيه حكمه حكم البدن الحسّيّ في أنّ له جميع الحواسّ الظّاهرة والباطنة |ط : وأنّ[١] المدرِك فيها[٢] هو النّفس النّاطقة| |إلاّ أنّها|[٣] يدرك في هٰذا العالم بآلات جسمانيّة وفي عالم المثال بآلات شبحيّة .

وممّا يدلّ علىٰ وجود هٰذا العالم |--أعني عالم المثال--| اعتراف الأنبياء والأولياء |و| المتألّهين من الحكماء :

أمّا الأنبياء--عليهم الصّلوٰة والسّلام--فلإخبار النّبيّ--عليه السّلام--|مثلاً عن[٤] | البرزخ وتجسّد الأعمال |فيه .|

وأمّا الأولياء ، فلقول الشّيخ المحقّق |المكاشف الكامل المكمّل|[٥] محيي الدّين ابن العربيّ--رضي الله عنه--مثلاً ، فإنّه ذكر في |الباب الثّالث والسّتّين[٦] الثّالث والسّتّون| من الفتوحات |٥م| المكّيّة «في معرفة بقاء النّاس[٧] في البرزخ بين الدّنيا والبعث» حقيقة البرزخ ، وقال[٨] :

<كلام ابن عربي في البرزخ>

١٢ ط : «يتحقّق أيضًا .»
١٣ ط : «تنعّم .»
١ ش ٥١٨ : «فإنّ .»
٢ ش ٥١٨ : «فيهما .»
٣ ط : «لأنّها .»
٤ ط : «من .»
٥ ط : «الكاشف المكمّل .»
٦ م ، فم ؛ ط : «الكتاب الثّالث .»
٧ ط ، فم ؛ م : «النّفس .»
٨ ابن عربي ، الفتوحات المكّيّة (بيروت : دار الصّادر ، ب . ت .) ١ : ٣٠٤-٣٠٥ .

إنّه حاجز معقول بين متجاورَيْن ليس هو عين أحدهما[١]، وفيه قوّة كلّ[٢] منهما.. كالخطّ الفاصل بين الظلّ والشمس.. وليس إلاّ الخيال.. كما يدرك الإنسان صورته في المرآة ويعلم قطعًا أنّه أدرك صورته بوجهٍ، و[٣] أنّه ما أدرك صورته|[٤]، لمّا يراها في غاية الصّغر بصغر جرم المرآة والكبر لعظمه[٥]، ولا يقدر أن ينكر أنّه رأى صورته ويعلم أنّه ليس في المرآة صورته، ولا هي بينه وبين المرآة.. فليس بصادق ولا كاذب في قوله |إنّه|[٦] رأى صورته ما[٧] رأى صورته.

فما تلك الصّورة[٨] المرئيّة، وأين محلّها، وما شأنها؟ فهي منفيّة ثابتة موجودة معدومة معلومة مجهولة، أظهر الله سبحانه هٰذه الحقيقة لعبده ضرب مثال ليعلم ويتحقّق أنّه إذا عجز وحار في درك حقيقة هٰذا وهو من العالم ولم يحصل عنه[٩] علم[١٠] بحقيقته، فهو[١١] بخالقها أعجز وأجهل وأشدّ حيرةً، ونبّه بذٰلك أنّ تجلّيات الحقّ له أرقّ وألطف معنىً من هٰذا الذي قد حارت العقول فيه وعجزت عن إدراك |١٧٤ط| حقيقته إلىٰ أن بلغ[١٢] عجزها أن تقول: «هل لهٰذا ماهيّة، أو لا ماهيّة له؟» فإنّ العقول[١٣] لا تلحقه

---

١ فم: «فذٰلك الحاجز المعقول هو البرزخ، فإن أدرك بالحسّ، فهو أحد الأمرين ما هو البرزخ، وكلّ أمرين يفتقران إذا تجاورا إلىٰ برزخ ليس هو عين أحدهما...»
٢ فم: «كلّ واحد.»
٣ فم: «ويعلم قطعًا.»
٤ فم: «صورته بوجه.»
٥ ط: «لعظمته.» فم: «لما يرى فيها من الدّقّة إذا كان جرم المرأة صغيرًا ويعلم أنّ صورته أكبر من الّتي رأى بما لا يتفاوت، وإذا كان جرم المرأة كبيرًا فيرى صورته في غاية الكبر ويقطع أنّ صورته أصغر ممّا رأى، ولا.»
٦ م، فم.
٧ م، فم؛ ط: «وما.»
٨ ط، فم؛ م: «الصّوَر.»
٩ م؛ ط: «له.» فم: «عنده.»
١٠ م، فم.
١١ م، فم؛ ط: «فمن.»
١٢ م، فم؛ ط: «يبلغ.»

بالعدم المحض، وقد أدرك البصر شيئًا مّا، ولا بالوجود المحض، وقد علمت أنّه ما ثَمّ شيئ، ولا بالإمكان البحت.[1]

وإلىٰ مثل هٰذه الحقيقة يصير الإنسان[2] في نومه وبعد موته فيرىٰ الأعراض صوَرًا قائمة بأنفسها تخاطبه ويخاطبها أجسادًا حاملة أرواحًا[3] لا شكّ فيها، والمكاشف يرىٰ في يقظته ما يراه النّائم في حال نومه والميّت بعد موته كما يرى في الآخرة صوَر[4] الأعمال توزن مع كونها أعراضًا، ويرىٰ الموت كبشًا أملح مع أنّ[5] الموت نسبة مفارقة عن اجتماع...

ومن النّاس [من][6] يدرك هٰذا المتخيّل بعين الحسّ، ومن النّاس من يدركه بعين الخيال، وأعني[7] في حال اليقظة، وأمّا في النّوم فبعين الخيال قطعًا.

---

١٣ فم: «فإنّها.»
١ فم: «المحض.»
٢ م، فم؛ ط: «من.»
٣ «حاملةً أرواحًا» غير موجود في فم.
٤ م، فم؛ ط: «صوَر صوَر.»
٥ م، ط: «مع أنّ»؛ فم: «بذبح و.»
٦ فم.
٧ م، فم: «أعني.»

<تتمة كلام ابن العربيّ>

ثمّ قال بعد أن ذكر النّاقور والصّور ووصف [الصّور] بالقرن النّوريّ١ :

بعد ما قرّرناه فليعلم أنّ الله--سبحانه و تعالىٰ--إذا قبض الأرواح من هٰذه الأجسام الطّبيعيّة حيث كانت والعنصريّة أودعها صوَرًا جسديّة في مجموع هٰذا القرن النّوريّ ، فجميع ما يدركه الإنسان بعد الموت في البرزخ من الأمور [إنّما يدركه]٢ بعين الصورة٣ الّتي هو فيها في القرن٤ وبنورها . . .

قال في آخر الباب٥ :

وكلّ٦ إنسان في البرزخ مرهون بكسبه محبوس في صوَر أعماله إلىٰ أن يبعث يوم القيامة في النّشأة الآخرة ، والله يقول الحقّ وهو يهدي السّبيل !

<كلام الحكماء>

وأمّا الحكماء فلأنّ أفلاطن وسقراط٧ وفيثاغورس و أنباذقلس٨ وغيرهم من الأقدمين المتألّهين٩ كانوا يقولون بالمثل الخياليّة المعلّقة لا [ط : في] محلّ المستنيرة والمظلمة ويذهبون إلىٰ أنّها جواهر مجرّدة مفارقة للموادّ ثابتة قي الفكر والتّخيّل النّفسيّ١٠ ،

---

١ فم : ص ١ :٣٠٧ .
٢ م ، فم ؛ ط : « المدركة . »
٣ م ، فم ؛ ط : « الصّور . »
٤ م ، فم ؛ ط : « القرآن . »
٥ فم ، ص ١ :٣٠٧ .
٦ ط : « كلّ . »
٧ م ، ش ٥١١ ؛ ط : « أفلاطون وبقراط . »
٨ ش ٥١١ ؛ م : « وأندباذقلس . » ؛ ط : محذوف .
٩ ش ٥١١ : « كما يقول بالمثل النّوريّة العقليّة الأفلاطونيّة كذلك يقولون . »

بمعنى[١١] [أنّها][١٢] مظاهر لهٰذه المثل المعلّقة[١٣] الموجودة في الأعيان لا في محلّ، وإلىٰ[١٤] أنّ العالَم عالمان: عالم المعنىٰ[١٥] المنقسم إلىٰ عالم الرّبوريّة وإلىٰ عالم العقول والنّفوس، [٦م] وعالم الصّوَر المنقسم إلىٰ الصّوَر الحسّيّة، وهي عالم الأفلاك والعناصر بما فيها[١٦]، وإلىٰ الصّوَر الشّبحيّة، وهي عالم المثال المعلّق.

ومن هٰهنا يُعلَم أنّ الصّوَر المعلّقة ليست مثل أفلاطن، لأنّ هٰؤلاء العُظَماء [من الحكماء] كما يقولون بهٰذه الصّور[١٧] يقولون بالمثل الأفلاطونيّة، والفرق بينهما أنّ المثل الأفلاطونيّة نوريّة عقليّة[١٨] ثابتة في عالم الأنوار العقليّة، وهٰذه مُثل معلّقة في عالم الأشباح المجرّدة، منها ظلمانيّة يتعذّب بها الأشقياء، وهي صوَر زرق سود بشيعة[١٩] مكروهة يتألّم [١٧٥ط] النّفس بمشاهدتها، ومنها مستنيرة يتنعّم بها السّعداء، وهي[٢٠] صوَر حسنة بهيّة بيض مرد[٢١] كأمثال اللّؤلؤ المكنون.

وكذا جميع السّلّاك من الأمم المختلفة يثبتون هٰذا العالم، فقد تحقّق ممّا[٢٢] ذكرنا اجتماع المحقّقين والمكاشفين علىٰ وجود هٰذا العالم.

---

١٠ م، ش ٥١١؛ ط: «النّفس.»
١١ م، ش ٥١١؛ ط: «يعني.»
١٢ ط، ش ٥١١؛ م: «أنّهما.»
١٣ غير موجود في ش.
١٤ م، ش ٥١١؛ ط: محذوف.
١٥ م، ش ٥١١؛ ط: «العقل.»
١٦ ط: «فيها.»
١٧ط؛ م: «الصّورة.»
١٨ ط: «عظيمة.»
١٩ ط: «صور سود وزرق بشيعة»؛ ش ٥١١: «صور شنيعة.»
٢٠ م، س ٥١١؛ ط: «وهي.»
٢١ يعني: «كغلمان بيض مرد.»
٢٢ ط: «بما.»

|ه: دليل عقليّ عليه|

وأمّا الدّليل العقليّ عليه، فهو أنّا بيّنّا في شرح حكمة الإشراق[٢٣] أنّ الإبصار ليس بانطباع صورة المرئيّ في العين علىٰ ما هو رأي المعلّم الأوّل ومَن اقيفىٰ أثره من القائلين بالانطباع، ولا بخروج الشّعاع من العين إلىٰ المرئيّ كما هو مذهب القائلين به من أرباب العلوم الرّياضيّة |سيّما أصحاب علم المناظر|[٢٤]، فليس الإبصار إلاّ بمقابلة المستنير للعين السّليمة لا غير، إذ بها يحصل[٢٥] للنّفس إشراق حضوريّ علىٰ المستنير فتراه.

وكذا هٰهنا[٢٦] أنّ صوَر المرايا ليست في المرآة، ولا في الهواء، لأنّه يدرك[٢٧] في الهواء ما هو أعظم من الهواء كالسّماء، |ط: وليست في البصر لامتناع انطباع العظيم في الصّغير،| وليست في صورتك أو صورة ما رأيته بعينها[٢٨] |علىٰ أن ينعكس الشّعاع من المرآة إلىٰ وجهك، والكلّ(كذا) ما يُرىٰ في خلاف جهة المرأة،| كما ظنّه بعضهم، فإنّا قد أبطلنا كون الإبصار بالشّعاع فضلاً عن كونه بانعكاسه.

وإذا نبيّن أنّ الصّورة ليست في المرآة، و لا في جسم من الأجسام، ونسبة الجليديّة إلىٰ المبصرات كنسبة المرآة إلىٰ الصّور [٢٩] الظّاهرة منها، لأنّ الجليديّة |أيضًا مرآة للنّفس بها تدرك صور الأشياء وأشباحها الحادثة عند مقابلتها للجليديّة|[٣٠] فحال الصّورة الّتي فرضها بعض النّاس في الجليديّة كحال صورة المرآة، فكما أنّ صورة المرآة ليست فيها كذٰلك

---

٢٣ ش ٢٦٧-٢٧٠.
٢٤ ط: «وأصحاب المناظر.»
٢٥ ط، ش ٣٣٦؛ م: محذوف.
٢٦ ط: «بيّنّا.»
٢٧ م: «تدرك»؛ ط: «لا يدرك.»
٢٨ ط: «بعينهما.»
٢٩ ط: «الصّورة.»
٣٠ م، ش ٢٧٣؛ ط: محذوف.

الصّور[٣١] التي تدرك النّفس الأشياء بواسطتها ليست في الجليديّة، بل تحدث عند المقابلة كما ذكرنا، وحينئذٍ يقع من النّفس إشراق حضوريّ علىٰ ذلك الشيء المستنير إن كان له هويّة[٣٢] في الخارج فتراه، وإن كان شبحًا محضًا[٣٣] فيحتاج إلىٰ مظهر آخر كالمرآة، فإذا وقعت الجليديّة في مقابلة[٣٤] المرآة التي |ظهر فيها|[٣٥] صوَر الأشياء المقابلة، وقع من النّفس أيضًا إشراق حضوريّ، فرأت تلك الأشياء بواسطة مرآة الجليديّة والمرآة الخارجة، لكن عند وجود الشّرائط وارتفاع الموانع.

هٰذا في عالم الحسّ وفي اليقظة، وأمّا في النّوم أو فيما بين النّوم واليقظة فسنتكلّم عليه، وبمثل ما امتنع به انطباع الصّوَر في العين كذٰلك يمتنع انطباعها في موضع من الدّماغ، فإذن الصّوَر الخياليّة لا تكون موجودة[٣٦] في الأذهان لامتناع انطباع[٣٧] الكبير |٧م| في الصّغير، ولا في الأعيان وإلاّ لراها[٣٨] كلّ سليم الحسّ، وليست عدمًا محضًا وإلاّ لَما كانت متصوّرةً[٣٩] ولا مميّزًا (كذا) بعضها |١٧٦ط| عن بعض، ولا محكومًا عليها بأحكام مختلفة. وإذ هي موجودة وليست في الأذهان ولا في الأعيان ولا في عالم العقول لكونها صوَرًا جسمانيّة لا عقليّة، فبالضرورة تكون موجودة في صقع آخر، وهو عالم المثال والخيال[٤٠]، وهو متوسّط بين عالمي[٤١] العقل والحسّ لكونه بالمرتبة فوق عالم الحسّ ودون عالم

---

٣١ م، ش ٢٧٣؛ ط: «الصّورة.»
٣٢ ط، ش ٢٧٣؛ م: «هويّته.»
٣٣ ش ٢٧٣: «كصور المرايا.»
٣٤ م، ش ٢٧٣؛ ط: «مقابلته.»
٣٥ ط، ش ٢٧٣؛ م: «بها ظهر.»
٣٦ م: «لم تكن موجودة»؛ ط: «لا تكون»؛ ش ٤٧٠: «لا يكون (كذا) موجودة.»
٣٧ م، ش ٤٧٠؛ ط: محذوف.
٣٨ ش ٤٧٠: «يشاهدها.»
٣٩ م، ش ٤٧٠؛ ط: «كان متصوّرًا.»
٤٠ ش ٤٧٠: «وهو عالم يسمّى بالعالم المثاليّ والخياليّ.»
٤١ م، ش ٤٧٠؛ ط: «عالم.»

العقل لأنّه أكثر تجريدًا من الحسّ وأقلّ تجريدًا من العقل.

وفيه جميع الأشكال والصّوَر والمقادير والأجسام وما يتعلّق بها من[٤٢] الحركات والسّكنات والأوضاع والهيآت وغير ذلك قائمة بداتها معلّقة لا في مكان ومحلّ، فصوَر[٤٣] المرآة والتّخيّل مظهرها المرآة والتّخيّل، وهي معلّقة لا في محلّ ومكان[٤٤]، وكذا جميع ما يراه |النائم| في المنام من الجبال والبحور والأرضين[٤٥] والأصوات العظيمة والأشخاص الإنسانيّة والحيوانيّة والنّباتيّة والمعدنيّة والعنصريّة والفلكيّة والكوكبيّة وغيرها، |كلّها مُثل|[٤٦] قائمة بذاتها لا في محلّ ومكان، وكذا الرّوائح وغيرها من الأعراض كالألوان والطّعوم وأمثالها هي أيضًا مُثل قائمة بذاتها لا في محلّ ومادّة في ذلك العالم، وإن كانت عندنا لا تقوم إلاّ بمادّة لعدم المادّة هناك، إذ لو كانت هناك مادّة وانطبعت فيها الأعراض كانت أجسامًا ذوات موادّ وصوَر[٤٧] وأعراض وكانت متحيّزة في هٰذا العالم وشاهدها كلّ سليم البصر.

فالصّوَر والأعراض المشاهدة في العالم المثاليّ في النّوم واليقظة أشباح محضة[٤٨] والتذاذنا في النّوم بمآكل ومشارب ذوات طعم |ولون ورائحة|[٤٩] ليس لانطباع[٥٠] هٰذه الأعراض في تلك[٥١] الأشباح، بل لتمثّلها فيها علىٰ سبيل التّخيّل، فكلّ[٥٢] ما في هٰذا العالم

---

٤٢ م، ش ٤٧٠ ؛ ط : «و.»
٤٣ م، ش ٤٧٠ ؛ ط : «بصور.»
٤٤ م؛ ط : «مكان ومحلّ»؛ ش ٤٧٠ : «مكان ولا في محلّ.»
٤٥ ط، ش ٥٣٥ ؛ م : «الأرض.»
٤٦ م : «كلّها»؛ ط : «وكلّها مثل»؛ ش ٥٣٥ : «كلّها مثل.»
٤٧ م، ش ٥٣٦ ؛ ط : «مادّة والصّورة.»
٤٨ م، ش ٥٣٦ ؛ ط : «محض.»
٤٩ م، ش ٥٣٦ ؛ ط : محذوف.
٥٠ م : «كانطباع.»
٥١ ط : «ذلك.»
٥٢ ط : «وكلّ.»

المثاليّ جواهر بسيطة لقيامها بذاتها وتجرّدها عن الموادّ، فلا يزاحم بعضها بعضًا، ولا بتمانع على محلّ و٥٣مكان.

وكما أنّ النّائم والمتخيّل ومن بين النّوم واليقظة إذا انتبه من٥٤ النّوم أو عاد٥٥ عن المشاهدة ما تخيّل أو ما رأى بين النّوم واليقظة، فارق العالم المثاليّ دون حركة محوجة إلىٰ قطع مسافة، ولم يجد ذلك العالم علىٰ جهة منه، فكذا من مات عن هٰذا العالم يشاهد عالم النّور دون٥٦ حركة، [وهو هناك]٥٧ إلّا أنّه إن كان من الكاملين يشاهد عالم النّور المحض، وإن كان من المتوسّطين يشاهد عالم النّور المثاليّ وإن كان من النّاقصين يشاهد ما يليق بحاله، وسنشير إلىٰ ما له.

[ه: أحوال النّفوس الإنسانية بعد المفارقة]

وإذا عرفت ذلك فلنشير إشارةً خفيفةً إلىٰ أحوال النّفوس الإنسانيّة بعد المفارقة، [١٧٧ط] ثمّ نشتغل بأجوبة المسائل٥٨، فنقول:

هي٥٩ لا يخلو عن٦٠ أقسام خمسة٦١ لأنّ النّفس إمّا أن تكون كاملة في الحكمتين العلميّة٦٢والعمليّة [أو متوسّطة فيهما أو كاملة في العمليّة دون العلميّة أو في العلميّة دون العمليّة]٦٣ أو ناقصة فيهما٦٤، والأوّل هو الكامل في السّعادة ومن [٨م] السّابقين

---

٥٣ ش ٥٣٦: «أو.»
٥٤ ش ٥٣٦: «عن.»
٥٥ م، ش ٥٣٦؛ ط: «حاد.»
٥٦ م، ش ٥٣٦، ح ٢٤١؛ ط: محذوف.
٥٧ م، ش٥٣٦، ح ٢٤١؛ ط: محذوف.
٥٨ عنوان في ه: «أجوبة المسائل.»
٥٩ه: أجوبة المسائل
٦٠ م، ش ٥٠٨؛ ط: «من.»
٦١ م، ش٥٠٨؛ ط: «خمسة أقسام.»
٦٢ م، ش ٥٠٨؛ ط: «النّظريّة.»

المقرّبين[٦٥] ، والثاني والثالث والرّابع من المتوسّطين في السّعادة ومن أصحاب اليمين، والخامس هو الكامل في الشّقاوة ومن أصحاب الشّمال المقيمين في «الهاوية وما أدريٰك ما هيه نار حامية؟»[٦٦]

أمّا الأوّل فلأنّ النّفس إذا تحلّت بلاطّلاع علىٰ حقائق الموجودات للحكمة النّظريّة وتخلّت عن رذائل الملكات بالحكمة[٦٧] العمليّة عشقت ينبوع[٦٨] النّور ، وكان شوقها إلىٰ العالم النّورانيّ أكثر ⌈منه⌉[٦٩] إلىٰ الظّلمانيّ لزوال المانع بالتّخلية عن الجهل والرّذائل المشوّقين إلىٰ الظّلمانيّ والمفرّقين عن النّورانيّ، ووجود المقتضى بالتحلية بالعلم والفضائل المميلين إلىٰ النّور⌈انيّ⌉ المزيلين عن الظّلمانيّ، مع أنّ النّور بطبعه[٧٠] مشتاق إلىٰ سنخه[٧١] ، فإذا شاهدت عالم النّور المحض بعد موت البدن تخلّصت من البدن[٧٢] بالكلّيّة إلىٰ ذلك العالم لكمال قوّتها وشدّة انجذابها إليه دون العالم الظّلمانيّ إذ لا نزوع لها إليه ولا التياع لأنّها قهرت الظّلمات لا الظّلمات قهرتها ، فإذا[٧٣] اتّصلت بذلك العالم «رأت ما لا عين رأت ولا أذن سمعت ولا خطر علىٰ قلب بشر[٧٤] .»

وأمّا الثاني والثّالث والرّابع وهم المتوسّطون في السّعادة ف⌈قد⌉ يتخلّصون إلىٰ عالم[٧٥]

---

٦٣ م ؛ مثله موجود في ش ٥٠٨ .

٦٤ م ، ش ٥٠٨ ؛ ط : «فيها .»

٦٥ انظر سورة الواقعة .

٦٦ سورة القارحة ٩-١١ .

٦٧ ط : «للحكمة .»

٦٨ م ، ش ٤٩٦ ؛ ط : «تنوع .»

٦٩ م ، ش٤٩٦ ؛ ط : محذوف .

٧٠ م ، ش ٤٩٧ ؛ ط : «بصر .»

٧١ م ، ش ٤٩٧ ؛ ط : «اسحه .» ؟؟

٧٢ ط : «عن النّفس» ؛ انظر ش ٤٩٧ .

٧٣ ط : «وإذا .»

٧٤ صحيح البخاري : بدء الخلق ٨ :٥ .

٧٥ ط ؛ م : «العالم .»

المُثل المعلّقة التي مظهرها بعض الأجرام الفلكيّة، لكن يختلف مظاهرها بحسب اختلاف هيئة نفوسهم، فإنّه كلّما كانت النّفس أشرف وأسنىٰ كان مظهرها أصفىٰ وأعلىٰ، وفي معراج النّبيّ--عليه الصلوٰة والسّلام--إشارة إلىٰ هٰذا حيث شاهد الصّوَر المثاليّة التي للأنبياء في السّمٰوات وشافههم، وفيه سرّ فنبّه[٧٦] له ورُمِز حَلّه إن أطقت[٧٧].

وللثاني والثالث--أعني للمتوسّط في العلم والعمل والكامل في العمل--إيجاد المُثل |الرّوحانيّة| المعلّقة لا في محلّ والقوّة علىٰ إيجادها، فيستحضران من الأطعمة اللّذيذة والصّوَر المليحة والسّماع الطّيّب[٧٨] وغير ذلك من الأشربة اللّطيفة والملابس الشّريفة علىٰ ما يشتهي الأنفس وتلذّ الأعين، وتلك الصّوَر أتمّ ممّا عندنا من صوَر هٰذا العالم، فإنّ مظاهر[٧٩] هٰذه الصوَر وحواملها ناقصة، لأنّها هيولىٰ عالم الكون والفساد، |و|المشتركة وهي متبدّلة[٨٠] دائمًا من حالة إلىٰ حالة[٨١] تخلع صورة وتلبس[٨٢] أخرىٰ، ومظاهر تلك الصّوَر[٨٣]|١٧٨ط| كاملة لأنّها الأجرام الفلكيّة التي لا تتكوَّنْ ولا تنفسد[٨٤].

ثمّ اختلف المتقدّمون في أنّهم يخلّدون تلك الأجرام أبدًا أو زمانًا طويلًا، ثمّ يتخلّصون إلىٰ عالم النّور |ط: المحض|، فذهب الأقدمون إلىٰ أنّ المتوسّط في العلم والعمل والكامل في العمل دون العلم يخلّدانِ في بعض الأفلاك إذ|ا| لم يكن لهما[٨٥] استعداد الخلاص إلىٰ عالم النّور المحض ولا التّرقي إلىٰ فلك أعلىٰ ممّا تعلّقانه، وأنّ الكامل في العلم دون

٧٦ م؛ ط: «فتنبّهْ.»
٧٧ م؛ ط: «أطلقت.»
٧٨ م؛ ط: «الطّيّبة.»
٧٩ م، ش٥٠٩؛ ط: «مظهر.»
٨٠ ش ٥٠٩: «الفساد المشتركة والمتبدّلة.»
٨١ م، ش ٥٠٩؛ ط: «حال إلىٰ حال.»
٨٢ ط؛ ش ٥٠٩؛ م: «لبس.»
٨٣ م، ش ٥٠٩؛ ط: «الصّورة.»
٨٤ م، ش ٥٠٩؛ ط: «لا تكوّن ولا تفسد.»
٨٥ م؛ ط: «فيهما»؛ ش ٥٠٩: «له.»

العمل لا يخلد فيه، بل يرتقي[٨٦] من الأدنىٰ إلىٰ الأعلىٰ إلىٰ أن يصل إلىٰ المحدّد ثمّ يتخلّص [إلىٰ عالم النّور إن كان لها استعداد التّخلّص][٨٧].

وذهب أفلاطن إلىٰ أنّهم لا يخلدون في[٨٨] الأجرام السّماويّة التي دون المحدّد، بل ينتقلون[٨٩] من البعض إلىٰ البعض، فإنّ النّفوس التي مظاهرها الفلك الأدنىٰ الذي للقمر--كإسمٰعيل، عليه السّلام--علىٰ ما أخبر الصّادق--عليه الصلوٰة والسّلام--عن رؤيته في السّماء الأولىٰ ليلة الإسراء--[ط: لكن] يمكث فيه زمانًا قصيرًا أو طويلاً حتّىٰ يزول عنها بعض الهيآت، ثمّ ترتقي إلىٰ فلك عطارد وتقوم فيه زمانًا كذٰلك، ولا تزال ترتقي من فلك أدنىٰ إلىٰ فلك أعلىٰ علىٰ التّرتيب مقيمةً في كلّ فلك بحسب هيآتها المحمودة والمذمومة زمانًا طويلاً أو قصيرًا حتّىٰ تصل إلىٰ المحدّد، [فإن كان استعداد الارتقاء إلىٰ عالم العقل المحض ترقت إليه ولا يخلد في المحدّد][٩٠].

وذهب بعضهم إلىٰ أنّه لا بدّ من المرور علىٰ[٩١] الأفلاك والخلاص منها إلىٰ عالم النّور المحض، وإليه ميل صاحب إخوان الصّفاء.

والحقّ أنّ النّفوس المرتقية إلىٰ الفلك الأعلىٰ إذا مكثت فيه المكث اللائق بها، تنتقل[٩٢] علاقتها عن هٰذا العالم إلىٰ عالم[٩٣] المُثل النّورانيّة، لأنّه مصاقب له، وترتقي فيه من مرتبة إلىٰ مرتبة حتّىٰ تصل إلىٰ الفلك الأعلىٰ من عالم المثال، ثمّ منه تنتقل إلىٰ عالم النّور المحض لمجاورته إيّاه.

---

٨٦ م، ش ٥٠٩؛ ط: «تترقّي.»
٨٧ م، ش٥٠٩.
٨٨ م، ش ٥٠٩؛ ط: «من.»
٨٩ م؛ ط: «ينتقل.»
٩٠ م؛ ش ٥٠٩.
٩١ ش ٥١٠: «إلىٰ.»
٩٢ ش ٥١٠: «ينفكّ، نسخة: ينتقل.»
٩٣ م، ش ٥١٠؛ ط: «العالم.»

مع أنّ أكثر النّفوس المستعدّة للوصول إلىٰ عالم العقل يترقي في العالم الحسّيّ والمثاليّ علىٰ التّرتيب من مرتبة إلىٰ مرتبة أعلىٰ منها حتّىٰ يصل إلىٰ عالم العقل، ثمّ تدوم فيه أبدًا من غير تغيّر، لأنّ هٰذه العوالم منازل ومراحل إلىٰ الله تعالىٰ، ويستحيل[٩٤] الوصول إليه دون قطع الجميع، وإلىٰ عالم النّور دون قطع عالم المثال لاستحالة الوصول إلىٰ المقصد وبينك وبينه منازل لا تقطعها كما هو سنّة [الله] في الأرض والسّماء، «وَلَنْ تَجِدْ لِسُنَّةِ اللهِ تَبْدِيلاً[٩٥]».

٩٤ م، ش ٥١٠؛ ط: «وليستحيل.»
٩٥ ط، سورة الإسراء ٧٧: «تحويلاً.»

أمّا القسم الخامس وهو ⌈النّاقص⌉[١] في العلم والعمل--أعني أصحاب الشّقاوة الّذين كانوا «حَوْلَ جَهَنَّمَ جِثِيًّا[٢]» «وَأَصْبَحُوا فِي دَارِهِم جَاثِمِينَ[٣]»--أي مائلين إلىٰ الحيوانيّات[٤] إذا تخلّصوا ⌈١٧٩ط⌉ عن أبدان الحيوانات، إن كان التّناسخ حقًّا، أو[٥] عن الأبدان الإنسانيّة، إن كان باطلاً، فإنّ الحجج علىٰ طرفيْ النّقيض في التّناسخ ضعيفة--يكون لها ظلال مثاليّة هي صوَر[٦] خياليّة معلّقة لا في محلّ علىٰ حسب هيآتها[٧] المناسبة لها إذ ليس لها ما للكاملين ليتخلّصوا عن[٨] الصّياصي إلىٰ عالم النّور، ولا ما للمتوسّطين ليصير الأفلاك مظاهر نفوسهم[٩]، وما فيهم من الهيآت الرّديّة تلجئهم[١٠] إلىٰ التّعلّق، فيتعلّقون بالصّوَر المثاليّة اللّائقة بها، إذ لكلّ خُلق من الأخلاق المذمومة والهيآت[١١] الرّديّة المتمكّنة في النّفس أبدان أنواع يختصّ ⌈بذلك الخُلق كخلق التكبّر⌉[١٢] والشجاعة المناسبة[١٣] لأبدان الأسُود ونحوها، والخبث[١٤] والرّوغان لأبدان الثعالب ⌈وأمثالها⌉[١٥]، والمحاكات والسّخريّة لأبدان القردة وأشباهها والسّلب[١٦] واللّصوصيّة لأبدان الذّئاب[١٧] وأشكالها، والعجب للطّواويس،

---

١ ط: «التّناقص.»
٢ سورة مريم ٦٨.
٣ سورة الأعراف ٩١؛ انظر ش ٥١٠-٥١١.
٤ م؛ ط: «الحيوانات.»
٥ م؛ ط: «و.»
٦ م؛ ط: «صورة.»
٧ ط؛ م: «هيآته.»
٨ ط؛ م: «إلىٰ.»
٩ ط؛ م: «لقومهم.»
١٠ م؛ ط: «تلحقهم.»
١١ م، ش ٤٨٥؛ ط: «له الهيآت.»
١٢ م، ش ٤٨٥؛ ط: «بذلك الخُلق الكبير.»
١٣ م، ش ٤٨٥؛ ط: «المناسب.»
١٤ ش ٤٨٥: «الجبن في مخطوطة.»
١٥ م، ش ٤٨٥.
١٦ ش ٤٨٥: «القتل والسّلب.»
١٧ ش٤٨٥: «ذياب مخطوطة.»

والحرص[١] للخنازير ، إلىٰ غير ذلك .

ولكلّ بدنٍ جزء[٢] من الخُلق الّذي يتعلّق بذلك [البدن] وعلىٰ قدره ، مثلاً للحرص أبدان [١٠م] [كالخنزير والنّمل لئلا[٣] يكون حرص النّمل كحرص الخنزير][٤] ، بل يكون لكلّ بدنها جزء مقسوم من الحرص بحسبهما ، ولا حرص بعض أفرادهما كحرص الباقي ، بل لكلّ فرد منها حرص خاصّ لا يشاركه[٥] فيه غيره ، والسّبب [فيه][٦] أنّ بحسب شدّة كلّ خُلق مذموم في النّفس وضعفه وما ينضمّ إليه من باقي الأخلاق المذمومة والمحمودة[٧] القويّة الضّعيفة واختلاف تراكيبها الكثيرة--[التي][٨] لا يمكن حصرها إلاّ الله--يختلف تعلّق النّفوس الموصوفة بخُلق مخصوص ، كالحرص مثلاً ببعض[٩] الأنواع من الحيوانات الموصوفة به دون البعض ، وكذا ببعض[١٠] أفراد نوع منها دون الباقي ، فلكلّ[١١] خُلق [مثلاً] كالشر[١٢] مثلاً حدّ معيّن من الشّدّة والضّعف إذا بلغت [النّفس[١٣] إليه تعلّقت ببدن نوع[١٤] من الحيوانات المناسبة للشّرّ كالكلب وأشباهه ، ثمّ بحسب شدّة الشّر وضعفه وما ينضمّ إليه ممّا[١٥] ذكرنا يختلف تعلّقها بأبدان أشخاص الكلاب الشّديدة الشّرّ والضّعيفة الشّرّ

١ ش ٤٨٥ : «الحرص والشّهوة .»
٢ ش ٤٨٦ : «جزء مقسوم .»
٣ م ؛ ش٥٨٦ : «فلا .»
٤ م ، ش ٥٨٦ ؛ ط : «كان كخنزير والنّمل كحرص الخنز(ير ؟) .»
٥ م ، ش ٤٨٦ ؛ ط : «مشارك .»
٦ م ، ش٦٨٦ .
٧ م ؛ ط ، ش٤٨٦ : «المحمودة والمذمومة .»
٨ م ، ش٤٨٦ .
٩ ط ، ش ٤٨٦ ؛ م : «بعض .»
١٠ ط ، ش ٤٨٦ ؛ م : «بعض .»
١١ م ، ش ٤٨٦ ؛ ط : «فكلّ .»
١٢ م ، ط ؛ ش ٥٨٦ : «كشره» ، وكذا أينما ذكر الأصل «الشّرّ ذكر ش «الشّره» .
١٣ م ، ش ٤٨٦ .
١٤ ط ، ش ٤٨٦ ؛ م : «بدن بنوع .»
١٥ ش ٤٨٦ : «كما .»

المتعذّبة١ ككلاب السّوق والمنعّمة٢ ككلاب الصّيد .

ولاختلاف النّاس٣ في الأخلاق المحمودة والمذمومة وشدّتها وضعفها واختلاف تراكيبها يختلف ظلالها المثاليّة المعلّقة لا في محلّ ، ولكنّ من فيه هيآت رديّة يتعلّق بعد المفارقة |بأعظم بدن حيوان يناسب|٤ أقوىٰ تلك الهيآت ، ثمّ نزل فيه علىٰ التّرتيب من الأكبر إلىٰ الأوسط ومنه إلىٰ الأصغر٥ إلىٰ أن تزول تلك الهيئة [١٨٠ط] الرّديّة ثمّ يتعلّق بأعظم بدن يناسب الهيئة التي تلي الهيئة الأولى في٦ القوّة متدرّجًا في النّزول إلىٰ أن تفنىٰ |كلّ|٧ تلك الهيآت ، وحينئذٍ يتّصل بعالم العقول ، مثلاً أصحاب الحرص والشرّ٨ والحرص أقوىٰ ، ينتقلون٩ أوّلاً |في أبدان|١٠ أنواع كثيرة ذوات هيئة حرص متقاربة المقدار في العظم والصّغر ، هي طبقات النّيران ودركاتها كالخنزير والنّمل ، بالتّرتيب والتّدريج حتّىٰ ينتهي | النّقل|١١ في الأخير إلىٰ الأبدان النّمليّة ثمّ إلىٰ ما هو أصغر منها إن كان ذا هيئة حرص ، فإذا بلغوا إلىٰ أصغر |الحيوانات في الحرص ١٢ وزالت تلك الهيئة |الرّديّة|١٣ عن النّفس بالكلّيّة |انتقلوا إلىٰ باقي|١٤ أبدان أنواع ذوات هيئة شر علىٰ الوجه المذكور ، فيلجؤن

---

١ ش ٤٨٦ : « المعذّبة . »
٢ م ، ش ٤٨٦ ؛ ط : « والمتنعّمة . »
٣ م ، ش ٤٨٦ ؛ ط : « النّفس . »
٤ ط : « بأعظم الحيوان يناسب » ؛ ش ٤٨٧ : « بأعظم بدن حيوانيّ ويناسبه . »
٥ م ، ش ٤٨٧ ؛ ط : « الأدنىٰ . »
٦ م ، ش ٤٨٧ ؛ ط : « من . »
٧ م ، ش٤٨٨ .
٨ ط : « السّرقة . »
٩ ط : « يتعلّقون . »
١٠ ط : « بأبدان . »
١١ ط ، ش ٤٨٨ .
١٢ ط : « الجسم » ؛ ش ٤٨٨ : « الحيوانات . »
١٣ م ، ش ٤٨٨ .
١٤ ط ؛ م : « انتقلواها بباقي » ؟ غير واضح . »

أوّلاً النّمور والذّئاب ثمّ الكلاب ثمّ ما هو أقلّ منها شرّا وأصغر |منه| جرمًا إلىٰ أن يزول تلك الهيئة الرّديّة عن النّفس بالكلّيّة أيضًا ، وكذا غيرها من الهيآت الرّديّة إن كانت ، وحينئذٍ يفارق عالم المُثل المعلّقة١ إلىٰ عالم أفلاكها٢ لها إن كان لها استعداد الترقي إليها .

وقوله--عزّ وعلا--«كُلَّما نَضِجَتْ جُلودُهُمْ بَدَّلْناهُمْ جُلودًا غَيْرَها٣» إشارة إلىٰ تبديل جلودهم بالوجه المذكور .

وكذا٤ قوله «كُلَّما أرادُوا أنْ يَخْرُجوا مِنْها |ط : أعِيدُوا فيها٥ »--أي في| النّيران المختلفة التي هي دركات جهنّم--يعني أبدان الحيوانات المثاليّة أعيدوا فيها ، أي في تلك النّيران الّتي هي |ا|الأبدان أيضًا ، وكذا قوله «رَبَّنا أخْرِجْنا مِنْها٦ فَإنْ عُدْنا فإنّا ظالِمُون٧» ، وكذا قوله في الأشقياء «رَبَّنا أمَتَّنا إثْنَتَيْنِ وَأحْيَيْتَنا إثْنَتَيْنِ |ط : فَاعْتَرَفْنا٨ بِذُنوبِنا| فَهَلْ إلىٰ خُروجٍ مِنْ سَبيلٍ٩ »--يعني من أبدان الحيوانات من سبيل حتّىٰ لا نموت مرّة أخرىٰ أو مرّات ، وفي السّعداء «لا يَذوقونَ فيها الْمَوْتَ إلاّ الْمَوْتَةَ الأولىٰ وَوَقَهُمْ عَذابَ الجَحِيم١٠» لاستحالة انتقال نفوسهم إلىٰ المُثل |١١م| الحيوانيّة لغلبة الأخلاق الفاضلة والصّفات المرضيّة ، فإذا لم تنتقل إليها فلا يذوقون إلاّ الموتة الأولىٰ ، وكذا قوله «وَنَحْشُرُهُمْ يَوْمَ القِيامَةِ عَلىٰ وُجُوهِهِمْ١١ »--أي علىٰ صوَر الحيوانات المنتكسة الرؤس .

---

١ ش ٤٨٨ : « عالم الكون والفساد . »
٢ ط : « الأفلاك لها . »
٣ سورة النّساء ٥٦ .
٤ ط : « وأمّا . »
٥ سورة السّجدة ٣٢ .
٦ م ، القرآن ؛ ط : « فيها . »
٧ سورة المؤمنون ١٠٧ .
٨ القرأن : « اعترفنا . »
٩ سورة غافر ٤٠ .
١٠ سورة الدخان ٥٦ .

والأحاديث الواردة في أنّ النّاس يُبعَثون علىٰ صوَر مختلفة بحسب أخلاقهم كثيرة ، كقوله--عليه الصّلوٰة والسّلام--«يَحشرُ النّاسُ يَوْمَ القِيامَةِ عَلىٰ وُجوهٍ مُختَلِفَةٍ» وقوله «كَما يَعِيْشونَ يَمُوتُونَ يُبْعَثونَ» ، ولهٰذا قال--عليه الصّلوٰة والسّلام--ما معناه أنّه يحشر من خالف الإمام في١ أفعال الصّلوٰة ورأسه رأس حمار ، [فإنّه]٢ إذا عاش في المخالفة التي هي عين البلاهة والحماريّة [١٨١ط] تمكّنت فيه ولتمكّن البلادة فيه يحشر علىٰ صور[ط : ة] الحمار إلىٰ غير ذلك ممّا يطول ذكره .

قال فيثاغورس :

> اعلم أنّك ستعارض بأفكارك وأقوالك وأفعالك ، وستظهر من كلّ حركة فكريّة أو قوليّة أو فعليّة صوَر روحانيّة٣ أو جسمانيّة ، فإن كانت الحركة غضبيّة [ط : أو] شهويّة صارت مادّة لشيطان يؤذيك في حيوٰتك ويحجبك عن ملاقات النّور بعد وفاتك ، وإن كانت الحركة أمريّة عقليّة صارت تلتذّ٤ بمنادمة في دنياك وتهتدي بنور[ها] في أخراك إلىٰ جوار الله وكرامته .

وأمثال هٰذا ممّا يدلّ علىٰ تجسّد الأعمال في كلام الأوائل كثيرة ، وهٰذا أنموذج [منها] ، والأولىٰ الاقتصار عليه حذرًا من الإطناب المؤدّي إلىٰ الإسحاب ، وإذا تقرّرت هٰذه المسائل] فلنرجع إلىٰ المقصود و[هو] تتبّع ألفاظه وتصفّح أقواله .

---

١١ سورة الإسراء ٩٧ : «علىٰ وجوههم عميًا وبكمًا وصمًّا .»
١ ط : «من .»
٢ ط : «زمانه .»
٣ ط : «صوَرًا روحانيًّا .»
٤ ط : تمتدّ .»

‹أجوبة المسائل›١

فنقول٢ :

أمّا قوله--أدام الله فضله وكثر في الأفاضل مثله--٣

قد وعدَنا الشّارعُ٤ . . .فتوعّدنا بأحوال٥ البرزخ وتجسّد الأعمال ، فهٰذه الصّوَر إن كان يتصوّر٦ الجوهر٧ الرّوحانيّ مجرّدًا عن علائق الأجسام ، فكيف يحصل من مثله هٰذا التّصوّر المحدود مع كونه مجرّدًا ؟

فلأنّه إن أراد بتجرّده عن علائق الأجسام جميع الأجسام--أعني الحسّيّة والمثاليّة--فليس كذٰلك ، لأنّه وإن تجرّد عن الحسّيّة لم يتجرّد عن المثاليّة كما سبق تحقيقه ، وإن أراد [به] بعض الأجسام--وهي الحسّيّة دون المثاليّة--[ط : فهو] مسلّم لكن٨ لا استبعاد فيه لِما سبق أيضًا بيانه .

أمّا قوله٩ :

وإن كان موضوع تخيّله جسمه . . .

فلأنّه إن أراد بجسمه جسمه الحسّيّ صحّ اختلاله بالموت ، وإن أراد جسمه المثاليّ فلا يصحّ لأنّه لا يختلّ به .

أمّا قوله١٠ :

---

١ انظر ص 236 ، حاشية ..
٢ ط : « ونقول . »
٣ ص 236
٤ ط : « الشرع . »
٥ م ، ص 236؛ ط : « أحوال . »
٦ ص 236 « يتصوّرها . »
٧ ص 236 « الجواهر . »
٨ ط : « لكنّه . »
٩ ص 236

إن كان موضوع التّخيّل جسمًا آخر من فلك أو غيره إلىٰ الآخر .

فلأنّ موضوع تخيّل البعض و[هم] المتوسّطون جرم الفلك ، وقد بيّنّاك[1] تعلّقهم به دون غيره من الأجسام المثاليّة لترقيهم من[2] عالم المثال وعدم لحوقهم بعالم الأنوار لفقدان الكمال ، فبالضّرورة يتعلّقون ببعض الأفلاك [بفلك أعلىٰ إن كان أصفىٰ ، وإلاّ فبالأدنىٰ .

وأمّا قوله:[3]

أو غيره .

فإن أراد به غير الفلك] من أجسام هٰذا العالم ، والظّاهر أنّه مراد لقوله[4] :

فإنّه بنسبةٍ[5] حدثت بالموت بينهما الىٰ الآخر .

فهو غير مراد ، ولا حاجة إلىٰ بيان مناسبة بينهما ، [وإن أراد من أجسام [١٢م] عالم المثال ، فهو المراد ويحتاج إلىٰ بيان مناسبة بينها ،] وقد بيّنّا أنّها مناسبة ثبتت بينهما قبل الموت بسبب تمكّن ملكات فيه مناسبة لذلك البدن المثاليّ لا بعده حتّىٰ يقال «فإنّه بنسبة حدثت بالموت بينهما .»

وأمّا قوله[6] :

ثمّ هٰذا الجوهر الرّوحانيّ ، إن تمّ علىٰ ما هو عليه من التّخيّل بواسطة[7] الجسم ، لزم اجتماع المفارقات كلّها علىٰ أجسام [١٨٢ط] العالم ، [فتجب نهاية تلك الجواهر أو عدم نهاية الأجسام ، وكلّ واحد من القسمين يحتاج إلىٰ برهان .

---

١٠ ص 236
١ ط : « قدّمناك . »
٢ ط : « عن . »
٣ ص 236
٤ ط : « مراده بقوله . » ص . .
٥ ط : « لنسبة . »
٦ ص 236
٧ م ، ص236 ؛ ط : « لواسطة . »

فلأنّا لا نتكلّم لزوم اجتماع المفارقات كلّها علىٰ أجسام العالم| سواء أراد بها أجسام الأفلاك أو[١] أجسام عالم المثال، إذ لا تعلّق لمفارق بغيرهما، بل يتعلّق بعضها--أي بعض المفارقات--بالأفلاك، وبعضها بأبدان عالم المثال، ولا اجتماع لمفارقين علىٰ بدن مثاليّ، وأمّا علىٰ جرم فلكيّ، وإن أمكن علىٰ ما أخبر النّبيّ--عليه الصّلوٰة والسّلام--من كون عيسىٰ ويحيىٰ--عليهما السّلام--في السّماء الرّابعة، فلا ثمّ اجتماع المفارقات غير متناهية علىٰ فلك واحد، وإن سلم[٢] فلا نسلّم[٣] استحالته، إذ الصّوَر المثاليّة لا تتزاحم علىٰ المحلّ، لأنّها ليست في محلّ، ويجوز[٤] أن تشاهد في فلكٍ صوَر كذلك كما تشاهد في المرآة كم كانت |وكيف كانت| من غير تزاحم ولا استحالة، وعلىٰ هٰذا لا تلزم نهاية تلك الجواهر ولا عدم نهاية الأجسام.

ثمّ قوله[٥]:

> وكلّ[٦] واحد من القسمين يحتاج إلىٰ برهان...

غير مناسب لسياق الكلام، بل |كان| المناسب له أن يقول: «وكلّ واحد من القسمين محال» أو «باطل» ونحوهما.

أمّا قوله[٧]:

> أو يتخلّص في آخر الأمر من علاقته إلىٰ السّعادة[٨]، فيلزم أن يكون له بعد الموت ترقٍّ[٩]، فيتعيّن بيانه...

---

١ ط: «و.»
٢ الكلمت: «فلا ثمّ اجتماع...علىٰ فلك واحد، فإن سلم» مكرّرة في ط.
٣ ط: «ثمّ.»
٤ ط: «فيجوز.»
٥ ص..
٦ ط: «كلّ»؛ ص236: «فكلّ.»
٧ ص 236
٨ م، ص 236؛ ط: «السّواد.»
٩ ص 236: «آخر.»

فلأنّا قد بيّنّا اختلاف الأوائل في هٰذا الترقي وما هو الحقّ فيه.

وأمّا قوله[١] :

فإنّ[٢] التّحقيق[٣] بالشّقاوة لزم[٤] انحطاطه، ولعلّ هٰذا الحال مناف لما يُرجىٰ من الجود[٥] الإلهيّ...

فلأنّه إنّما كان ينافيه لو كان مادّته قابلة لذلك، وليس كذلك، وإلاّ لما يختلف ما يرجىٰ من الجود عنه إذ لا بخل في[٦] الفاعل، فإن كان قصور[٧]، فهو في القابل.

وأمّا قوله[٨] :

أو لا إلىٰ سعادة ولا إلىٰ شقاوة، فيلزم التّعطيل[٩]، أو إليهما معًا[١٠]، فيكون جمعًا بين الضّدين.

فلأنّ كون الإنسان سعيدًا من وجه شقيًّا من |وجه| آخر لا يقتضي اجتماع الضّدّين إلاّ في اللّفظ دون الحقيقة.

وأمّا قوله[١١] :

إن كان كما زعم قوم أنّ لكلّ واحد وجودين: عينيّ، وهو الظاهر، وذهنيّ... |هو| موجود في علم الله...

فلأنّهم |إن| أرادوا بوجود|ه| الذّهنيّ الموجود في علم الله وجوده المثاليّ الموجود في عالم المثال علىٰ سبيل التّجوّز، فهو حقّ علىٰ ما سبق تقريره، وإن أريد به ظاهره، فهو

---

١ ص 236
٢ ط، ص 236: «وإن.»
٣ ص 236: محذوف.
٤ ط، ص 236؛ م: «ولزم.»
٥ م، ص 236؛ ط: «مناف للجود.»
٦ ط: «عن.»
٧ ط: «قصورًا.»
٨ ص 236
٩ ص 236: «التّعطّل.»
١٠ م، ص 236؛ ط: «معانٍ.»
١١ ص 237

باطل لِما ذكر من [تعالي] علمه تعالىٰ عن أن يكون محلاً للحوادث، لا لما ذكر من اجتماع الوجود الذّهنيّ [للرّوح] والوجود العينيّ علىٰ الوجود الذّهنيّ للجسم لأنّه لا استحالة فيه.

أمّا قوله في الفصل الأوّل[١]

ويكون جميع ذلك أعراضًا تبطل بالانحلال.

فلأنّه إن أراد ببطلانها بالانحلال زوال آثارها عن النّفس، فهو ممنوع لجواز تمكّنها فيها بحيث لا يزول عنها إلاّ بالانتقال في الصّوَر المثاليّة، [١٨٣ط] وإن أراد [ط: به] زوالها [١٣م] عن البدن الحسّيّ، فهو مسلّم وغير بعيد.

وأمّا قوله في الفصل الثّاني[٢]

فإذن هو عرضيّ يعرض بمطالبة الجسم، فعند عدم المطالبة يبطل ذلك كلّه.

فلأنّه لا يلزم من كون نزوعه إلىٰ الجسم والاهتمام بمصالحه [ط: كونه] عرضيًّا[٣] يعرض بمطالبة الجسم بطلان ذلك كلّه عند عدم المطالبة، وإنّما كان يلزم ذلك لو لم يتمكّن [في النّفس من ذلك العرضيّ][٤] ما يقتضي النّزوع إلىٰ الجسم والاهتمام بمصالحه المقتضين للتّصوّرات والتّخيّلات.

وأمّا المذكور في الفصل الثّالث[٥]، وهو أنّ الأرواح الحيوانيّة هل تفنىٰ بفناء أجسادها[٦] أم لا، فنقول: لأنّا بيّنّا في شرح [حكمة] الإشراق[٧] أنّ كلّ من يدرك ذاته [ط: فهو نور مجرّد، ولا شكّ أنّ الحيوان يدرك ذاتهم] كالإنسان، ومنكر إدراك الحيوان ذاته معاند مكابر

---

١ ص 238؛ م: «الثّاني.»
٢ ص 239؛ م: «الرّابع.»
٣ ط: «عرضًا.»
٤ ط: «من ذلك العرضيّ في النّفس.»
٥ ص 239؛ م: «الرّابع.»
٦ ط: «أجسامها.»
٧ انظر ش ٢٩٠ وما يليه.

[كمنكر إدراكه]١ الكلّيّ، ومن أراد الاطّلاع علىٰ براهين هٰذه المسئلة، فليراجع٢ ذلك الشرح.

وأمّا قوله٣:

> فقد تحدّس الإنسان من مثل هٰذا الحيوان ترقّيه إلىٰ جهة الكمال، فإن كان له ارتقاء، فكيف ذلك؟ وإن لم يكن له، فهو غير لائق بالجود الإلٰهيّ أن يمنع المستعدّ للكمال عن٤ كماله.

فلأنّه لا يلزم من مشاهدة الإنسان في القرد بعض٥ القوىٰ العمليّة بحدسه ترقيه إلىٰ جهة الكمال، إن أراد به الكمال الّذي يتعلّق [بالمعاد، وإن أراد به الكمال الّذي يتعلّق] ببعض القوىٰ العمليّة، فهو لازم ومعقول ومشاهد في القرد وفي كون بعضها أكثر حدسًا وأرقّ عملاً إلىٰ غير ذلك، بل القرد الواحد يتكامل فيه القوىٰ العمليّة بحسب مرور الزّمان عليه ومباشرة الأعمال ومزاولة الحركات والسّكنات وغيرها، وعلىٰ هٰذا ينتهي كلّ منها إلىٰ كماله بحسب حاله، ولا يمنع واحد منها عمّا استعدّ [له] من الكمال في هٰذا العالم، وكذا إن استعدّ في عالم المثال لا يمنع عنه وإن لم يستعدّ له فيه، لا يكون له ارتقاء، ولا يلزم منه كونه غير لائق بالجود الإلهيّ، لأنّه لم يلزم منه منع المستعدّ للكمال٦ عن كماله.

فهٰذا ما سنح للخاطر العليل في الحال وسمح به الذّهن الكليل علىٰ سبيل [الاستعجال]، فإن وٰافق الصّواب، فقد أدرك طلبتي، وإلاّ فليعذرني إذ قدّمت معذرتي، والمرجوّ ممّن حسن حتمه وسلم من الحليم أدبه٧، [أنّه] إذا عثر منّي [علىٰ] سهوان يسترني بذيل تجاوز

---

١ ط: «كمثل إدراك.»
٢ ط: «فيرجع.»
٣ ص 239
٤ ص 240: «من.»
٥ ط: «وبعض.»
٦ ط: «لكمال.»
٧ م: «أديمه.»

وعفو، فإنّي للخطايا لَمعترف وبالقصور والعجز لَمقترف.

زادنا الله اعترافًا بالعجز وإيّاك، فالعجز عن درك الإدراك إدراك.

[و]هٰذا آخر الجواب، [والله أعلم بالصّواب.]

<كلام ناسخ مخطوطة مشهد>

علىٰ يد الفقير الحقير المعترف بالقصير

عبد الأوّل بن محمود بن محمود العبّاسيّ

جعله الله عارفًا بحقائق الأشياء كما هي

بحرمة سيّد العارفين وأكمل العالمين

محمّد المصطفىٰ الأمين

آمين، ربّ العالمين.

في الثامن والعشرين من رمضان المبارك

سنة ثمانٍ وتسعمائة[١] .

---

١ ٢٧ آذار ١٥٠٣

<كلام ناسخ مخطوطة تهران>

تمّ.

رسالة في جواب أسؤلة بعض الأفاضل
في تحقيق عالم المثال وغيره
للعلامة الشيرازيّ
رحمه الله

قد اتّفق الفراغ في خامس شهر ربيع الأول
سنة اثني وعشرين وألف[1] في دار الفضل شيراز.

قد تمّت الرّسالة الشريفة
علىٰ يد أقلّ خلق الله
عبد القادر الأردوبادي.
م

---

١ ٢٥ نيسان ١٦١٣.

<u>رموز وعلامات</u>

[ ] موجود في أحد النّسخ دون السّائرين

< > زيادة المصحّح

ش: موجود في شرح حكمة الإشراق لقطب الدّين الشيرازي

ح: موجود في كتاب حكمة الإشراق للسّهروردي

ص: صفحة في هٰذه الرّسالة

ط: موجود في مخطوطة تهران

م: موجود في مخطوطة مشهد

فم: موجود في كتاب الفتوحات المكيّة لابن عربيّ

ه: موجود في هامش مخطوطة تهران

Bibliography

HISTORICAL, BIOGRAPHICAL, AND BIBLIOGRAPHICAL SOURCES

Abulfedae annales Muslemici. Edited by Jacobi Reiskii. 5 vols. Copenhagen, 1794.

al-Asnawī, Jamāl al-Dīn ʿAbd al-Rahīm. *Ṭabaqāt al-Shāfiʿīya.* Edited by ʿAbd Allāh al-Jubūrī. 2 vols. Baghdad, 1391.

Brockelmann, Carl. *Geschichte der Arabischen Literatur.* 5 vols. Leiden: E. J. Brill, 1937–49.

Browne, E. G. *A Literary History of Persia.* Vol. 2: *From Saʿdī to Jāmī.* London: Cambridge University Press, 1928.

Cambridge History of Iran. 8 vols. Vol. 5: *The Saljūq and Mongol Periods.* Edited by J. A. Boyle. Cambridge: Cambridge University Press, 1968– .

al-Dalajī, Aḥmad b. ʿAlī. *Al-Falāka wa'l-Maflūkūn.* Cairo: Maṭbaʿat al-Shaʿb, 1322.

Ergin, Osman. *Ibni Sina Bibliografyasi.* Istanbul, 1937.

al-Fārābī. *Fuṣūl al-Madanī.* Edited with an introduction and comments by Fawzī Mitrī Najjār. Beirut: Dar El-Mashreq, 1971.

Farmer, Henry George. *History of Arabian Music.* London, 1929.

Ḥājjī Khalīfah. *Lexicon bibliographicum et encyclopaedicum.* 7 vols. Edited by G. Flügel. Leipzig and London, 1835–56.

Hirschberg, J. *Die arabischen Lehrbücher der Augenheilkunde.* Abhandlung der preussischer Akadamie, no. 93. Berlin, 1905.

Honigman, Ernest. *Die sieben Klimata.* Heidelberg, 1929.

Ibn Abi'l-Wafā' Muḥyi'd-Dīn. *al-Jawāhir al-Muḍī'a fī Ṭabaqāt al-Ḥanafīya*. Hyderabad: Niẓāmīya, 1352.

Ibn al-Fuwaṭī. *al-Ḥawādith al-Jāmi'a*. Baghdad: al-Maktabat al-'Arabīya, 1932.

———. *Talkhīṣ Majma' al-Ādāb fī Mu'jam al-Alqāb*. Volume 4, pt. 4. Damascus: Mudīrīyat Iḥyā' al-Turāth al-Qadīm, [1967].

Ibn al-Wardī. *Tatimmat al-Mukhtaṣar fī Akhbār al-Bashar*. Cairo, 1285.

Ibn Ḥajar al-'Asqalānī. *al-Durar al-Kāmina fī A'yān al-Mi'a al-Thāmina*. Hyderabad, 1350.

Ibn Rāfi' al-Sallāmī. *Tārīkh 'Ulamā' Baghdād*. Abridged by al-Taqī al-Fāsī. Baghdad, 1357/1938.

Ibn Taghribirdī, Jamāl al-Dīn Yūsuf. *al-Nujūm al-Zāhira fī Mulūk Miṣr wa'l-Qāhira*. Cairo, n.d.

Iqbāl, 'Abbās. "'Allāma-yi Quṭb al-Dīn Shīrāzī." *Majalla-yi Armaghān* 16 (1311): 659–68.

I'tiṣāmī, Yūsuf, et al. *Fihrist-i Kitābkhāna-i Majlis-i Shūrā-i Millī dar Ṭihrān*. 19 vols. Tehran, 1305/1927–1353/1973.

Ivanow, Wladimir, et al. *Catalogue of the Arabic Manuscripts in the Collection of the Royal Asiatic Society of Bengal, 1st Supplement*. 2 vols. Calcutta, 1939–49.

Kennedy, E. S. "Late Medieval Planetary Theory." *Isis* 57 (1966): 365–78.

Jāmī, 'Abd al-Raḥmān. *Nafaḥāt al-Uns min Ḥaḍarāt al-Quds*. Edited by Mahdī Tawḥīdīpūr. [Tehran]: Sa'dī, 1336.

Kaḥḥāla, 'Umar Riḍā. *Mu'jam al-Mu'allifīn*. Damscus, 1380/1960.

Khwāndamīr, Ghiyāth al-Dīn. *Tārīkh Ḥabīb al-Siyar*. [Tehran]: Khayyām, 1333.

Khwānsārī, Mīrzā Muḥammad-Bāqir. *Rawḍāt al-Jannāt fī Aḥwāl al-'Ulamā' wa'l-Sādāt*. Edited by al-Ḥājj Sayyid Sa'īd al-Ṭabāṭabā'ī. Tehran, 1304–6.

Krause, Max. "Stambuler Handschriften islamischer Mathematiker." *Quellen und Studien zur Geschichte der Mathematik, Astronomie, und Physik*. Abt. B, Studien 3 (1936): 507 ff.

al-Laknawī, Muḥammad 'Abd al-Ḥayy. *al-Fawā'id al-Bahīya fī Tarājim al-Ḥanafīya*. India, 1236.

Leclerc, L. *Histoire de la Mèdicine arabe*. Paris: Librairie des Sociètès Asiatiques, 1876.

Mīnawī, Shādrawān. "Mullā Quṭb al-Shīrāzī." In *Yād-Nāma-yi Īrānī-yi Mīnūrskī*. Edited by Mujtabā Mīnawī and Īraj Afshār. Ganjīna-yi Taḥqīqāt-i Īrānī. Tehran: Dānishgāh-i Tehran, 1348/1969.

Mīr, Muḥammad-Taqī. *Pizishkān-i Nāmī-yi Pārsī*. Shiraz: Pahlavi University, 1348/1969.

———. "'Allāma-yi Quṭb al-Dīn Shīrāzī." *Khirad wa-Kūshish* 2 (1349): 451–65.

———. *Sharḥ-i Ḥāl wa-Āthār-i 'Allāma-yi Quṭb al-Dīn . . . Shīrāzī*. Intishārāt, no. 91. Shiraz: Pahlavi University, 2535.

Mishkāt, Muḥammad. Introduction to *Durrat al-Tāj li-Ghurrat al-Dubāj* by Quṭb al-Dīn al-Shīrāzī. Edited by Muḥammad Mishkāt. Tehran: Majlis, 1317.

Munzawī, Aḥmad. *Fihrist-i Nuskha-hā-i Khaṭṭī-i Fārsī*. 6 vols. Tehran: Mu'assasa-i Farhangī-i Manṭiqi'ī, 1348/1969– .

Mustawfī Qazwīnī. *Tārīkh-i Guzīda*. Edited by 'Abd al-Ḥusayn Nawā'ī. Tehran, 1336.

al-Nadwī. *Tadhkirat al-Nawādir*. Hyderabad, Deccan: Dā'irat al-Ma'ārif, 1350.

Nansen, Fridtjof. *In Northern Mists*. 1911.

Nasr, Seyyed Hossein. "Quṭb al-Dīn al-Shīrāzī." *Dictionary of Scientific Biography*.

Qazwīnī, Muḥammad b. 'Abd al-Wahhāb. *Yād-Dāsht-hā-yi Qazwīnī*. Edited by Īraj Afshār. Tehran: Tehran University Press, 1332–42.

al-Qurashī, Muḥyī al-Dīn 'Abd al-Qādir. *al-Jawāhir al-Muḍī'a fī Ṭabaqāt al-Ḥanafīya*. Hyderabad: Niẓāmīya, 1332.

Qurbānī, Abū al-Qāsim. "Quṭb al-Dīn Shīrāzī." *Rāh-Numā-yi Kitāb* 11: 429–33.

Rashīd al-Dīn Faḍl Allāh Abū al-Khayr. *Kitāb-i Makātīb-i Rashīdī*. Edited by Muḥammad Shafī'. Lahore: Punjab Educational Press, 1364/1945.

Rāzī, Amīn. *Tadhkirat-i Haft Iqlīm*. 3 vols. Tehran, 1340.

Rāzī, Fakhr al-Dīn. *Kitāb al-Arba'īn fī Uṣūl al-Dīn*. Hyderabad, Deccan: Maṭba'at Dā'irat al-Ma'ārif al-'Uthmānīya, 1353.

Riḍawī, Mudarris. *Aḥwāl wa-Āthār-i . . . Khwāja Naṣīr al-Dīn al-Ṭūsī.* Intishārāt, no. 282. Tehran: Tehran University Press, 1334.
Saliba, George. "The First Non-Ptolemaic Astronomy at the Maraghah School." *Isis* 70 (1979): 571–76.
———. "The Original Source of Quṭb al-Dīn al-Shīrāzī's Planetary Model." *Journal for the History of Arabic Science* 3 (1979): 3–18.
Sarton, George. *An Introduction to the History of Science.* Vol. 2. Baltimore: Carnegie Institution, 1941.
Seippel, Alexander. *Rerum normannicarum fontes arabici.* Part 1. Christiania, 1896.
Sezgin, Fuat. *Geschichte des arabischen Schriftums.* Leiden: E. J. Brill, 1970– .
Sharif, M. M. *A History of Muslim Philosophy.* 2 vols. Wiesbaden: Otto Harrossowitz, 1963–66.
al-Shawkānī, Muḥammad b. ʻAlī. *al-Badr al-Ṭāliʻ bi-Maḥāsin Man Baʻd al-Qarn al-Sābiʻ.*
Storey, C. A. *Persian Literature.* London: Luzac, 1958.
al-Subkī, Tāj al-Dīn. *Ṭabaqāt al-Shāfiʻīya al-Kubrā.* Edited by Aḥmad b. ʻAbd al-Karīm al-Qādirī al-Ḥasanī. Cairo: Maṭbaʻat al-Ḥusaynīya al-Miṣrīya, n.d.
Suter, H. *Mathematiker und Astronomer der Araber und ihre Werke.* Leipzig: H. G. Teubner, 1900.
al-Suyūṭī, Jalāl al-Dīn. *Bughyat al-Wuʻāt fī Ṭabaqāt al-Lughawīyīn wa'l-Nuḥāt.* Edited by Muḥammad Abū al-Faḍl Ibrāhīm. 1st ed.; Cairo: Maṭbaʻat ʻIsā al-Bābī al-Ḥalabī, 1384/ 1965.
Ṭāshküprüzāda. *Miftāḥ al-Saʻāda.* Hyderabad, 1328.
al-Ṭihrānī, Āghā Buzurg. *al-Dharīʻa ilā Taṣānīf al-Shīʻa.* Tehran, 1355/ 1936– .
Wiedemann, E. "Quṭb al-Dīn al-Shīrāzī." *Encyclopedia of Islam,* 2nd ed., 2:1166–67.
Wüstenfeld, F. *Geschichte der Arabische Ärtze.* Göttingen, 1840.
Zarkūb Shīrāzī. *Shīrāz-Nāma.* Ed. Bahman Karīmī. Tehran: Aḥmadī, 1310/1350/1931.
al-Ziriklī, Khayr al-Dīn. *al-Aʻlām.* 3d ed; Damascus, 1960.

PHILOSOPHICAL SOURCES

Afnan, Soheil. *A Philosophical Lexicon in Persian and Arabic.* Beirut: Dar El-Mashreq, [1968].

Aristotle. *The Basic Works of Aristotle.* Edited with an introduction by Richard McKeon. Random House Lifetime Library. New York: Random House, 1941.

Avicenna. *Avicenna's Psychology.* Translated by Fazlur Rahman. London: Oxford University Press, 1952.

———. "Fī Aqsām al-'Ulūm al-'Aqlīya." In *Majmū'at al-Rasā'il,* 192–203. Edited by Muḥyī al-Dīn Ṣabrī al-Kurdī. Cairo: Kurdistān al-'Ilmīya, 1328.

———. *Kitāb al-Najāt.* Edited by Mājid Fakhrī. Beirut: Dār al-Āfāq al-Jadīda, 1985.

———. *Kitāb al-Shifā'. al-Ilāhīyāt.* Edited by Ibrāhīm Madkūr. Cairo: al-Hay'a al-Āmma li-Shu'ūn al-Maṭābi' al-Amīrīya, 1380/1960.

———. *Kitāb al-Shifā'. al-Ṭabī'īyāt.* Vol. 6, *al-Nafs.* Edited by Ibrāhīm Madkūr. Cairo: al-Hay'a al-Miṣrīya al-'Āmma li'l-Kitāb, 1975.

———. "Tafsīr Kitāb Uthūlūjiyā." In *Arisṭū 'Ind al-'Arab.* Edited by 'Abd al-Raḥmān Badawī. Cairo: al-Nahḍat al-'Arabīya, 1947.

Çapak, Miliç. "The Eternal Return." In *The Encyclopedia of Philosophy.* New York: Macmillan, 1967.

Chittick, William C. "Mysticism versus Philosophy in Earlier Islamic History: The al-Ṭūsī, al-Qūnawī Correspondence." *Religious Studies* 17 (1981):87–104.

Encyclopedia of Philosophy. 1967 ed.

Corbin, Henry. *Spiritual Body and Celestial Earth.* Translated by Nancy Pearson. Bollingen Series no. 91:2. Princeton: Princeton University Press, 1977.

———. *En Islam iranien.* 4 vols. Vol. 2, *Sohravardī et les Platoniciens de Perse.* Paris: Gallimard, 1971.

de Vaux, B. Carra. "Tanāsukh." *The Encyclopedia of Islam.* 4:648–49.

al-Fārābī. "The Letter Concerning the Intellect." Translated by Arthur

Hyman. In *Philosophy in the Middle Ages*. Edited by Arthur Hyman and James J. Walsh. Indianapolis: Hackett, 1974.

Goichon, Amèlie-Marie. *Lexique de la langue philosophique d'Ibn Sīnā*. Paris: Desclèe de Brouwer, 1938.

Gutas, Dmitri. *Avicenna and the Aristotelian Tradition*. Islamic Philosophy and Theology: Texts and Studies, vol. 4. Leiden: E. J. Brill, 1988.

Ḥaqqī, Ibrāhīm. *Ma'rifat-Nāma*. Būlāq, 1251, 1255.

Harawī, Muḥammad Sharīf b. Niẓām al-Dīn b. *Anwārīya*. Ed. Hossein Ziai. Tehran: Amīr Kabīr, 1358/1980.

Ibn 'Arabī. *al-Futūḥāt al-Makkīya*. Beirut: Dār al-Ṣādir, n.d.

Ibn Taymīya. *Naqḍ al-Manṭiq*. Edited by Muḥammad b. 'Abd al-Razzāq al-Ṣanī' et al. Cairo: Maṭba'at al-Sunna al-Muḥammadī, 1370/1951.

Izutsu, Toshihiko. *The Concept and Reality of Existence*. Studies in the Humanities and Social Relations. Tokyo: Keio Institute of Cultural and Linguistic Studies, 1971.

Kātibī Quzvīnī, Najm al-Dīn, and Ṭūsī, Naṣīr al-Dīn. *Muṭāraḥāt Falsafīya*. Edited by Shaykh Muḥammad Ḥusayn Āl Yāsīn. Nafā'is al-Makhṭūṭāt, no. 7. Baghdad: Dār al-Ma'ārif, n.d.

The Koran Interpreted. Translated by A. J. Arberry. New York: Macmillan, 1955.

Lang, J. Bruce. "Reincarnation." *Encyclopedia of Religion and Ethics*. New York: Macmillan, 1987.

al-Muthul al-'Aqlīya al-Aflāṭūnīya. Ed. 'Abd al-Ra'ḥmān Badawī. Cairo: Dār al-Kutub al-Miṣrīya, 1947.

Nasr, Seyyed Hossein. *Three Muslim Sages*. Cambridge, Mass.: Harvard University Press, 1964.

———. *An Introduction to Islamic Cosmological Doctrines*. Revised edition; Boulder: Shambhala, 1978.

Pearson, A. C. "Transmigration (Greek and Roman)." In *Encyclopedia of Religion and Ethics*. 1958 ed.

Peters, F. E. *Aristoteles Arabus*. Leiden: E. J. Brill, 1968.

———. *Aristotle and the Arabs*. New York Studies in Near Eastern Civilization, no. 1. New York: NYU Press, 1968.

———. "The Origins of Islamic Platonism: The School Tradition." In

Islamic Philosophical Theology, pp. 14–45. Edited by Parviz Morewedge. Studies in Islamic Philosophy and Science. Albany: State University of New York Press, 1979.

Plato. *The Collected Dialogues.* Edited by Edith Hamilton and Huntington Cairns with an introduction and prefatory notes. Bollingen Series, no. 71. New York: Bollingen Books, 1961.

Plotinus. "The Theology of Aristotle." Translated by Geoffrey Lewis. In *Plotini Opera.* Edited by Paul Henry and Hans-Rudolf Schwyzer. Museum Lessianum series philosophica, no. 34. Paris: Desclèe de Brouwer, 1959.

Quṭb al-Dīn al-Shīrāzī. *Durrat al-Tāj li-Ghurrat al-Dubāj.* 8 vols. in 2. Vol. 1 edited by Muḥammad Mishkāt. Vol. 2 edited by Ḥasan Mishkān Ṭabasī. Tehran: Majlis, 1317–24.

———. *Sharḥ Ḥikmat al-Ishrāq.* Edited by Asad Allāh Harātī. [Tehran]: 1313–15.

Rahman, Fazlur. "Dream, Imagination, and 'Ālam al-Mithāl." *Islamic Studies* 3 (1964): 167–80.

———. *The Philosophy of Mullā Ṣadrā.* Studies in Islamic Philosophy and Science. Albany: State University of New York Press, 1975.

Sabziwārī. *The Metaphysics of Sabziwārī.* Translated by Mehdi Mohaghegh and Toshihiko Izutsu. Wisdom of Paris, vol. 10. Delmar, N. Y.: Caravan Books, 1977.

Shahristānī. *Kit'ab al-Milal wa'l-Niḥal.* Ed. Muḥammad b. Fatḥ Allāh Badrān. Cairo: Maṭba'at al-Azhar, 1910.

Shīrāzī, Ṣadr al-Dīn (Mullā Ṣadrā). *al-Ḥikma al-Muta'āliya fī al-Asfār al-Arba'a.* Tehran: Shirkat al-Ma'ārif al-Islāmīya, 1387.

Shīrāzī, Zarkūb-i, *Shīrāz-Nāma.* Edited by Bahman Karīmī. Tehran: Ahmadi, 1310/1331, 131–32.

Smart, Ninian. "Reincarnation." In *Encyclopedia of Philosophy.* New York: Macmillan, 1967.

Suhrawardī, Shihāb al-Dīn Yaḥyā. *Œuvres philosophiques et mystiques.* 3 vols. Edited by Henry Corbin. Bibliothèque Iranienne, n.s. Tehran: Academie Imperiale Iranienne de Philosophie, 1976–77.

Taylor, J. C. "Essence and Existence." *New Catholic Encyclopedia.* 1967 ed.

Thomas Aquinas. *Commentary on the Metaphysics of Aristotle.* Library of Living Catholic Thought. Chicago: Henry Regnery Co., 1961.

Werblowsky, R. J. Zwi. "Transmigration." In *Encyclopedia of Religion*. New York: Macmillan, 1987.

Wolfson, Harry Austryn. *The Philosophy of the Kalam*. Cambridge, Mass.: Harvard University Press, 1976.

Ziai, Hossein. *Knowledge and Illumination: A Study of Suhrawardī's "Ḥikmat al-Ishrāq."* Brown University Judaic Studies Series 97. Atlanta: Scholars Press, 1990.

Index of Passages Cited

The number in the first column refers to the page or section number of the passage being discussed. The number in the second column is the page number in the present book.

Index of Names and Subjects